Ann Morrow is a former Court Correspondent of the *Daily Telegraph*. She was born in Ireland and lives in Pimlico, London.

Her previous book, *The Queen*, was a bestseller and was described as:

'A brilliantly informed, witty portrait . . . reveals more vividly than ever before the Queen as a woman, as a wife, as a mother'
Daily Express

'A popular book on a popular Queen'
Sunday Telegraph

'An excellent book'
Daily Telegraph

By the same author

The Queen

ANN MORROW

The Queen Mother

PANTHER
Granada Publishing

Panther Books
Granada Publishing Ltd
8 Grafton Street, London W1X 3LA

Published by Panther Books 1985

First published in Great Britain by
Granada Publishing 1984

Copyright © Ann Morrow 1984

ISBN 0-586-06075-8

Printed and bound in Great Britain by
Collins, Glasgow

Set in Baskerville

Contents

List of Illustrations

The Queen Mother on her 80th birthday (Camera Press)
In the paddock at Cheltenham, 1981 (Keystone Press)
Greeting a bearded Prince Andrew back from the Falklands (Rex Features)
With playwright Ben Travers (Anwar Hussein)
The Queen Mother walking alone (Tim Graham)
With Lady Sarah Armstrong-Jones (Keystone Press)
After the royal wedding, 29 July 1981 (Tim Graham)
At the christening of Prince William (Syndication International)

COLOUR PLATES

The Queen and the princesses at Windsor Castle during the war (BBC Hulton Picture Library)
Fishing in New Zealand (Popperfoto)
'Around the world under the umbrella' (Anwar Hussein)
A celebration photograph of the Queen Mother on her 80th birthday (Camera Press)
Mother and daughter in St Paul's Cathedral (BBC Hulton Picture Library)
In the robes of the Order of the Garter (Tim Graham)
With the cast of *Underneath the Arches* (Photographers International)
At the Castle of Mey (J. McDonald Photographers, Wick)

Acknowledgements

The book is based on many conversations with people close to the Queen Mother, and I should like in particular to thank her Private Secretary Sir Martin Gilliat for much skilled guidance and kindness.

It is difficult to name all the people who have helped, and some of the most vital sources have requested no acknowledgement of any kind, wishing their contributions to be 'off-the-record'. I owe a debt of gratitude to Lord Wigram for access to his mother's elegant letters, and I much appreciate his trust.

My special thanks to the following for their help: Gordon Adam; Lady Elizabeth Anson; Sir Frederick Ashton; Lord Astor of Hever; Tom Barnett; Lady Elizabeth Basset; Brother Benet; Charles Bisset; Michael Bloch; Lord Boothby; Lady Bowes Lyon; Malcolm Brown; BBC; Doris Cadmay; Mrs Patrick Campbell-Preston; Sir Hugh Casson; Lord Charteris; Deirdre Cordwell; Lady Donaldson; Charles Drew; Lord Drogheda; Evelyn Elliott; Gavin Fenn-Smith; Oliver Ford; Dick Francis; Major-General G. J. Hamilton; Lord Harlech; Archbishop Bruno Heim; Bevis Hillier; Lord Home; Tom and Beatrice Hughes; M. M. Kaye; Ludovic Kennedy; Rosamond Lehmann; Martin Leslie; Virgina Letcher; Sarah Locock; Sir Douglas Logan; Dame Vera Lynn; Bette McCardle; Angus McGill; Sir Claus Moser; Nigel Nicolson; Michael Noakes; Jack O'Donoghue; Norman Parkinson; Sir Peter Pears; Sir Eric Penn; John Piper; Jane Prior; Joy Quested-Nowell; Bill Rees; Kenneth Rose; Royce Ryton; Malcolm Scott; Sir Geoffrey Shakerley; David Shepherd; Sir John Sinclair; Richard Stone; The Countess of Strathmore; William Tallon; Edda Tasiemka; Lord Thurso; Group-Captain Peter Townsend; John Tullis; Trevor Turner; Fulke Walwyn; Huw Wheldon; John Williams; Brigadier J. H. Woodroffe; Howard Wright; Sir Woodrow Wyatt; Lady Zetland.

My thanks are also due to historian Denis Judd for his helpful and entertaining comments on the manuscript; to Janice Robertson, Richard Johnson and Mike Shaw; to Anne Charvet and Marianne Taylor for their work on the manuscript and photographs; to Rita Marshall who unstintingly keyed in thousands of words on her word processor; and to Terry Keeler, *Daily Telegraph* sub-editor, for his careful checking of the finished manuscript.

Finally to G. F. S. who took the flattering photograph of me on the jacket – my thanks and much more.

1

The Heart of a Young Girl

A weekend guest at Royal Lodge, Windsor, is puzzled when he sees a woman vigorously weeding the Queen Mother's flower beds one Saturday morning. When she straightens up, he can hardly believe his eyes. It is the Queen.

'Mummy couldn't find a gardener,' she says airily as she takes off her gloves, explaining that she cannot stay long because she has a large party at the Castle for lunch.

The thought of the Queen Mother not being able to find a gardener makes everybody smile. Most able-bodied men in the county of Berkshire would gladly leave their racing or football to dig up her entire garden if that was what she wanted. 'So good of you, darling,' the Queen Mother bubbles.

Mother and daughter kiss goodbye and the Queen Mother turns back to the handful of friends standing in the main Saloon at her Windsor home, its inoffensive green walls perfectly complementing the early nineteenth-century Gothic style of the house.

The motherly figure swathed in feminine layers of lilac and blue chiffon takes off an oyster shell of a hat which had been sitting on grey curls. Lively eyes of Mediterranean blue light on you with a brightness and a readiness to be amused. There is a roundness about the softly powdered face and her mouth turns up at the edges as if she has never known a day's sulkiness or petulance in 84 years.

'Shall we go in?' The inimitable voice invites you to follow. A plumpish hand with very little jewellery and squarish pink varnished nails puts down a crystal glass of gin and Dubonnet and, with a slightly rolling walk, moves into the dining-room, a favourite corgi, Geordie, scurrying ahead.

It is a lunch of delicate pale green and pink: mousse, fresh salmon and strawberries, with white wine from a decanter shaped like a silver leaping trout and, with the cheese, claret cascading from the acorn held in a silver squirrel's paws. In the afternoon it is the Queen Mother who is longing to go for a walk, 'so refreshing', in Windsor Great Park: nothing too strenuous, just about two miles.

She has no time for class distinction; there are – for her – 'only real people'. She sabotages any attempts to make her cut down on engagements; her style is royal but warm. People lose all nervousness when they are with her, convinced that they, maybe, have been the one person who has brightened her day.

Her proper title is Queen Elizabeth, the Queen Mother – but everyone calls her the 'Queen Mum'. She is also the most loved person in Britain today. The Princess of Wales is a close second in popularity, but her appeal is ephemeral youth and a shy prettiness. The Queen Mother has a shyness still; she never wanted to be royal and still possesses an appealing diffidence as if she has been thrust to the front unexpectedly, even though it is now nearly half a century since the Abdication.

The Queen Mother has never been able to forgive Mrs Simpson, blaming her for 'blowing in from Baltimore' and stealing Edward VIII's heart so that he gave up the throne to marry her. Her husband, Bertie, the pale, withdrawn Duke of York, was catapulted on to the throne. But together, George VI and his Queen were to save the monarchy.

The King died in 1952, worn out by the war and the 'intolerable honour' of monarchy. His daughter Elizabeth, the present Queen, succeeded at the age of 26. Her mother, after a period of intense grief, came back into public life to become a Queen Mother unlike any other in history.

She has been unique and she can hardly have been impelled by any previous example. Queen Mary, whom she described as a 'sweet mother-in-law', was a prim, remote public figure and, before her, Queen Alexandra in widowhood was deaf, slightly dotty, beautiful but dithery. Kings' widows stayed quietly at their needlepoint and were brought out on the balcony at Buckingham Palace for weddings and flypasts.

What surprises people who like to see the Queen Mother as a Neapolitan ice-cream, or an eiderdown of baby blue, is to discover that under the charm there is such strength and self-control.

But, as one friend of the Queen Mother explained: 'She is a splendid old bird; there is never an iciness or sharpness, but the interesting thing is that underneath the charm there is granite – the nicest sort of granite.' The smile will never leave her face but that hint of steel, of royal apartness is one of her great attractions. She believes in the magic of monarchy and beware anyone who tries to debase it.

There is never a superfluous gesture. She has a magnetic charm which she never uses cynically. She has a zest for life like Arnold Bennett, for whom 24 hours in any day were never enough. Sir

Woodrow Wyatt says she has the heart of a young girl. One of her ladies-in-waiting, Frances Campbell-Preston, says men fall over like ninepins for her. She is a man's woman and loves to be surrounded by clever men.

'She is the epitome of style,' says Sir Roy Strong, Director of the Victoria and Albert Museum. 'The sweet thing is that the Queen Mother is totally unaware about style; she has ignored it and created her own.'

It is behaving as if laying a foundation stone were a new and exciting way of spending an afternoon. It is making rain seem fun. It is giving someone the feeling that they have shone in her company, and it is that incomparable voice, the warmth and the strength.

Her style is royal but quite informal. The artist David Shepherd, who painted her portrait for the King's Regiment, wore his jeans to work in Clarence House. When, on the last of the eight sessions, she spotted him in a dark suit she said, 'You look terribly smart, Mr Shepherd.' 'Well yes, Ma'am, I am having lunch with you today.' She held out her arms. 'You shouldn't have bothered; it's quite informal – it's only us and Princess Alice, Duchess of Gloucester.'

The Queen Mother – what is she really like? Say her name and people go 'aaah', or 'she's lovely'. 'I don't like the word lovely,' says Sir Douglas (Jock) Logan, former Principal of London University. 'She's a marvellous woman.'

It is her way of dressing, the marvellous shabbiness of Clarence House; this is all true style, confident and inviolable. It is sailing into the wrong cocktail party in a Mayfair hotel, talking animatedly to several guests: 'How nice to see you' and then being rescued by a flurried courtier. 'Wrong party, Ma'am, frightfully sorry.' A gliding exit, a little wave, 'Bye, such fun,' leaving behind a flattered host.

Her grandson, Prince Charles, put it best: 'Ever since I can remember, my grandmother has been a most wonderful example of fun, laughter and warmth and, above all, exquisite taste in so many things. For me she has always been one of those extraordinary, rare people whose touch can turn everything to gold . . . She belongs to that priceless brand of human beings whose greatest gift is to enhance life for others through her own effervescent enthusiasm for life.' He admitted he was biased.

She has all the warmth and kindness of self-indulgent people. One friend says: 'People who know how to please themselves can please other people.'

She loves good food and wine; parties; witty men; singing out loud on long walks; watching *Dad's Army* on television; trips to France, 'my little jaunts', staying with the Rothschilds; writing thank-you letters by hand; the ballet; opera by Puccini and Verdi; and going to church. She is extremely religious, but not in a pious, sanctimonious way.

Sir Huw Wheldon thinks the Queen Mother an able, clever woman. He has to admire her resistance to television appearances, although he has been the loser in this, but she hates the sound of her own voice on television and radio. Time and again, Prince Philip and Prince Charles have tried to make her change her mind and give an interview, but always at the last minute she reneges: 'I'm sorry, I really can't. I am sorry to disappoint everyone, but I can't bring myself to do this.'

She has a funny mixture of modern and old-fashioned attitudes; one never sees her at the wheel of a car or wearing trousers. But she loves helicopters and has sophisticated video equipment so that the drone of racing results is often heard at Clarence House. She was the first member of the royal family to fly round the world. The younger members of the family give her pop records and she loves to dance to some of them, but she does not understand the new pound coins and still thinks in a world of half-crowns.

She is doted on and cherished by the royal family who, young and old, value her strength and her experience. The bond between the Queen and her mother is close, and they are equally proud of each other. The Queen will tell you, 'It's extraordinary, my mother doesn't need glasses at all and here I am fifty-two, fifty-six, well whatever age I am, and can't see a thing'.

Early on in her reign, the Queen was complimented by one of her father's courtiers who thought she had done something 'frightfully well'. 'Ma'am,' he said, 'if I may say so, you did that superbly,' to which the young Queen replied: 'Yes, I did do that very well, but nowhere near as well as Mummy would have done it.'

'I always have to drive myself to do things,' the Queen Mother once said, and she has little signs on her desk, urging her 'Do It Now', which makes her performance in public even more remarkable. She has as little liking for paperwork as Prince Charles. But she is very astute. Her advisers are few, the right mixture of old-fashioned courtesy and insistent efficiency.

The Queen Mother is not a stickler for punctuality and hates to be hurried. 'It's much more important not to miss anyone than to be five minutes late.' Waiting in the Garden Room, which is full of flowers and looks out over the lawns, you hear the 'advance guard', the corgis clattering down the stairs. The Queen Mother sails in full of apologies. 'So sorry I'm late, but I've been up the road having coffee with my daughter.' This is said in a perfectly natural way.

She is very fortunate in being able to start from the premise that everyone will like her. She likes most people, but dislikes official-dom; smoked salmon; television sound booms; starting engagements before 11 A.M.; flat shoes; being helped into cars; being touched; timetables; irksome security; spectacles; snobbery; being hurried; malingerers; caviare and cats.

She loves telling people she is as strong as a horse. She eats less these days, but in spite of a serious operation in 1966, has not had a day's illness since. She shares Prince Philip's attitude: 'Never cancel an engagement. If you have a headache, take an aspirin.' Tiredness in others and 'not feeling well' both make her irritable. She herself never tires, never flags. A courtier watching her at the end of a long day said solicitously, 'Always on her feet, but enjoying it; there she goes, giving again.'

The Queen Mother, according to one of her Household, is a 'jolly good sleeper, a tiny eater and a happy person'. Some of her favourite expressions are 'such fun' and 'quite delicious'. She never raises her voice and she never needs to assert herself; she will attract attention even from the younger, more glamorous, members of the royal family.

Fundamentally, she is not a solitary person. She prefers to have company to lunch, although she loves walking on her own.

Her friends are a catholic mixture: Dame Vera Lynn, the singer; Sir John Plumb, Master of Christ's College, Cambridge; Sir Wood-row Wyatt ('She worries about my not being a believer'); the choreographer Sir Frederick Ashton; Sir Roy Strong, who says, 'She never looks back, everything is now and tomorrow'; Jim Callaghan, former Labour Prime Minister; the 65-year-old Chris-tianne Bell, widow of the Rector at Mey; Lord Home, former Conservative Prime Minister; the Cassons; the Buccleuchs; Lady Diana Cooper; the Devonshires; Lord Boothby ('such a jolly man'); and Harold Macmillan, now the Earl of Stockton, an Edwardian like herself.

She much enjoys the company of jockeys, and of all the colourful figures of the racing world. Indeed her enthusiasm for National Hunt Racing and her eagerness to turn out in mackintosh and boots on wintry days has done a great deal for the popularity of the sport.

She is not the sort of woman who dislikes other women, but she does prefer the company of men. Ludovic Kennedy once described her as being 'extremely flirty'. She is clever, not intellectual, but with a sprightly mind and very well read.

Her attitude to reading is rather different from that of the Queen, who says in her dry way, 'I have no time to read large books now, only small ones.' The Queen Mother enjoys biographies and has read everything written by P. G. Wodehouse and Dick Francis. She loved it when Lord David Cecil used to read Jane Austen to her. She was a friend of the Sitwells and likes the novels of Ada Leverson, who used to turn up at parties in exotic gold turbans and was known as 'The Sphinx' by Oscar Wilde.

Once, at a race meeting at Ascot, she and Woodrow Wyatt were giggling at lunch about the 'Sphinx's' *The Little Ottleys*. A slightly pompous senior steward who had joined them for lunch put down his binoculars and found he could not quite get into the conversation which Her Majesty was clearly enjoying so much, laughing until the tears practically ran down her cheeks. 'The Ottleys?' the steward said gruffly. 'Are they Berkshire people?' Wyatt could not contain a guffaw. They had just been talking about how awful the husband had been in the book, not unlike the blundering steward, but the Queen Mother just smiled.

She is a good mimic, of accents rather than people, but she is modest about her popularity and her humour is never cruel. Her quick wit makes her exhilarating company and her interest in people would, Woodrow Wyatt thinks, 'have made her a lively journalist'. She once said, 'I'm not as nice as you think I am' – but everybody is waiting for some confirmation of this. Her eyes will express her anger, but she will never speak sharply.

She is broad-minded and jolly and, as one of her close friends said, never a condemning person. One of her ladies-in-waiting suggested: 'I doubt very much if she would know the meaning of the word homosexual. The word "gay" retains for her the alternative *Oxford Dictionary* meanings' ('bright' and 'merry').

She is not narrow-minded, but dislikes the 'smuttier' newspapers. She does like *Yes Minister* on television and wishes they would bring back old-fashioned comedies like *All Gas and Gaiters*, with Derek Nimmo playing the pigeon-toed cleric.

The television commentator, Richard Dimbleby, no lightweight, once stumbled as he ran down the steps from the commentary box at a race meeting. As he pitched forward with his arms outstretched, he ran straight into the Queen Mother. 'But I didn't know you cared,' she said dryly, moving on to the paddock.

She is intensely patriotic and loves things sometimes for 'being so English'. Rather right-wing, she has great sympathy for poor Mr Ian Smith in that dear place she will always think of as Rhodesia. She does worry about African countries, unaccustomed to democracy, being given their independence. Prince Philip made her laugh once when he said, 'Third World, why does everyone go on about it? What I want to know is, where is the Second World?'

She once lost her temper when someone suggested that there had been bungling at Dunkirk and questioned the bravery of the men. But the anger she felt at the time of the Abdication has set like a crystal and nothing would ever break this self-control again. Riding above every crisis, she says that, like many old people, 'The only regret one has as one grows older is that things do not matter so strongly.' But she wept in front of her Household when she told them about Princess Margaret's unhappiness as the marriage with Lord Snowdon came to an end. She will cry at friends' funerals, and often, as one of her Household said, 'it is at one of those unexpected little moments, not the great fanfares of "Lest we Forget" occasions'.

The photographer Norman Parkinson, an elegant man with his Kashmiri hat and whiskers, has been taking pictures of beautiful women for years. But still, he says, whenever he gets a summons to Clarence House, 'My heart takes a leap; she is such an amazing lady.'

Franta Belsky, the sculptor, was working on a bronze of the Queen Mother for the Queen Elizabeth Hospital in Birmingham. He tells how he left his studio in Kensington one day and went to South London to finish the cast in a bronze foundry. As he worked in the large workshop near the Oval, he remembers: 'At one point, a workman came in, somewhere behind me, and let go a terrific flow of swearing at the bosses. I noticed the abrupt interruption and silence, then I heard steps coming closer and a voice behind me: "Sorry, sir, I didn't realize you were working on Her Majesty."'

2

The Clubs Are in Gloom

At 21, Lady Elizabeth Bowes-Lyon looked adorable. Her hair was cut in a fashionable fringe, which later disappeared because her husband did not like it. 'Bertie likes me in fluffy frocks,' she explained, which is why, 60 years later, we still see her in the sort of clothes he appreciated when they were married in the twenties.

Of course, she followed fashion. Sir Frederick Ashton remembers meeting her shortly after she became Duchess of York. 'She was absolutely ravishing in brown velvet,' he said, 'wearing one of those hats with brushes . . . But I remember, too, that she was rather reserved.' Long-bodiced tea dresses were 'becoming' on her, always in dusty pastel shades. Looking back at the twenties, the Queen Mother says, 'funny, seeing one's clothes . . . funny hats . . . rather marvellous.'

In those flamboyant days, the Marquese de Casa Maury took tea at the Ritz wearing wistaria on her hat, and, when she married, she was dressed as a nun; Lady Ottoline Morrell dyed her hair purple; another extrovert beauty dressed for parties in black and was always followed by a turbaned, black manservant. In all this dedication to the outrageous Lady Elizabeth Bowes-Lyon was considered a beauty without any effort at all.

She moved with a grace that was perfect for slinky twenties' clothes; her manners were appealing and she was without snobbery. She was lively; never arch or coyly flirtatious. The Countess of Airlie thought her 'very unlike the cocktail-drinking, chain-smoking girls who came to be regarded as typical of the 1920s'. Her radiant vitality, she said, 'and a blending of gaiety, kindness and sincerity made her irresistible to men'.

Her life was divided between Glamis – 'so perfect here' – where she acted as hostess for her father, Lord Strathmore, after her mother became unwell, and The Bury, the family house in Hertfordshire built of soft red brick – 'so perfect here, too'. There were race meetings at Ascot and Goodwood; she wore white lace and broke more hearts. There were tennis parties and dances and fast motorcars.

When Queen Mary called at Glamis with her daughter, Princess

Mary, she noticed immediately what 'a well brought up' girl Elizabeth was, as she watched her pouring the tea and passing hot buttered scones and homemade strawberry jam.

Guiding was the common interest between the two girls. In personality they could hardly have been more different, one bubbling, the other earnest. But a friendship blossomed.

Even Queen Mary found her only daughter a bit bleak at times. 'My dear child, why can't you knit yourself a pretty jumper? Clothes are so expensive and a pretty jumper would be most becoming,' she once said as she watched Princess Mary knitting what could only be described as a 'particularly hideous sweater'.

But the King and Queen showered gifts on her: a pair of blond tortoiseshell and diamond hairpins, or an ermine muff. The boys were always given silver, so that, when they married, they would be 'suitably equipped'. It was mildly hilarious at Christmas to see the Princes, Henry and George 'staggering off with silver toast racks, salvers and tea strainers'. Later the more careful friends of the royal brothers were to scour their wedding lists for these little tokens, but, as a result of this comic thrift on the part of George V and his Queen, were obliged to choose a simple piece of Chippendale or a gold cigarette case. When Elizabeth Bowes-Lyon married, in 1923, at the age of 22, friends were advised that because of the post-war austerity there should be no expensive fur gifts, please – only squirrel or 'lapin', as they liked to call the humble rabbit.

While Princess Mary and Elizabeth Bowes-Lyon chatted about the Girl Guides, Queen Mary was astutely assessing her daughter's new friend. She liked Elizabeth's sparkle; her attitudes were right, though she was far from prim. Her second son, Prince Albert Frederick Arthur George, known as Bertie to the family, had been staying with the Airlies and had been invited with them to Glamis.

They had occasionally been at the same children's parties but really met at a London dance. It was the start of a diffident courtship. But Queen Mary already knew that Elizabeth was 'the one girl who could make Bertie happy', although she protested all through her son's romance that 'mothers should never meddle in their children's love affairs.'

George V had been secretly dreading his sons' wives, imagining they would lounge about on the priceless French furniture, smoking cigarettes through long holders, drinking cocktails, and being 'rather fast' – quite unlike his 'darling May'.

At 27, Bertie was striking, slim and lithe, the best athlete in the family. Group Captain Peter Townsend, who became his equerry later, recalls him as a marvellous looking man, with not a spare bit of flesh to be seen when he was in swiming trunks. Contemporaries agree that he was good looking but shy.

Having overcome every obstacle in the Navy he had joined the Royal Naval Air Service and became a Squadron Leader. He was a superb tennis player and was to win the RAF doubles at Wimbledon with Louis Greig. During a spell at Cambridge he had read political economy, civics and history and stayed, with his older brother David, in a house run by the Greigs. He rode a motorbike and one day asked a gardener not to keep calling him 'Your Royal Highness' all the time. 'Once a day is enough,' the young prince said, putting his foot down on the accelerator.

In 1920, Bertie, discovering girlfriends rather late in life, was amused by Grace Vanderbilt, daughter of the American hostess Mrs Cornelius Vanderbilt. The romance was not to last, for that same year he went to the RAF summer ball at the Ritz and saw a remarkably pretty girl dancing with his equerry, 23-year-old James Stuart, MC, son of the Earl of Moray. The next dance saw the Duke of York whirling Elizabeth Bowes-Lyon round the ballroom, both still smiling at his quick response to the 'Take your partners, please'.

When he fell in love with Elizabeth that evening Bertie was about to face one of the more tantalizing challenges in his life. In the war he had proved himself courageous and determined, but this peace-time manoeuvre would be more demanding than anything he had ever tackled.

That autumn Elizabeth showed him round Glamis Castle. He thought it was marvellous: she made him laugh and he was so relaxed that he hardly stuttered at all. He told her about his plans for underprivileged young people, a scheme which he was later to put into action.

In 1920 George V made Bertie Duke of York. His father considered he had earned this, the oldest Dukedom in the country. 'I feel this splendid old title will be safe in your hands,' he wrote, 'and that you will never do anything to tarnish it. I hope you will always look upon me as your best friend and always tell me everything. Your very devoted Papa'.

Rather impetuously, Bertie did tell his father about his plan to propose to Lady Elizabeth Bowes-Lyon. He had been even more captivated by her when he went to a dance at Glamis, at which she wore 'a rose brocade Vandyck dress with pearls in her hair'. The

King, in his usual outspoken way, blurted out, 'You'll be a lucky fellow if she accepts you,' rather undermining his son's confidence. The King was right. It was terrible for Bertie.

Lady Elizabeth, like Lady Diana Spencer many years later, had a pristine background. There was not a hint of scandal about her and she would have been a most acceptable daughter-in-law to the royal family. The only trouble was that, although she was the perfect choice in every way, she refused Bertie's proposals. Other eligible young men in London were mad about her, but she turned them down, too.

Bertie persisted. His mother kept her 'intent, questioning gaze' on Elizabeth when she visited the Palace to see her daughter. Nobody was quite sure why she had rejected two proposals of marriage from the Duke. But joining the royal family could be a thoroughly daunting prospect, even for someone as socially burnished as this Bowes-Lyon girl.

From an early age, Lady Elizabeth had enormous presence. She was taught the 'no looking down' technique by her mother, which to this day carries her into banquets, down the steps of St Paul's Cathedral or into Town Halls in long evening dresses. Her mother also insisted upon economy of movement and advised her 'never to use a superfluous gesture'. It is terribly gauche in royal circles to look down at your feet, and a sin to look back when sitting down. Those bred to the purple know that there is always a chair for them – those who are not are uncertain.

But the prospect of a lifetime of public spotlight appalled Elizabeth, although there was no thought at the time that Bertie would succeed to the throne; but clearly Prince Albert already saw in her an ideal wife who would never let him down.

Today, the Queen Mother does not care to be reminded of her reluctance to marry the man she loved. Dismay at the thought of royal life made her hesitate. In retrospect, there is sadness for the lost year they might have spent together had they married when Bertie first proposed.

There were other reasons too for her reluctance to marry the King's son. It is easy to see how a young girl's heart might not leap at the thought of Queen Mary as a mother-in-law, even though, once the Queen assured herself that the girl 'knew how to behave', she proved very kind. Queen Mary, like all the royal family, believed in a God-given destiny which made them different. She would talk about 'dear so-and-so' if it was family; anyone else was 'poor so-and-so' – aristocrat or commoner.

She could be terrifying and to meet her was to walk a tightrope. But she disliked sycophancy. An encouraging scene took place one evening at Windsor, and is described by a woman whom Queen Mary later liked and respected. Nora, wife of Lord Wigram, who was Private Secretary to George V, did well at an early encounter and was acquitted, as she later recalled:

After dinner, the King, of course, went out first and he walked straight into a further smoking room. The Queen sat down at once so it was quite restful. She produced some pink crochet work, so all the ladies fled for their horrid little bits of work. The Queen asked me if I never worked. So I said I simply hated working and was very bad at it, so she said it was quite refreshing to meet an honest woman. Then, when the King came in again, she said, 'Mrs Wigram is an honest woman. She says that working bores her to death. She is so wise not to do it.' She came and had a little talk to me ... I can't understand the people who think the Queen stiff. She was quite charming ... The little princess looked shy herself. She has a gruff manner, but is quite simple and unaffected, with a beautiful skin. [Which would not have been a bad description of her great-niece, Princess Anne.]

Everyone was relieved when 'the little princess' Mary became engaged to the suitable and unexcitable 6th Earl of Harewood. They were married on 28 February 1922 and later had two sons, the eldest being the musical Earl of Harewood whose first wife was Marion Stein, the concert pianist now married to the former liberal Leader, Jeremy Thorpe.

At the Harewood wedding the love match between the King's second son, Prince Albert, and Lady Elizabeth Bowes-Lyon, 'very lovely in a white and silver dress', was there for all to see. Yet by a curious irony, Lady Elizabeth was one of the bridesmaids for whom the artist, Frank Salisbury, could find no room when he painted the wedding group.

Chips Channon, the American social commentator, diarist and Tory MP — himself a little in love with Elizabeth and 'her curious sideways lilting walk', which is even more pronounced now — was at Glamis one rainy afternoon in 1922. The house guests, including the Duke of York, were playing cards. Channon pretended to read the cards intently and predicted 'a great and glamorous royal future for Lady Elizabeth'. It made her laugh, but only reminded the other guests, as they went off to change for dinner, how much the Duke was in love with her.

According to his mother, Bertie was 'always talking about Elizabeth'. The couple often called on Lady Airlie, a comforting woman who could give subtle advice. Sometimes she saw Elizabeth on her own, confused and abstracted. Lady Strathmore, with astute motherly eye, thought she had never seen her normally carefree daughter so withdrawn and 'really worried'. She felt, all during that winter of 1922, that Elizabeth was 'torn between her longing to make Bertie happy and her reluctance to take on the big responsibilities which this marriage must bring . . .'

You cannot have a lot of brothers and not be teased. One of the six Strathmore boys told the family: 'Courtings are as old as the hills, and just as obvious,' as his sister, in a tweed suit, long Fair Isle scarf and snug hat, set out for yet another walk with the Duke of York in his tweeds. He was genuinely interested in gardening, but this was ridiculous!

Even in January, The Bury is romantic and, walking in that 'enchanted wood' in 1923, the Duke of York proposed again. He was accepted, all misgivings gone. 'Oh, Bertie, yes,' she answered. Not feeling the cold at all, she put her hand in his and they walked back to the house.

On 13 January 1923, a Saturday, he sent his parents a rather economically worded telegram: 'All right, Bertie'. But this had been a pre-arranged code. When he arrived home at Sandringham after the weekend, Queen Mary thought she had never seen her son look so happy. 'We are delighted,' she wrote in her diary. 'He looks beaming.' And well he might for, according to Chips Channon, 'There is not a man in England today that doesn't envy him. The clubs are in gloom.'

Long before she had been given her ring, a large Kashmir sapphire and two diamonds, Elizabeth was skittishly telling friends that she feared their secret was out. 'The cat is now completely out of the bag and there is no possibility of stuffing him back,' she wrote. In the Strathmore family's new London home at 17 Bruton Street – an Adam house off Berkeley Square in Mayfair since rebuilt as the Lombard North Central Bank – Elizabeth was 'very happy, but quite dazed'. The engagement was announced in the Court Circular on Tuesday, 16 January.

Her only slip from the King's favour was when she innocently gave an interview to an enterprising reporter. Mr Cozens-Hardy from the *Star*, a popular evening newspaper – rather different from its earthy namesake, today's *Daily Star* – called at the house and was invited into the breakfast room.

Lady Strathmore had been anxious to help, but her daughter said firmly: 'Mother, leave this gentleman to me.' The reporter felt the elation of a scoop.

'Is it true that the Duke proposed three times?' he asked. Lady Elizabeth replied: 'Now, look at me, do you think I am the sort of person Bertie would have to ask twice?' When the King picked up the newspaper at Sandringham there were rumblings as loud as an elephant digesting fig leaves.

There would be no more interviews with the press: a rule the royal family has stuck to fairly rigidly ever since. There are photocalls of the young when they get engaged; Prince Philip will bark on about his favourite causes, like the preservation of wildlife or the need to control world population. And Prince Charles and Princess Anne have, in recent years, given the occasional interview. But the royal mistrust of these occasions has persisted. The Queen was rather appalled at the course of one television interview given by her daughter and Captain Mark Phillips. When her oldest son became engaged, the BBC and ITV arranged for the Prince of Wales to appear with Lady Diana Spencer on the lawn close to the back of Buckingham Palace. The Queen was seen peeping out at them uneasily from behind a curtain.

On Saturday, 20 January 1923, Elizabeth and Bertie went to Sandringham for a meeting with the King and Queen. As they left Bruton Street Lady Elizabeth, a fur wrapped round her throat, looked slightly apprehensive. The Duke, wearing a Homburg hat, hurried her into the waiting car. At Liverpool Street station, they were ushered into a special carriage attached to the 11.50 train to Norfolk. They were in Sandringham in time for lunch.

That meeting between the King Emperor and the spirited girl was to be the start of a tender and enduring bond between the two. In the King she found a wise friend. He was fun – even if his children thought him a martinet. He is alleged to have said: 'My father was frightened of his mother, I was frightened of my father and I am damned well going to see to it that my children are frightened of me.' But he did not scare Elizabeth, however much he boomed at his sons. They quivered with fear. The King upbraided David (later to become Edward VIII) for wearing fashionable turn-ups: 'Is it raining in *here*?' the King thundered, but it was hard not to laugh. He had his endearing ways. He would bring his parrot, Charlotte, to the table, much though Queen Mary disapproved. But his children were so nervous of him that they did not understand his humour until much later on.

The King often played games on the family when they were larking around after dinner. Sometimes they threw bread rolls at each other; sometimes they danced. The King would mischievously slot the National Anthem in the middle of some Charleston, the joke being how long it would take everyone to twig and be stunned into automatic stillness . . . But these were the lighter moments. He was a stickler for correct behaviour, obsessional about dress and the solemnity of monarchy, reminding his sons: 'We sailors never smile on duty . . .'

His future daughter-in-law passed all the tests. She made him laugh and he was thrilled with her. 'She is a pretty and charming girl. Bertie is a very lucky fellow.' He sounded surprised that the hesitant Bertie should have found such a winner.

Sir Eric Penn, a most experienced courtier and part of the Queen's Household until he retired in 1980, said that the King 'adored her'. A simple enough statement, but nobody in royal circles ever underestimates the achievement.

Not all that easy going today, then the royal household was intimidating. But Elizabeth Bowes-Lyon matched up to those impeccably high standards with 'her incomparable voice and manner'. She was, Sir Eric said, 'an absolute angel with that extraordinary magnetic charm'.

Queen Mary was delighted. She had always known that Bertie's choice was perfect for him – but almost as important – it was perfect for the family too. 'Elizabeth is charming, so pretty and engaging and natural – a great addition to the family.'

It was a relaxed time of the year at Sandringham, the men out shooting and Queen Mary carrying out a few engagements. If her future daughter-in-law could only have been a fly on the wall at the Sandringham Women's Institute she would have seen her daunting mother-in-law-to-be letting her hair down:

She was at a little table pouring out tea, then the room was cleared and they all played games, the Queen sitting down to 'Happy Families' with three old ladies. 'Please, Your Majesty, is Mr Bun the Baker at home?' This was varied by a prolonged game of musical chairs . . . if you could have seen H M rushing round . . . then Sir Roger de Courcy [*sic*] was danced. Meanwhile Queen Alexandra [the Queen Mother], Queen Maud of Norway and Princess Victoria had joined the party. Queen Maud got so elated by the proceedings that she jumped high in the air, with the result that the contents of her pockets flew in all directions, powder puffs, peppermints . . .

The royal tradition at the Women's Institute has been longstanding and, rather endearingly, the Queen Mother refuses to give up the presidency of the Sandringham branch which she inherited from Queen Mary. The Queen should be president now, but would never take away one of her mother's pleasures in life.

As the royal family do not care for long engagements, the wedding between Elizabeth and Bertie was fixed for Thursday, 26 April 1923, in Westminster Abbey. It was to be the first wedding of a king's son in the Abbey since 1382, when Richard II married Anne of Bohemia.

Elizabeth knew exactly what she wanted and designed the wedding dress herself. The discreet couturiers, Handley Seymour, made her a dress of medieval delicacy and decorum. There was a panel of silver lace from the neck to the hem, down the centre. The neck was square and the sleeves of Nottingham lace billowed as she put her hands to her throat in that familiar gesture. There was nothing flashy about the dress, and typically, it was a local woman who had worked for years sewing and mending for the vast family of Strathmores who was invited to help with the trousseau and the bridesmaids' dresses, too. Queen Mary insisted that 'darling Elizabeth' should have a train of Flanders lace, *point de Flandres*, which she had unearthed for her. There were six bridesmaids in white and green with silver shoes. Two nieces were train bearers: Elizabeth Elphinstone, daughter of sister Mary; and Cecilia Bowes-Lyon, daughter of brother Patrick. They wore white satin slippers.

The bride left Bruton Street at 11.12 A.M. on the arm of her father, the Earl of Strathmore, looking splendid in his scarlet uniform of Lord Lieutenant of Forfar. They rode at a stately pace in an open state landau escorted by mounted police.

It was a drizzling, grey morning as the Duke of York, solemn in his RAF uniform, with his supporters, David Prince of Wales and Prince Henry, set out in the Glass Coach at 11.13 A.M. As she entered the Abbey, the bride, slight and decorative, impulsively paused to lay her white bouquet, roses of York and heather from Scotland, upon the Tomb of the Unknown Soldier.

Once the wedding service began, the crowds had to content themselves with trying to keep warm outside and counting the silver bell decorations. On no account would the Abbey Chapter allow the wedding ceremony to be broadcast, although Buckingham Palace and the Dean had agreed that it could be. The fear was simply that unsuitable people might tune in: 'People might hear it while sitting in public houses, or with their hats on.' How different from the warm summer day of 19 July 1981, when millions in tee-shirts heard and saw the royal wedding in St Paul's.

The bride moved to the altar like a small Botticelli figure as the choir sang 'Lead us, Heavenly Father . . .' The guests could smell the scent of the white flowers in the bridesmaids' hair. The Archbishop of Canterbury, Cosmo Lang, read the wedding service. The Archbishop of York praised the couple: the groom for his commitment to the 'working people' and his bringing together of boys from the workshop and the public school in 'free and frank companionship'. This had been something Bertie had often talked to Elizabeth about in their early courting days, when both young people, matured by the war, had wanted to help the less privileged. One of the results had been the Duke of York's Boys Camps. The bride, her dark hair in little pressed waves, smiled slightly through her veil when the guests in the Abbey heard how 'very fitted' she was for her place in the people's life. The Archbishop of York's words were to be more apt than he knew.

When the bride was signing the register, Queen Alexandra – always a chatterbox – leant across to have a word with Queen Mary. Beneath the two regal matriarchs were the two terrified train bearers. They had been warned to follow the bride everywhere, but were now immobilized and almost smothered by this crescent of furs, Garters and diamonds. The Hon. Elizabeth Elphinstone remembers the moment vividly more than 60 years later. 'What were two shy little gels to do?' Fortunately, by the time the bride moved forward, her mother-in-law and Queen Alexandra had exchanged their confidences and parted.

On the way back to the Palace in the Glass Coach, the smiling stopped as the Duke and his bride paused at the Cenotaph. This girl, no longer a commoner, had become the fourth lady in the land, after the Queen, George V's sister the Princess Royal and Princess Mary. She was now Her Royal Highness.

When her husband became King, she would be the first truly British Queen Consort for centuries, without a recent drop of European blood. This did not seem important at the time of the wedding, but when the monarchy faced the crisis of the Abdication and the anathema of the Prince of Wales's interest in Nazi Germany, it became a reassuring, unmentioned, bonus. The Queen Consort is not a Constitutional Queen but is crowned alongside her husband. Before Elizabeth Bowes-Lyon the last Queen Consort with a British father was Elizabeth, daughter of Edward IV and wife of Henry VII – 450 years ago.

Once outside the Abbey, the Duke and Duchess of York showed a great sense of relief: the pageantry over and the pleasant surprise of seeing ordinary people in ordinary clothes – no robes, mitres or tiaras – and a great sound of cheering. In the Glass Coach, the new Duchess of York waved her open palm up and down, as if sand was slipping through her fingers, in that early wave of hers before she changed to the enveloping style she cultivated as Queen.

'There was a sea of waving handkerchiefs . . . everyone was so happy,' was all the bride remembered of her first time on the famous balcony at Buckingham Palace. It was chilly, and it was Queen Mary who gently wrapped a shawl round Elizabeth's shoulders.

When the royal party went inside for a staggering wedding breakfast, the menus, in scarlet and gold, were engraved with the King's cipher above and the crests of the couple below. There were eight courses: Consommé à la Windsor; Suprêmes de saumon Reine Mary; Côtelettes d'agneau Prince Albert; Chapons à la Strathmore; Jambon et langues découpées à l'aspic; salade royale; asparagus et crème mousseuse sauce; Duchess Elizabeth strawberries; pâtisseries in spun sugar baskets, and bowls of grapes. For such a vast amount of food, the guests ate remarkably rapidly – and were ready to wave the couple off after 90 minutes. The wedding cake, nine feet high and weighing 800 pounds, had been baked by McVitie and Price in Edinburgh. The couple had been there a month before their wedding and arranged that the cake should be filled with gold charms.

Typically, their wedding cake was shared. So while blue-blooded lips barely nibbled their portions, 100,000 underprivileged children round the country enjoyed the same cake and drank the couple's health in fizzy lemonade through straws.

The King and Queen did the newly-weds handsomely, even though the occasion may have lacked the informality of Prince Charles's wedding breakfast in the ballroom at Buckingham Palace, when his brothers, Prince Andrew and Prince Edward, whirled rattles and announced each guest: 'One Earl-in-Waiting; One King of Norway' – enter the jolly King Olaf.

In the formal wedding pictures Lady Strathmore, the bride's mother, looking feathery and soft, seemed the only one daring enough to smile in public. One could never be 'too earnest' was Queen Victoria's maxim. What on earth would she have made of the

Prince and Princess of Wales's wedding picture, with bride and groom and bridesmaids falling against one another with laughter as the royal snapper, Patrick Lichfield, told a funny story to make them relax.

When the couple left for the honeymoon, the bride had changed into a long-waisted, soft mushroom coloured dress, with a string of beads and a close-fitting hat. There was the hint of a pussy-cat smile as she looked over her shoulder and a flirty wave at the guest who threw a shoe at the open landau. The swoop of feathers on the back of her hat bobbed as she turned to the right, but more often to the left to say something to her husband, as they laughed and enjoyed the drive to Waterloo Station. The Prince of Wales saw them off – and then they were alone.

The special carriage was so full of white carnations, lilies of the valley and white roses that there was scarcely any room for the honeymooners. The journey to Bookham in Surrey took 35 minutes and there were people cheering along every bit of track. At Bookham Station the locals even managed an address of welcome.

It is a tradition of the royal family to spend the honeymoon in the countryside at the pleasant house of a friend. The Queen, and later her son Prince Charles, chose 'Broadlands', a warm dreamy house by the River Test in Hampshire, home of the late Earl Mountbatten. The Duke and Duchess of York selected Mrs Ronnie Greville's Regency home, Polesden Lacey, set in pines and overlooking mossy green lawns in the Surrey hills.

Prince Charles and his bride were able to enjoy a re-run of their wedding on television. The Duke and Duchess of York had only the excitement of the 'wireless receiver', specially installed. The newly-weds relaxed in wickerwork chairs or strolled in the grounds where the crocuses were just opening, or did a little leisurely putting with golf clubs on the lawn. Thank-you letters were sent off quickly, a courteous practice which has not been lost. (People were amazed to receive letters from the Princess of Wales at Broadlands, dated 30 July 1981 – the day after her wedding – thanking them for some small kindness.)

The Duke of York had also written instantly to his mother: 'I do hope you will not miss me very much – though I believe you will, as I have stayed with you so much longer really than my brothers.' But he was the first to marry.

The couple then moved to Glamis where the Countess of Strathmore had created a special and romantic trio of rooms for them.

There was a sitting-room of charm, with latticed windows, blue and white Delft tiles set in the carved chimney, squashy pale yellow sofas and a white runner on the back of one with the embroidered words, 'where friends meet'. At the end of a spring afternoon walk through the woods and shrubberies around the Castle, nowhere was more cosy than this sitting-room: the coral curtains drawn, tea brought in and the light of the fire on the Chinese porcelain figures.

The bedroom was in gentle colours. The four-poster bed, with fluted columns and gilt woodwork, had the remarkable embroidery of Lady Strathmore, with the names of all her children hanging in nine bubbles in rainbow-coloured stitching below the richly pleated creamy satin canopy. Typical of the times, and of a draughty castle, there was only a jug and bowl and, of course, a chamber pot decorated with ornamental roses. There was a small dressing-room for the Duke of York looking out over some of the turrets and a little bit spooky. These rooms are still so lovingly kept that you feel the couple might walk in at any moment.

The excitement and her resistance to warm heavy clothes, which has persisted until today, combined to give the Duchess a bad bout of whooping cough. The Duke was solicitous, but he thought it was 'not very romantic'.

Elizabeth, propped up against pillows in the four-poster bed, had a chance to read all the letters in the spring sunshine. The King, who liked to hide his emotions, had written to his son:

Dearest Bertie, You are indeed a lucky man to have such a charming and delightful wife as Elizabeth and I am sure you will both be very happy together. I trust you both will have many, many years of happiness before you, and that you will be as happy as Mama and I are after you have been married for 30 years. I can't wish you more . . . Ever, my dear boy, your most devoted Papa, G. R.

The King had given Bertie's bride an ermine fur coat as a wedding present. The young Duchess of York, in turn, was to give the royal family a gift beyond value.

3

Responsive as a Harp

The day Princess Margaret was born in Glamis Castle, parlourmaid Janet Fox remembers that it was so hot the road had melted as she cycled into Forfar during a thunderstorm. Like the other villagers, she knew that the Duchess of York had come back to her family home in Scotland for the birth of her second child, on 21 August 1930.

In that part of Scotland they think of Queen Elizabeth, the Queen Mother, as a Scottish princess and of her marriage to a King as only fitting for a direct descendant of their King Robert II. When the Duke of York's engagement was announced, disgruntled dowagers had wondered why their daughters, who had worked so hard to catch the royal eye, had been pipped by the gentle girl from Forfar. They may have been attractive but she had a sweetness which was not cloying, with a spirit shaped by Scottish good sense and a remarkable mother.

To this day, Glamis has a compelling charm for the Queen Mother. The Queen, Princess Margaret, Prince Charles and Prince Andrew will often drive over for lunch from Balmoral. On those days the old retainers are rustled up to help in the kitchen and dining-room and to make sure the cushions are plumped in the pink and pale gold drawing-room. The miniature of the Queen Mother's grandmother – white curls and rosy cheeks in a gold frame – is dusted, as are the de Laszlo paintings of the Earl and Countess of Strathmore and Kinghorn. Their daughter did not inherit her parents' angular bone structure.

Her soft, rounder features are more flattering in old age and quite unlike those of her own mother, who looked a little stern and long-faced in later years: a misleading impression of this warm woman who taught her children that nobody in life, rich or poor, is boring. 'If you find somebody or something a bore the fault lies in you . . .' To this day, if she is being told by a slow-speaking Lord Mayor how many tons of cement went into the making of a flyover her look will betray only rapt fascination. 'Oh, really, how hard it must have been for the lorry drivers to cope,' or some similarly soothing remark will make everybody in the group feel it has all been quite riveting for her.

Janet Fox, now a spry 73-year-old, still works for the Queen Mother's family. The present Countess of Strathmore, the Queen

Mother's niece by marriage, says she is the best parlourmaid she has ever known. Janet has not much time for flowery compliments as she hurries home through the village at Glamis to light the fire in her tiny cottage. Smoke curls up from the chimney as her wiry back stoops over the twigs. 'Aye, my mother used to work at the Castle – doing cleaning when the pay was six old pence an hour. That was when Bobo was a young nursery maid.' 'Bobo', Miss Margaret MacDonald, is a legend amongst the castle staff since she went to London, where she has been the Queen's personal maid for some fifty years.

The village of Glamis is still fairly feudal. Mrs Mary Simpson, the elderly widow of the foreman forester, nearly died of fright and thought she would be evicted if she spoke to the 'nice girl from the BBC' who was sent to do research for a television programme. The choice of researcher was a cunning one; Lady Jane Wellesley, daughter of the Duke of Wellington and once a girlfriend of Prince Charles, was sent to chat up the ageing tenants.

Bert Tosh, Hogg the tailor, and Frank McNicol, the wood carver, never thought of the Queen Mother as anybody but 'our Lady Elizabeth'. Their children live in the same flinty spare ways of their parents and grandparents before the beginning of the century. They are proud that their village produced a Queen – but not surprised. After all, 'their' family of Glamis is descended from the first of Scotland's Stewart Kings, Robert II, whose daughter Princess Joanna married Sir John Lyon of Glamis in the fourteenth century.

The Queen Mother was born in London on a Bank Holiday Saturday, 4 August 1900, the ninth child of Lord Glamis, 45 years old and a countryman at heart. He was a gentle soul with a droopy moustache and a weakness for a Scottish version of plum pudding. 'Shooting pudding' was something he would willingly dip his whiskers into every day, he was so partial to the heavy mix.

The voice more often heard was that of his wife, the spirited Cecilia, who would come striding into the village in her swishing skirts and high-necked decorative lace blouses, asking, 'Anyone seen those little rascals?' Lady Elizabeth and her brother, David, were usually 'hiding in the smithy' or buying 'striped balls', bullseyes, in the 'sweetie shop'.

'Cecilia,' a member of the Bowes-Lyon family said, 'definitely wore the trousers'. Christened Nina Cecilia, she was the daughter of the Reverend Charles Cavendish-Bentinck and the great-granddaughter of the third Duke of Portland, who was twice Prime Minister and a distinguished Home Secretary under Pitt. The Queen Mother escaped the prominent Bentinck nose and was described as a 'bundle of prettiness' when only a few weeks old. She reminded her father, not usually an effusive man, of nothing so much as a small angel. His youngest daughter lacked that pink squashed baby look and her arrival had made up for the disruption of his weekend. A Saturday and Sunday in London for most aristocrats was unthinkable. Once the good reason for his presence in town arrived, Lord Glamis raced away from his town house, 20 St James's Square, to the family home at St Paul's Walden Bury in Hertfordshire. 'St Paul's' because the land once belonged to the Chapter of the cathedral in the City of London, 'Walden' for the woods that the Queen Mother came to love so much.

His wife and baby followed in the next few days to the mellow red Queen Anne house covered with ivy that to the family was always 'The Bury' and to the Queen Mother that 'dear, friendly old house; we all loved it dearly.' The other children were waiting to see the baby, with sisters Rose, aged 10, and Mary, 17, the first allowed near the cot. The last of the family, David, was born two years later, on 2 May 1902. He was like a twin to his sister Elizabeth. They chased each other round the beech trees. 'Buffy, Buffy, wait for me.' He could never get his tongue around his sister's name so Elizabeth became 'Elizabuff' and he was always to call her 'Buffy'.

Elizabeth's christening was on 23 September 1900 in the small, pretty twelfth-century village church on a hill near the house. The vicar, Tristram Henry Valentine, called out her names, 'Elizabeth Angela Marguerite', in his best oratorical Sunday voice as he poured the water on the baby's head. In Balmoral, old Queen Victoria was enjoying one of her last carriage rides in the Highlands. When she died the following January, 1901, her great-grandson 'Bertie', later the Duke of York, was four years old and being so intimidated by a succession of nannies that he developed digestion problems and a stutter.

As the early autumn light brightened the medieval window and the colours shone on the robes of the fourteenth-century Virgin and Child, there was a conspiracy of silence between the baby's father, possibly the vicar and a few close family friends.

For some quirky reason Lord Glamis had registered the baby's birth as taking place at the St Paul's Walden Bury house and not in London. This harmless but inexplicable deception only came to light during the Queen Mother's 80th birthday celebrations. A beady-eyed parishioner threw the organizers of the local festivities into a tizzy by asking why they were not making more of the fact that the plaque in the church said the Queen Mother was born in the parish. Surely this pleasant piece of history could only enhance the village? Nobody could quite explain Lord Glamis's little lapse. The Queen Mother has always had the reticence of her generation about anything remotely connected with matters of health or intimate details of any sort, even about a tooth extraction. Her household at Clarence House echoes this Victorian sensibility: 'It doesn't matter where she was born or if there were inaccuracies.' Possibly the family was leaving London for St Paul's Walden Bury when the baby started to arrive. The only person who could explain the discrepancy is the Queen Mother, but for her the subject is a closed book, like the Abdication. Nevertheless, she was born in London.

To this day, in the cherished church with its tapestry kneelers in blues and greens with doves and harvest festival fruit, there is a stone plaque which says in bold letters that the Queen Mother was 'born in this Parish August 4 1900 . . . and here worshipped'. Nobody is arguing about the worshipping, for it was after all the family's church and Lady Glamis was keen that the children should be devout. This is where the eldest child, a wistfully pretty creature called Violet Hyacinth, is buried, with a tablet marking her death in 1893 at the age of 11 from the old-fashioned killer, diphtheria. The grieving Countess, who had just had another baby, later christened Michael, designed two cherubs holding a wreath for Violet which rests over the pale green and cream rosebud carvings of the chancel.

Until Lord Glamis inherited his father's title in 1904 the warm house in Hertfordshire which came to the Lyon family with their Bowes ancestors in 1767 was the family home. The house and the unhappiness of the widow of the 9th Earl of Strathmore who made a disastrous second marriage is said to be the inspiration for Thackeray's *Barry Lyndon*. The Bury always smelled of polish, of fresh flowers and pot-pourri. The Adam ceilings were picked out in blue, white and yellow; in the hall there was a bunch of edible-looking carved bananas, attached to some ruby damask drapes.

The Queen Mother's brother David, a man 'of great charm', lived there until his death at the age of 59 in 1961. He married Rachel Spender-Clay, a niece of Lord Astor and a girl who looked uncannily like his sister. She remembers today being a little nervous when she met that huge Bowes-Lyon family for the first time; but the old Countess cast her eye over her with a brisk cheerfulness. Apart from the three sisters, David had five older brothers: Patrick born in 1884; John Herbert in 1886; Alexander Francis, 1887; Fergus, 1889; and Michael, 1893. Rachel first met Lady Elizabeth 'at the Café de Paris, somewhere in Piccadilly, I think.'

Now an elderly widow, Lady Bowes-Lyon has on her desk a favourite, yellowing photograph of her late husband, David, who was Lord Lieutenant of Hertfordshire, with his sister Elizabeth. They were aged about three and five and dressed in smocks like the cherubs in *The Magic Flute*.

'David and Elizabeth were thrown together because they were so close in age. You see them looking angelic here, but actually David was trying to wrestle with his sister to get back his favourite toy, a small wheelbarrow, and she was not letting go.'

'They are my two Benjamins', Lady Glamis would say, relishing the biblical reference to the youngest of Jacob's twelve sons.

Earliest descriptions of the youngest daughter of the family, Elizabeth, were of a baby with lots of dark hair and big blue eyes. Her pram, which has been given to a museum in Hitchin, used to be pushed round the rose gardens by a local girl. A gawky, willing creature, named Clara Knight, one of twelve children from the village of Whitwell, she became the much loved nursemaid, 'Alla'. She devoted her life to babies of distinction and achieved the final honour of buttoning the shoes and straightening the white ankle socks of the Princesses Elizabeth and Margaret. In the nursery at The Bury, with its brass fender, coal fire, scrap book screens and the smell of toasting bread Elizabeth, Alla reported, was 'an easy, happy baby, running at thirteen months and speaking very young'.

When Lady Elizabeth was still a small child, the factor – or land agent – at Glamis was asked by the small creature: 'How do you do, Mr Ralston? I haven't seen you look so well, not for years and years.' He tried to keep a straight face and was given a gloomy bulletin. 'I am sure you will be sorry to know that Lord Strathmore has got toothache.'

The Strathmore upbringing aimed at giving the children poise without precociousness. Lady Strathmore did not believe in the green baize door, which separated the family from the servants and meant that children remained with nanny, except when allowed to join their parents in the drawing-room for tea and stuttering attempts at 'conversation'. She was not a disciplinarian but a warm, practical woman of great energy. Her homes were hospitable, full of gaiety and the sound of piano music. Furniture was well worn.

Once, when water gushed down a drawing-room wall, Lady Strath-more asked, 'Would someone be very kind and move the sofa?' and then went off to sort out Barson.

Barson was the valet who was constantly making sure that the claret and port were fit for drinking. He was fired once or twice for being 'inebriated', but was always taken back. The last straw was when he stumbled and upset a boiling kettle over his master.

The Queen Mother has spoken of her childhood to her children and grandchildren, about 'the bottom of the garden where there was the wood, the haunt of fairies, with its anemones and ponds and moss-grown statues'. There were two pet pigs called Lucifer and Emma and a wickerwork house for the ring doves to make their comforting cooing sounds; amongst them her favourites, 'Caroline Curly Love' and 'Rhoda Wriggly-Worm'.

Looking back, the Queen Mother said: 'Here were all the things that children could desire, dogs and tortoises, Persian kittens and Bobs the Shetland pony. Hay to make, chickens to feed, a garden . . . and on wet days the books that are best read on the floor in front of the fire.' Even today her happiest memories are of early summer mornings getting up at six, mushrooming, collecting bantam eggs for tea in the place they called the Flea House, where they used to hide from Alla striding along in her flat shoes, vainly searching for the 'Benjamins' snuggled behind mossy statues. The wood, still shaped like a star, has all the flair of the French architect, Le Nôtre, who was certainly its inspiration if not the actual designer of the grounds.

It was a winsome childhood. The Strathmores were a devoted couple, with strong moral values, commonsense and a lack of snobbery. The church on the hill saw the family and staff every Sunday.

If you go to St Paul's Walden Bury today the house remains full of charm. There is still a feeling of the warmth and even of the vitality of the nine Bowes-Lyon children who grew up there, coaxing their ponies to come up the steps into the drawing-room, giggling at the manly discus-thrower statue known to them as the 'Bounding Butler'. In the summer the children collected wild strawberries and in the autumn ran through leaves as crisp as cornflakes to jump a stream which they called the 'Zambezi'.

'You don't have to go through Welwyn Garden City,' Lady Bowes-Lyon tells the visitor today, as she gives instructions on how to get to the house from London. Once you leave the A1 and the rolling lorries rattling on to their industrial estates, reaching Walden is like finding a secret village nestling among the chalky uplands untouched by Stevenage and Luton. You drive past the Strathmore Arms and the church, past hedges red with holly berries to the gates of the house. The kitchen garden is overgrown, now used only for grazing the ponies. Only a few red apples bob from the old trees year after year; the mellow walls have a few whiskery creepers, but there are no espalier pears or peaches any more; the gates are held with a horseshoe. Pheasant scoot onto the railings and, in the spring, the yellow crocuses surround the tiny lake where a fleet of ducks head towards the white temple where the initials 'D' and 'R' (David and Rachel) are entwined, marking the year 1961.

Like many a stately home in Britain today, St Paul's is divided. Lady Bowes-Lyon is glad of the friend who has a flat on the nursery floor, the top part of the house. Her son, John Bowes-Lyon, lives with his wife and four children in what his mother calls 'the backside of the house'. 'I sleep in what we call the Duchess's room,' she says; it is where Lady Elizabeth slept as a child. It is still a pretty room with pink curtains and a fireplace decorated with rosebuds.

Today, you can see the scribbles where all the children had their height recorded. In the middle of the parchment coloured stone the mark in pencil shows David, 13 months, 1903; Elizabeth, October 1902 aged 2, and in amongst her aunts and uncles is Margaret Rose, 1932. Princess Margaret was an almost exact contemporary of David's only daughter, Lavinia, and they played around the rather formal long walks, the French style *allées* between lime and beech trees.

Lord Gorell, briefly Secretary for Air in Lloyd George's Coalition government, was so taken by Lady Elizabeth as a child that he dashed off a letter to Lady Cynthia Asquith full of praise for this youngest Strathmore girl, whom he thought 'small for her age, responsive as a harp, wistful and appealing one moment, bright eyed and eager the next, with a flashing smile of appreciative delight . . . quick of intelligence, alive with humour, able to join in any of the jokes and hold her own with the jokers, and touchingly, and sometimes amusingly, loyal to her friends'. But what struck this amateur poet and author of detective stories most was that the child had, even then, that 'blend of kindness and dignity that is peculiar to her family . . .'

It was 1904 when 'Claudie' Glamis became the 14th Earl of Strathmore. Now the family would spend more time than simply summer-to-autumn holidays at Glamis, 12 miles north of Dundee, the castle set below the Grampian Mountains, which on a spring day can have a rim of smoky blue. At other times the black clouds are so menacing that you expect a biblical figure, a hoary old man with a white beard, to come shooting down with the navy blue rods of rain. But it was a perfect place for the children to play spooky games, looking out for the ghost of the smiling Grey Lady or even the Monster of Glamis. It is hard to imagine how any serious monster or ghost could really have thrived in noisy, happy Glamis, which today is richly polished and cherished. It remains the Strathmores' home but is open to the public in the summer months and attracts 77,000 visitors a year, with tea provided by a Mrs Jolly.

There is a newish theory about the Monster at Glamis. The writer Paul Bloomfield suspects that intermarriage in the 1820s between Strathmore cousins resulted in the birth of a child with water on the brain. Surprisingly, the child hydrocephalic lived for some years. A second son became the heir. But the theory goes that the eldest was kept in a special room, and sometimes embarrassingly appeared in the corridors and startled the guests. The eldest son in each generation is allegedly told the secret on his 21st birthday.

'How nice to see you again,' the Queen Mother will say to the old villagers she recognizes. Few have worn as well as herself.

They had all known the shy Duke of York. He often drove from Balmoral, over the spectacular Cairn O'Mount where the great pine trees at dusk look like clumps of black velvet and in winter parties of skiers are sometimes snowed up at the Spittal of Glenshee. They also knew Edward the Prince of Wales, who liked to order his kilts in the village from Hogg the tailor. One day soon after Lady Elizabeth's engagement there was a meeting of the Glamis and Eassie Girl Guides. One of them recalls: 'We were all standing by the cricket pavilion just over by the castle and I always remember Lady Elizabeth was so happy – she just jumped over the gate, didn't take time to open it, so she could show us her beautiful sapphire ring.'

The young Guides clubbed together and bought the bride a silver inkstand. Those who did not get to the wedding – there was only room for the Guide Captain and a few senior Guides – received a piece of cake. When Janet Fox moved house three years ago she found her silver and white frilled wedding cake box, 'yellow with age'; sadly, 'the cake was like a little stone' and had to be thrown away.

On her annual summer visits the Queen Mother likes to sleep in the famous bedroom where turbulent weather heralded Princess Margaret's arrival in this world on 21 August 1930. It is a pretty room, all done in soft mushroom colours with flowery, chintzy bed covers, gold dressing-table mirrors and on the wall by the window the famous Desiderata prayer of 1692 found in St Paul's church, Baltimore:

Go placidly amidst noise and haste
And remember what peace there may be in silence . . .

The bedroom faces south and when the Queen Mother wakes she can see the trees where branches have been trained to droop tent-like to the ground, hiding children from the open of the green lawns.

A young Bowes-Lyon relative complained recently about the length of the train journey from London to Glamis. 'Why, I remember once making a banana last the whole journey,' the Queen Mother remarked. Nursemaids, valets, footmen and lady's maids all loved the adventure of the 400-mile trip north on the 'Flying Scotsman'.

The younger Lady Elizabeth and her brother David, when they were not at the 'sweetie shop', enjoyed being frightened by the big game trophies of elk and stag, their surprised brown eyes pugnacious in the Castle's murky light, and the impala and buffalo in the crypt above the gleaming heavy Jacobean furniture. There was the secret chamber, or Monster Room, where the Lord of Glamis is said to have played cards with the Devil on the Sabbath . . .

Everything in Glamis is worth a second look. Elizabeth and her brother loved hearing more about the visits to the Castle by ill-starred members of the Stewart family like Mary, Queen of Scots and Bonnie Prince Charlie; and the legend of Duncan's murder by Macbeth. Sir Walter Scott confessed to feeling nervous when he stayed there. But to the children, the vast kitchen with large black ranges and great copper jelly moulds and saucepans was more inviting than reading – whether history books, bound volumes of *Punch*, Dr Johnson's *Highland Journey* or Shakespeare's plays.

In Lady Elizabeth's childhood the cook and her helpers still had a bed set in under the kitchen table for naps between meals. And no wonder, if an earlier Strathmore menu was an indication. It was just a simple picnic lunch in 1866 for Elizabeth's grandfather, Claude, the 13th Earl. Rabbit and beefsteak; mutton pies; 2 chickens; shoulder of lamb in pastry – and Prince Albert pudding. In the evening for dinner they had green pea soup; pourbelle of hare; beef olives; roast ducks; cheese cakes; cherry water ice. For the servants, roast mutton – but on certain days they were allowed gooseberry tarts.

The housekeeping was on a vast scale but it was done with a Scottish thrift which the Queen Mother has passed on, particularly to the Queen, in its meticulous detail. A late-eighteenth-century Factor went to terrible lengths to explain why there seemed to have been such reckless buying of citrus fruit. 'A fever raged,' he said. 'Dr Farquharson prescribed lemons and oranges among sick people to drink as they were all very poor.' The five dozen fish and lobster seemed to pass without a query – being a reasonable 20 pence in all.

The Strathmores had an income of £20,000 a year from their tenant farmers in Scotland. But by the time of their Golden Wedding celebrations in 1931, the Earl admitted publicly that they were finding it hard to make ends meet. 'Out of every £100 local and imperial taxes absorb £80,' he complained.

The Earl and his wife were liked by the locals – some say they were a 'homely' couple, others found the Countess slightly forbidding. The tenants gave them a set of gates for the Castle to mark their 50 years of marriage.

The Countess, even in her last years, was very much the châtelaine, a bustling, white-haired woman who was not the daughter of a clergyman for nothing and resourcefully tightened up the housekeeping. Pleasant chores for the daughters of the house included carrying baskets around the greenhouses while their mother astutely questioned the gardeners about the prospect of decent figs and grapes.

Their sprigged cotton dresses were patched and mended and Lady Elizabeth's shoes at a tennis party looked 'distinctly secondhand', a '*nouveau*' type reported. And as for her racquet, 'it was full of holes' and had obviously been handed down. Although the Strathmores were not by any means really hard pressed, the Earl was always a bit tight with pocket money for his children. Lady Elizabeth found an engaging way of wringing some money from her father. She sent him a telegram: 'SOS LSD RSVP Elizabeth'.

The Queen Mother remembers now that in her childhood some of the best fun involved digging into a 'wonderful chest full of period costumes and wigs that went with their gorgeousness'. The Strathmore family was the last in Scotland to keep a private jester, and Lady Elizabeth and her brother David often dressed up in the harlequin jester clothes of shocking pink and yellow candy-striped satin. This early fun and dabbling in amateur dramatics helps to explain the Queen Mother's flair today for timing and mimicry which she has passed on to her daughters, particularly Princess Margaret. She has always had a feeling for mood – like an actress her entrances are always perfectly timed. She has a real talent for mime and is a terror at a game called Clumps, foxing an entire party with a skilled impression of 'a rolling stone gathering no moss'.

There were no videos or television sets, so the family made their own entertainment and an evening round the piano was always the 'greatest fun'. Sheets of music with favourite numbers, 'The Vamp' and 'You Hold Me in the Hollow of your Hand', are dog-eared now and the piano looks well worn; the music for a rather apt piece by Mendelssohn, 'Scotch Maiden's Dream', tumbles out. As the Countess swayed at the piano, fingers flying, her eyes – roaming to the royal coat of arms, with green thistle and rose motif over the fireplace – would rest on the comical figures in slightly bad taste on either side of the chimney-breast. Years later, the two princesses, Elizabeth and Margaret, would sit like bookends in their miniature chairs on either side of the log fire.

The long days of summer were spent picnicking, playing tennis or learning about flowers. Lady Strathmore had introduced elegant Italian-type gardens at Glamis, rather out of keeping with the wildness of Scotland. The Queen Mother's childhood was a cloudy mist of delicate lady-like pursuits, music lessons and hours helping her mother to re-embroider the counterpane of the bed where the harassed Bonnie Prince Charlie slept.

By the time Lady Elizabeth was four she could recite several psalms and enjoyed reading her *Little Folks* magazine. But Lady Strathmore felt it was time to employ a governess. Too many days spent gathering strawberries or playing tennis in summer would not give her daughter any feeling for the classics.

The Strathmore boys went to Eton and the Queen Mother thinks it is a splendid school. She still feels that Gordonstoun was a harsh place for Prince Charles, although she agrees with the Queen and Prince Philip that he has turned out to be a credit to this bleak, slightly Teutonic, Highland institution.

A French governess, Mademoiselle Lang, arrived in 1904 and was welcomed by Lady Elizabeth with a 'I do hope you will be happy here'. 'Madé', as she became known to the two young children who could not pronounce 'Mademoiselle', was very happy with the family, leaving only when 'Postie' brought a letter with a proposal of marriage. Leaving for France, she opened the card with her present and smiled. 'We hope Edmund will be kind to you' signed 'David and Elizabeth'; with it was a silver teaspoon so that she could make good tea. She was replaced by a German governess, Fräulein Kathie Kuebler, who was also a success.

Fräulein Kuebler thought it was like being home in Germany again in the winter at Glamis, when the Grampians were white with snow, the tree trunks seemed dark red and everyone tobogganed. She was a good teacher and coached Lady Elizabeth for her Junior Oxford Local, which she passed with distinction in the spring of 1914. Lady Elizabeth also briefly attended a girls' school in London, Dorothy and Irene Birtwhistle's 'select classes for girls' in South Kensington. This showed mother and daughter's enterprising spirit. Girls of the same aristocratic background were content at that time to stay at home and just cultivate socially acceptable colloquial French and Italian. But Lady Strathmore worried because she thought too much studying had made her daughter pale and ill. Perhaps it was time for another holiday in Italy?

From the age of 11 Lady Elizabeth had been on rather sophisticated jaunts to her maternal grandmother, Mrs Caroline Scott, who lived in a Medici villa in Arcetri, outside Florence. There were visits to galleries in Florence, often with her grandmother's unmarried daughter. It was a grand adventure for a child, travelling on the Rome Express overnight and then being spoilt by an exotic grandmother and her friends, and the first trip served as a distraction to take her mind off the death of her brother Alec when he was 24.

A bone-shaking carriage, drawn by a skinny pony 'much thinner than Bobs', would take grandmother and granddaughter to church, trotting through the dusty avenues of cypress, the shutters of pink and sand-stoned villas closed against the midday sun, when the wild roses drooped on the terracotta steps.

An early introduction was made to the 'Bloomsbury Set', as one of Mrs Scott's nieces was Lady Ottoline Morrell. 'Oh, it is all far too High Church for me,' Lady Ottoline would say, excusing herself from church and stretching out on a *chaise-longue*.

Good results in her exam called for a celebration for Lady Elizabeth's 14th birthday. Her treat was a visit to the London Coliseum with her mother to watch a hilarious evening of vaudeville; the 'Palace of Entertainment' that evening was showing 'acts from all over Europe'. There were Lipinsky's Dog Comedians;

Moran and Wise, jugglers; and a Russian ballerina. On the programme Elizabeth saw Pinoli's Restaurant in Wardour Street advertising a special 'Parisian Dinner' for two shillings, served from 5 until 9 P.M.

The next morning when she woke up in her parents' house in St James's Square, she found that Britain was at war with Germany. All the vulnerability of adolescence was heightened a year later, when her brother Fergus was killed at Loos. The indefatigable Lady Strathmore's health was to break down, and the running of the Castle would be left to the youngest unmarried daughter who was still at home – Lady Elizabeth.

4

A Stern Greeting

Instead of pleasant visits she might have expected to art galleries and concerts with her governess or enjoyable fittings for her first evening dresses, Lady Elizabeth was catapulted into war. The first inkling she had of it was on the morning of 29 June 1914, when her father, Lord Strathmore, hurled the *Morning Post* across the breakfast table towards the governess. 'This means war,' he said, as Fräulein Kuebler read about the assassination of the Archduke Ferdinand at Sarajevo.

When war broke out Lady Strathmore tried to keep up the pretence that things were normal. She pleaded with Fräulein Kuebler to come back to England after her parents' silver wedding celebrations in Germany in two weeks' time. It was a sensitive way of making bearable what must be a permanent parting between a popular governess and her pupil.

George V had been on the throne since 1910, the *Titanic* had sunk with the loss of 1,500 lives, Scott had reached the South Pole, and Glamis was to be turned into a hospital for wounded soldiers. The bookshelves were now crammed with hand-knitted scarves and vests for the Front instead of Moroccan-bound volumes on India. The family drawing-room had 16 white hospital beds and in them were the 'boys in hospital blue' sent to convalesce from the Dundee Royal Infirmary. Their recovery was helped by the capable Lady Strathmore and her daughter Rose, who was ward sister, but above all by the youngest daughter of the house – 'the lassie', Lady Elizabeth.

It was remarkable how Elizabeth coped with the trauma of war. She had enjoyed a specially innocent and charmed childhood but, as one soldier who was at Glamis during the war, said: 'We were all amazed; for her fifteen years she was very womanly, kind hearted and most sympathetic.'

Of course, Elizabeth was extremely pretty in a wistful way, with long dark curly hair and a tiny waist. But there was something else about her; she could make any mood of despair – that 'intimate enemy' – disappear.

Soon after the outbreak of war, she was coping with the ribald humour of the soldiers one minute, and their tears of depression the next. She knew them by their Christian names and wrote letters for them to their families on what was left of the engraved Strathmore writing paper – 'Dear Mum, you'll never guess where I am . . .' And mothers would be delighted with the clear legible handwriting which tends to this day to start well into the page, the hallmark of the Queen Mother's distinctive style.

The child in her would make the soldiers laugh as they dozed on the Castle lawn, for she would ride her bicycle wildly amongst them, with eyes shut and hands crossed before falling into a flowerbed. She took them on at billiards, often won at cards, played the piano and sang the Boer War song 'Goodbye Dolly, I Must Leave You' and 'There's a Long, Long Trail a Winding' with them.

Christmas, Lady Strathmore said, would not be gloomy, but like a large, jolly houseparty. Everyone gathered round the huge Christmas tree with a hundred candles, and there were presents for all.

At what the Queen Mother later described as 'the start of those awful four years', three of her brothers were serving in the Black Watch and one with the Royal Scots Greys.

Two of them were newly married, Fergus to Lady Christian Dawson-Damer, and John to the Hon. Fenella Hepburn-Stuart-Forbes-Trefusis. The first casualty in the family was Fergus, before the war had hardly seemed to begin. He had come home to celebrate his first wedding anniversary in September 1915, and to see, for the first time, his two-month-old baby daughter. The day after his return to France he was dead.

When she was not writing letters for the soldiers, it was Elizabeth's job to keep in touch with her brothers at the Front, Jock, Michael and Patrick. In the family they used to say: 'We leave the letter writing to Elizabeth; she will always know what they want to hear.' What they did not want to hear at Glamis was the news that now Michael was missing, believed dead. This marked the time when Lady Strathmore's health began to deteriorate. Finally, the War Office confirmed her worst fears of the dark, sleepless, early hours, that Michael had also been killed.

The Strathmores always believed in a quality among themselves of 'second sight', or what was called in Scotland then, 'the giftie'. Lady Elizabeth refused to believe that her brother was dead – and her brother David was even more adamant. He was only a schoolboy at the time and had been brought home from Eton to be with the family when the War Office telegram confirmed the death of Captain Michael Bowes-Lyon at the Front.

'Michael is not dead,' the youngest insisted. 'I have seen him twice. He is in a big house surrounded by fir trees. I think he's very ill. I don't care what the War Office says, I know he's alive.' David refused to wear a black tie, he was so convinced that he was right.

But although 'the giftie' was taken seriously by the family and they longed to think David was right, they found it hard to believe his dream.

Three months later they were hugging him and apologizing for their cynicism. Michael was alive, but severely wounded, in a place surrounded by fir trees. He had been shot through the head, then taken as a prisoner of war to Germany. He was so ill he had been offered the chance of coming home, but he had behaved in a way which made his mother doubly proud; he had offered his place to another soldier.

A mixture of mythology and her descent from the Kings of Scotland may help explain the Queen Mother's interest in the supernatural. She was to bring to the stout Hanoverian House of Windsor a cheerful feyness.

In 1916, Rose married the Hon. William Leveson-Gower and the duties of ward sister passed to Lady Strathmore and Rose's youngest sister. But not long after the wedding, Lady Strathmore became too strained to cope. One of the many soldiers she cared for showed on leaving Glamis an uncanny talent for foretelling the future. In the autograph book of the girl who had made sure every patient had tobacco and who had willed some of them to go on living, W. H. Harrup, Eighth Seaforths, wrote, '12th September, 1917. For Lady Elizabeth. May the owner of this book be hung, drawn and quartered. Yes, hung in diamonds, drawn in a coach and four and quartered in the best house in the land.'

On the Queen Mother's 80th birthday, BBC Scotland, with producer Malcolm Brown and narrator Tom Fleming, presented a special programme full of affection for her, called *In This Your Honour*. The present Countess of Strathmore had been watching the programme at Glamis; her daughter, Lady Elizabeth Bowes-Lyon, who works as a secretary for a firm of London publishers, had referred to the autograph while narrating some of her great-aunt's life. In the middle of the film the telephone rang and a man with a Midland accent said: 'This is W. H. Harrup's son. I just wanted to tell you Mum and I have just been watching the programme about the Queen Mother and . . . Dad is dead, but . . .' There was a snuffle on the line. He was in tears.

At last the war was over. Brother Michael was home; the soldiers had gone from the Castle, all 1,500 of them. It was time to catch up on a lost season. Marriage was not on Elizabeth's mind. The war had deprived her of parties and dances, and now she had to make up for the lack-lustre years. In the words of her future husband's biographer, Sir John Wheeler-Bennett, 'She took London by storm.'

During the war, at the 'best house in the land' Queen Mary had tried to economize. Lunch at York Cottage, Windsor, during the war years was often 'simply – just pheasant and chocolate *soufflé*'. George V gave up wine and spirits. He abhorred the middle-class habit of using napkin rings. 'I quite refuse to use one,' he grumbled. 'I like a clean napkin every day.' From her end of the table the Queen remarked, rather tartly, 'You don't encourage me at all in my war efforts.'

Theirs was a good marriage, although often misunderstood by the outside world. Although the King and Queen were exactly the same height, 5 feet 6 inches, her toques and furs made her look form-idable. The Americans joked about the King and Queen of England as 'George and the Dragon'. The French had a titter about '*Soutien-Georges*', a Gallic play on the word for brassière – and support – *soutien*. But, if the truth were known, Queen Mary was a most biddable, dutiful wife. When she married she became more and more inhibited and coldly hid her feelings. But there was no doubt that the King loved her and she him.

Their courtship had hardly been impetuous. And their marriage, on 6 July 1893, was really all Queen Victoria's idea. The royal family had been appalled by the sudden death of the heir presumptive to the throne, Prince 'Eddy', Duke of Clarence, at the age of 26, in 1892. His fiancée, Princess May of Teck, would have been a most suitable wife. A cold-eyed assessment of potential wives for the royal princes was unremarkable then. Queen Victoria's devious plot would hardly work today. One could not imagine the spirited Lady Diana Spencer agreeing to marry either of Prince Charles's brothers had anything happened to him. But whether he knew it or not, Prince George was going to marry his dead brother's fiancée.

The wily old Queen Victoria wrote to her grandson George. 'Have you seen May, and have you thought more about the possibility, or found out what her feelings might be?' she suggested artfully, nudging along the sluggish suitor.

Princess May was in Cannes with her parents when she received a letter from Prince George. He was coming to the South of France to

Cap Martin, to recover from a nasty bout of typhoid and to come to terms with the fact that he was now the heir presumptive.

'Papa and I are coming over to Cannes towards the end of the week for a few days (incog.),' Prince George wrote to May, 'and we hope one day you will give us a little dinner. We are going to stay at a quiet hotel, only don't say anything about it . . . Goodbye, dear Miss May, ever your loving old cousin, Georgie.'

At about this time Princess May was coping with her feckless brother Frank. He had been expelled from Wellington College for throwing the headmaster over a hedge. He was a compulsive gambler who had lost £10,000 at an Irish race course. She was relieved to see him off to India, and happy that she no longer had to put up with his wicked jokes about the royal family.

Princess May was no great beauty, but her complexion won praise. It was compared to alabaster and the perfect line of her neck and shoulders was also much admired. She brought to the royal family a cultivated taste in music and literature and an ability to speak fluent French and German.

Prince George and Princess May were surprisingly well suited, but shy with each other. Their engagement was announced on 3 May 1893. Through the courtship they had tried to explain to each other how they felt. Rather humbly, Prince George explained that he might 'appear shy and cold'. 'I think it unnecessary to tell you how deep my love for you, my darling, is,' he wrote to Princess May in reply to a letter from her complaining bitterly about her own personality and for being 'so stupid, so stiff'.

They married two months later, and the closeness remained until the King's death in 1936. But their children inherited much of the same nervousness and shyness and were too much in awe of their parents to enjoy their humour.

Prince Albert ('Bertie') was born on 14 December 1895, at Sandringham. Princess May's first son, Prince Edward – 'Eddy' after his dead uncle but known later as David within the family and eventually the Duke of Windsor – was then a captivating 17 months. Although there were four more babies, she never lost her distaste for childbirth, finding labour highly embarrassing and undignified.

All the remaining children were born at Sandringham: Princess Mary, 1897; Prince Henry (Duke of Gloucester), 1900; Prince George (Duke of Kent), 1902; and the gentle John, the youngest, in 1905. John was epileptic and brought up mostly in Balmoral from the age of 12, on his own, separated from his brothers and sisters.

Lady Elizabeth Bowes-Lyon, aged four, and her brother David, aged two – called the
'two Benjamins' by their mother, Lady Strathmore. David feels he is the rightful
owner of the wheelbarrow

Edwardian prettiness. Lady Elizabeth
Bowes-Lyon, aged seven, posing with
apple blossom and pearls – which she
loves to this day

Lady Elizabeth and her brother David in
candy-striped jester costumes at Glamis
in 1909. The Strathmores were the last
family in Scotland to retain a private
jester

With a girlish smile, Lady
Elizabeth and her older sister
Rose say goodbye to a soldier
who has been convalescing at
Glamis during the First World
War

Still shades of the country girl:
Lady Elizabeth Bowes-Lyon
giggles with the Duke of York
at an interval in a tennis
match during their courting
days

The bride leaves her London home for her wedding at Westminster Abbey on 26 April 1923, looking calm and graceful. Her father, the Earl of Strathmore, in his uniform as Lord-Lieutenant of Forfar, watches from the doorway of 17 Bruton Street

On honeymoon at Polesden Lacey in the Surrey hills, the Duke of York smiles indulgently at his wife as they stroll through the woods

A stylish couple, the Duke and Duchess of York arrive for a house-party at the Earl of
March's home in 1925. The Duke was rarely without a cigarette

The close bond between the Duchess of York and her brother David was strengthened when they both had daughters in the summer of 1930. Princess Margaret is on her uncle's lap and Lavinia Bowes-Lyon gives her aunt the Duchess of York a gentle push by the swing at St Paul's Walden Bury

The Duke and Duchess of York prayed for strength to help them through their Coronation on 12 May 1937 at Westminster Abbey

The newly crowned King and Queen wave to the people

One of the first major tours abroad after the Coronation was to Canada and the United States in July 1939. The King and Queen are greeted by a 'papoose', a Red Indian child, at an encampment in Calgary, Alberta

Top Visiting homeless people in Sheffield in 1941. The Queen often felt that the suffering they endured during the war was 'almost too much to bear'

Centre Victory celebrations. On the balcony at Buckingham Palace on VE night 1945, the King and Queen and their daughters are cheered by the crowds. Later the princesses ran down amongst the people in the Mall and waved to their parents

Bottom Teatime at Buckingham Palace and life is back to normal after the war. Tea is a popular drink with the royal family. The Queen pours and the King often listens to his favourite programme on the radio – Tommy Handley's 'ITMA'

Top An offguard moment. Group Captain Peter Townsend and Princess Margaret seem apart from the royal group. The Queen admires her gift of a carved zebra and Princess Elizabeth looks uneasy

Centre Princess Anne in her mother's arms after her christening at Buckingham Palace in 1950. The Queen tries to stop Prince Charles from walking out of the group photograph; Prince Philip enjoys his son's determination while Queen Mary places a restraining hand on her great-grandson's head

Bottom The week before he died in February 1952, the King went to London Airport to wave goodbye to his daughter Princess Elizabeth and her husband Prince Philip as they took off for a five-month Commonwealth tour. The King looks strained and the Queen tries to stay cheerful

Epilepsy was more frightening in those days when it was not properly understood. In photographs of the royal family he was one of the best looking of the boys, staring out at the camera frankly, shoulders back in his sailor suit. But not much was heard about John in the family and, when he was 13, he died quietly at Wolferton, Norfolk, the privacy of his parents' grief echoing the stigma they felt at having an epileptic son. Prince Henry, later the Duke of Gloucester, was a willing but nervous child, with a quick temper and given to nervy giggling bouts. He showed little promise in the classroom, which irritated the King. He became a first-class soldier but never lost his fear of his father. Once, when he had been away in a campaign for several months, he arrived home in time for dinner just as the royal family was sitting down. 'Late as usual, Harry,' the King said grumpily. Prince George was the most attractive of the boys and seemed able to escape his father's wrath. Less was expected of Princess Mary as the only girl.

Each child had its own problems; in Bertie's case it was the psychological and physical upset of an unstable nursemaid. He tended to be 'easily frightened and somewhat prone to tears', and developed a stammer when he was seven. He had been left-handed but was forced to learn to write with his right. Lady Airlie, a close friend of his mother, saw in him the qualities which showed a sensitive, artistic child. There had been an unspoken belief that perhaps he was slow because of his stammer. But Lady Airlie, whose own roistering six children were 'like a pack of hounds in full cry perpetually at her heels', described how Bertie had waylaid her one morning with an Easter card when she came out of his mother's room: 'At the last moment his courage failed him, and thrusting the card into my hand without a word he darted away.' Later she caught up with the six-year-old and learnt that he had designed the card himself.

When his confidence had been gained, he 'talked to me quite normally, without stammering, and I found that far from being backward he was an intelligent child with more force of character than anyone suspected in those days.' This was the quality which made George VI a good king, surprising people who had been superficially deceived by the physical handicap of a stutter.

Unfortunately, while they were young the children stayed, frightened, behind the green baize door. As a result they were too deeply respectful and nervous of their parents to have much fun with them. Their father would chaff them and complain: 'My children are always trying to evade me and get lost purposely.' He would tell them jokes – his humour was bluff – some with faint undertones of the colour prejudice of the time. One favourite went like this: 'There was a little girl who wanted to take her doll to heaven. "Mummy, when I die I want to take my dolly to heaven . . ." "Oh, I am afraid you can't do that dear." "Well, then, may I take my old dolly?" "No, I am afraid, not even that." Whereupon, the little girl, losing all patience, said: "Very well then, I will take my golliwog to hell." '

As King, George V mellowed and later Queen Mary could tease him. He once gave his children a stern lecture on what bad form it was to clap when the band finished a dance. But, afterwards, in the drawing-room, Queen Mary, in a pale pink evening dress trimmed with silver and with a diamond choker round her neck, said, slipping lightly into French, the habit of fashionable folk at the time, 'Oh, don't take any notice. Papa is old fashioned – *autres temps, autres moeurs*.'

Nor was Queen Mary lacking vivacity; she enjoyed the jokes in *Punch* and *La Vie Parisienne* even when they were at her own expense; and she went to some trouble, when it was the song of the moment, to learn the words of 'Yes, We Have no Bananas'. Her sense of humour was on the dry side, though. When Admiral Sir John Fisher took the then Prince of Wales off to sea in a submarine, his young wife said with more than a touch of Lady Bracknell as she stood on the quayside: 'I shall be very disappointed if George doesn't come up again.'

George V disliked foreign travel, saying, 'I hate abroad. I know because I've been there,' but he agreed to endure essential State visits. Once, in Belgium in 1922, he complained about the accommodation at Laeken where the palace was so vast. 'May lives at one end of the Palace and I at the other. It is not very convenient.' Queen Mary was miserable too, disliking boring ceremonial dinners and missing the comfort of shared, overheard jokes at the end of a day. In the middle of the night she heard her bedroom door opening stealthily and, startled, sat up in bed, switching on the light. Peeking round the screen was the 'dear, sad little face' of the King.

He valued her opinions and would often stomp into his wife's sitting-room. It was hung with a soft shade of green brocade, always filled with masses of lilac and dark red roses. The Queen would be resting her head against some embroidered cushions, wrapped in a kimono of 'a lovely pale shade' as a lady-in-waiting read to her before dinner.

* * *

Almost from the start, as second son, Bertie seemed to be fighting obstacles. From the beginning Prince 'Eddy' was a more captivating child, while his brother, Bertie, was shy and withdrawn.

Queen Victoria was still alive and very much a presence in a whirl of black bombazine, and Bertie's birthday being 14 December, the anniversary of the other Prince Albert's death, he enjoyed some favour with his forbidding great-grandmama. Yet understandably, Bertie was frightened of the old lady and would burst into tears as soon as he saw her. On the other hand, David was not at all scared of her. She found him delightful, 'a most attractive little boy, and so forward and clever. He always tries at luncheon to pull me out of my chair, saying "get up Gangan" and, to one of the Indian servants, "man pull it", which makes us laugh very much.'

David was also quite perceptive about 'Gangan's' attitude. An artist, called Mrs Gertrude Massey, working on miniatures of the boys at Osborne, the Queen's house on the Isle of Wight, heard David ask: 'Are there kings and queens in heaven? Is everybody equal?' When he was told heaven was extraordinarily democratic and everyone was equal, he replied, 'Great Granny won't like that.'

While his sons were small, their father, then Duke of York, would boast about his ability to bath the princes, just as the Prince of Wales today has proudly told the world about his bathing Prince William. It is a funny admission by the prince and his great-grandfather, both so expert at controlling excitable horses, yet to them a slippery baby in a bathtub seemed much more of a challenge. But it was Edward VII and Queen Alexandra who gave their grandchildren most affection. Romping was certainly not for their mother, Princess May, who would have been far too inhibited to crawl about on the floor. The King, 'Grandpapa', would sit by the fire with the children at Sandringham, 'the Big House', and share their nursery food, cream cakes and toast oozing with butter and jam.

'Look at me. If that boy grows up to look like this it will be your fault,' the Prince of Wales said one day to the nursery footman, Frederick Finch, who had weakened the agonizing wooden splints imprisoning Bertie's knock-kneed legs. It was a fairly primitive cure but it worked, and it was understandable that the future King should want to ensure that his sons could walk at places like the Cenotaph in tight uniform trousers confidently.

York Cottage was small for such a big family, and there was always a smell of cooking – not of chopped garlic and *fines herbes* sautéeing in butter, but of greens and mash and game. If Princess May had a feeling for paintings, her husband did not share it. Growing up surrounded by a superb collection of Canalettos and Leonardo drawings, he really did not mind that the pictures at York Cottage were reproductions, presumably because he would inherit many of the originals. The furniture was not elegant French or English, it was from Maples. He did not read a lot, neither did his parents. When he became King, Asquith, Prime Minister at the time, suggested a telegram from the Palace might be appreciated by the author Thomas Hardy, who had reached his seventieth birthday. 'Old Hardy' would be thrilled – and with a prompt 'it shall be done' from a Palace official, an astonished Mr Hardy of Alnwick, a man the King did know and who specialized in fishing rods, received a telegram from the monarch. The contrast here is that at Glamis and Walden Bury the works of Thomas Hardy were all on the bookshelves and, more important, they were taken down and read.

Another telegram was sent to Prince Albert, still in the nursery and on the eve of his birthday. It was a stern greeting:

Now that you are five years old, I hope you will always try and be obedient and do at once what you are told, as you will find it will come much easier to you the sooner you begin. I always tried to do this when I was your age and found it made me much happier.

When George was born in 1902, a tutor was hired for the two older boys. The seven-year-old Bertie and his brother were in the schoolroom on the second floor of York Cottage every morning at 7.30 A.M.; icy in winter, sitting on hard wooden seats under the watchful eye of the rather bleak Mr Henry Peter Hansell. Unmarried, and fairly humourless, Mr Hansell taught the boys history and classics. He was a good athlete, which went down well with their father.

There were some faltering, agonizing moments, and reports made daily to 'Papa' were sometimes rather sarcastically phrased. 'Division by two seems to be quite beyond him' was one of the most caustic remarks. Bertie was inevitably summoned to his father's study. The Prince, in his abrasive Sea Lord manner, turned his back on the stamp collection which he had been enjoying to ask his pale, stuttering son Bertie why the sum had proved so difficult. Staring at the walls of his father's study – rather eccentrically lined in the red material used for making French soldiers' trousers – the boy was often unable to give a coherent answer. And, of course, this inability to express himself would be the trigger for another explosion of pent-up nerves. All the boy could do was stare hopelessly at the depressing *bons mots* on the wall: 'Teach me neither to cry for the moon, nor over spilt milk.'

Hansell found the atmosphere stifling. At exactly the same time every morning, the Prince of Wales would come out from his bedroom, tap the barometer and light his cigarette – all done on the same dot with the precision of a speaking clock. At Sandringham the telephonist's voice could have recorded 'at the third stroke the Prince will finish breakfast' – it was such an inflexible routine. Hansell often went across the meadows on his own after breakfast to stare at the countryside. This bewildered his charges, who probably thought the country was not for looking at but a place where you watched your father hunting and shooting. 'Freedom,' Hansell muttered when pressed for an answer as he shambled back to his charges, rubbing his hand over his unruly moustache. He was a good golfer and sailor, but a fairly hopeless teacher.

So despair would seize hold of Prince Albert as he failed to solve mathematical problems and he would burst into angry tears again. There was no question of extra coaching or a crammer. The nervous strain of getting through his entrance examination to the naval college at Osborne on the Isle of Wight was an unusually heavy burden for such a highly strung boy. Nevertheless, when he was 14, Bertie went to Osborne; and nobody could have prepared him for the bullying which his stammer invited. The fact that Bertie was royal did not save him; indeed, it seemed to exacerbate the cruelty. The boys pricked his skin with pins to see if his blood was blue; there was no favouritism shown and only by subterfuge could he meet his brother, David. They called Albert 'Bat Lugs'. Prominent ears are still a family characteristic; Prince Charles has sometimes been called 'Jug Ears', though rather more affectionately.

Bertie was beaten up and laughed at for his inability to say his Rs and because he always referred to his parents as 'Their Majesties'. Not surprisingly, his stomach began to play up. By the end of his first year at Osborne, he was so ill with whooping cough that he was moved into isolation, made even more miserable by missing the visit of Nicky – the Tsar of Russia – to his college.

All the royal family had been longing to see the Tsar, who was the King's first cousin. A visiting Danish diplomat had told the gossips of Windsor how much he was under the thumb of his wife. 'The Tsar is undependable in that he is so superstitious and if the Empress comes to him and says, "I dreamt such and such a thing and it succeeded," the Tsar is quite likely to go off and do this ... The Empress is mad.'

The Danes heard the latest from St Petersburg because the Tsar's mother was the sister of Queen Alexandra, both of whom were descended from the Kings of Denmark. There was a definite resemblance between the two cousins, George V and the Tsar. Today, now that Prince Michael of Kent has been allowed to keep his beard, he reminds the family of the hapless 'Nicky', assassinated by Bolsheviks in the summer of 1918 in the desolate town of Ekaterinburg in the Ural Mountains.

'Allowed' to keep a beard may seem a strange expression but Princess Margaret is not at all keen on beards and the Queen frankly hates them. One of her household came back from a fortnight's leave with a new hairy growth, and the Queen, hardly looking up from her Red Boxes, remarked: 'That's coming off.' When Prince Charles had to remove a beard, he divided it up and sent it in matchboxes to people 'who had been beastly about it', including 'Aunt Margaret', who had refused to kiss him until he was cleanshaven.

In 1910, bottom in a class of 68, Bertie went home to Christmas at Sandringham with a heavy heart – but a determination to stay in the Navy. Curiously, he began to change and develop with the death of the amiable Edward VII, who had been such a loving grandfather. He walked behind the coffin and saw the panoply of a king's funeral. When he went to Dartmouth Naval College, which was altogether different from Osborne, there was more respect for the new King's second son. In January 1913, he joined the County class cruiser *Cumberland*. The following September he became a 'snotty' (midshipman) – and was known as 'Mr Johnson'. (Today, Prince Andrew is called 'H' by the other helicopter pilots in his squadron.)

With the outbreak of war, 'Mr Johnson' joined the battleship *Collingwood*. In his diary in that late summer of 1914 his father wrote a prayer, 'Please God it may soon be over and that He will protect Bertie's life.'

But on 29 August 1914, Bertie was taken ashore from the hospital ship *Rohilla* on a stretcher with violent stomach pains. He was operated on for appendicitis and sent to convalesce at York Cottage, where he complained about feeling 'completely out' of the war. The King's medical advisers felt he should never go back to sea again.

But the spirit which was to carry the Prince through the trials in his life so impressed his father, who now saw his son in a new light, that by February 1915 he was back on board *Collingwood*, taking his place on watch at Scapa Flow. He told his brother, the Prince of Wales, how through the Battle of Jutland he had been on top of the turret, and never 'felt any fear of shells or anything else'. His bravery was rewarded by his father with the Order of the Garter when he became 21.

He was still dogged by stomach trouble, and doctors diagnosed a duodenal ulcer. But in 1917 he was reporting for duty to the battleship *Malaya*. Two months later he was in hospital again and the ulcer was removed by surgery. It was decided that perhaps he would be better off in the Royal Naval Air Service.

Throughout these troubled years a naval doctor called Louis Greig had been an outspoken friend. This red-haired, blunt Scot was no courtier but he had guided Bertie since Osborne days. He was once told off by the King for swearing in the royal box at Twickenham while watching a rugby match between Scotland and England. The air was blue, and the King told him: 'If you don't watch your language we will have to stop you being in the royal box.' But Greig disarmed the King with his straight-from-the-heart, 'But what canna do, y'Majesty, when Scotland plays so badly?' There were those at court who did not care for Dr Greig, later to become Sir Louis, thinking him a faintly nasty, vulgar man. But to his credit the King said: 'Greig has made a man of my son, he stays.' It was not until Prince Albert married that his reliance on Greig altered; his wife made sure that there was less need for Greig's presence.

The war had given Prince Albert a new confidence. He now spoke up and even disagreed, though gently, with his father. Lady Wigram, wife of the King's Private Secretary, tells the story of a picnic lunch during a shoot:

The King attacks me at one period and tells me Clive [Wigram] is tiresomely pessimistic about the general situation and don't I think so? A voice at my elbow, the Duke of York, consoles me by saying, 'Wiggy knows what he is talking about, that's why' . . . Lunch at last comes to an end and the company rises and we watch the Beaters going off, very picturesque figures in blue smocks with black, soft felt hats with a red band . . . The King invites me to stand beside him . . . driven partridges coming like bullets. The King got a brilliant right and left, with a 'well done, George' from the Queen. We have a great deal of walking through ploughed turnip fields, the Queen stomping along with the best of them being pushed through a hedge by two of the keepers . . .

Often Queen Mary would be wearing a very long dress, a very unsuitable feather toque and an 'absurd little tweed cloak wrap'. After lunch 'three shaggy old ponies' were provided for the ladies but most preferred to walk.

The Duke of York, Nora Wigram noticed, referred to his older brother as 'Little D'; indeed in the household in general there seems to have been a tendency to call the Prince of Wales by the affectionate, diminutive name, 'Little Prince'. It was surprising, because he was the witty, flamboyant one and, on the face of it, much more attractive to the sparkling Elizabeth Bowes-Lyon. But there was never a glimmer of romance between them. There is a view that she had been rather dazzled by him, and that this was partly the reason for her deeply embedded bitterness at the time of the Abdication. No two brothers could have been more different. Astute about character and matured by those war years at Glamis, Lady Elizabeth was never in love with the Prince of Wales.

But the brothers, Bertie and David, were close. Out walking with the whole royal family at York Cottage a courtier thought:

The Prince of Wales has filled out a good deal I think; nice looking boy and much more talkative and not such a baby stick; he and Prince Albert walking arm in arm singing comic songs, very cheerful and most typically English. . . the 'Little Prince' thinks fit to use the most appalling language . . . the correct thing in the Guards, I suppose.

David was still a family pet. His grandmother, Queen Alexandra, adored him and played childish tricks on him when he was almost grown-up – romping into his white bedroom and hiding his blue silk pyjamas. He was good with her too and gentle about her deafness. At a dinner party, for which he arrived late – and only got away with it because his left ear was 'bleeding profusely' after he cut it shaving – he kept tapping his entrée fork against a salt cellar. This was to illustrate to his very deaf grandmother that he had been playing golf.

But he could be remote and was not good at hiding ennui; sometimes he made no effort at all. Nothing could be less attractive to a girl like Elizabeth, brought up to believe that nobody in the world was dull. One guest, who sat next to the Prince at an Easter dinner at Windsor Castle, was appalled by his poor conversation. 'You take it from me that no one can speak worse than the Prince of Wales . . . he is the only member of the royal family I have found *difficile*. I couldn't make any headway. I don't know if it was shyness, or what it was . . .'

But even the less talkative Prince Albert was beginning to find the social life at Balmoral rather dreary and complained how everyone was getting older. 'There's no spring in it and no originality in the talk. No one has that exciting feeling that if they shine they will be asked again next summer – they know they will be automatically, as long as they are alive . . . Traditionalism is all very well, but too much leads to dry rot.'

Meanwhile, in London, eligible young men were 'swooning' over Lady Elizabeth Bowes-Lyon, 'quite mad' about her. When she focused her blue eyes on each one of them and listened with such interest to what he had to say, he felt he must be the most fascinating person in her world as they gossiped about the Prince of Wales 'not wearing gloves to the ball' at which the 'acknowledged belle', Lady Diana Manners – later to marry Duff Cooper the diplomat – was the 'creamiest of the cream'.

But in her life at Glamis something more important had happened. Lady Elizabeth, aged 21, had been made District Commissioner of the Girl Guides for the parishes of Glamis and Eassie. This brought her into contact with George V's only daughter, Princess Mary, also a keen enthusiast in the activities of Brown and Tawny Owls. Very often Queen Mary would drive across to Glamis with her daughter. Lady Elizabeth would act as hostess and it is no secret now that Queen Mary liked what she saw.

5

Our Happiness Complete

When the newly-wed Duke and Duchess of York were homeless, Queen Mary suggested they live at White Lodge, the tall, rambling house in Richmond Park. It was chilly; there was no central heating; the kitchens were bleak and institutional. But the setting was romantic, with spotted deer and forests where Charles I used to gallop for a good day's hunting, undisturbed by today's intrusive bumble of jets from nearby Heathrow Airport.

Even in the royal family, young couples are often hard pressed to find their first home. There may be large estates in Scotland, Berkshire and Norfolk, but there always seems to be a scramble to find somewhere for the newly-wed. The present Prince and Princess of Wales were squeezed into Kensington Palace, which Prince Charles calls the 'Aunt Heap' because Princess Margaret has apartments there as do Prince and Princess Michael of Kent.

White Lodge was gloomy and filled with rather solemn furniture, but the young Duchess tactfully described her new home as 'airy'. It had been granted to Queen Mary's parents by Queen Victoria in 1870, and it would have been unwise to grumble about the house in which the King and Queen had started their own married life and where Bertie's elder brother had been born.

The happiness of the Duke and Duchess of York and their special popularity prompted more questions about the heir to the throne's leisurely and apparently indifferent search for a bride. David was having fun, and seemed to prefer the company of married ladies: Thelma, Lady Furness or Freda Dudley Ward. The daughter of a rich Nottinghamshire industrialist, Freda had what Sir Cecil Beaton called 'a hot-house elegance and lacy femininity'. Queen Mary called this young woman, married to an MP, 'Miss Loom, the lacemaker's daughter' but in any case would not have received her. The King and Queen sneered at 'trade'. Nothing less than a princess was acceptable as wife to the future King of England. Edward had been attracted to Lady Rosemary Leveson-Gower, daughter of the Duke of Sutherland, but the King rejected her as not being grand enough to be a future Queen Consort. In 1919 she married Lord Ednam.

As early as 1925, Chips Channon had written in his diary: 'The Prince of Wales, one feels, would not raise his finger to save his future sceptre. In fact, many of his intimate friends think he would be only too happy to renounce it.'

Once the furniture, the ornate ormolu bureaux, the Sheraton bow-fronted chests of drawers and Chippendale mirrors and all their wedding presents had been moved into White Lodge by Currie and Co, the young couple invited the King and Queen Mary to lunch. Although the Duchess had staff she still felt nervous about the menu.

'Our cook is not very good but she can do the plain dishes well, and I know you like that sort,' the Duke sensibly advised his mother in advance. His young wife warned the chef not to attempt any fancy *soufflés* or *bombes glacées*: stewed fruit and custard would be perfectly acceptable. The lunch was a success.

Queen Mary thought there was something different about 'dear' White Lodge: 'They have made the house so very nice,' she remarked, 'with all their wedding presents.' This was a tactful way of saying that she knew perfectly well that furniture had been moved about since her day. There was an easy atmosphere now, with bowls of fresh flowers and the Duke's *petit point*.

The newly-weds were sociable, but at their happiest when they stayed at home. The Duke loved his needlework and made lots of chair covers. He was blissfully happy, knowing a peace and contentment which had eluded him until his marriage. The Duchess played the piano, sang to him, or read. Sometimes they went to the theatre and once, when he accompanied them, Duff Cooper told his wife, Lady Diana:

They are such a sweet little couple and so fond of one another. They reminded me of us sitting together in the box, having private jokes and, in the interval when we were all sitting in the room behind the box they slipped out and I found them standing together in a dark corner of the passage talking happily as we might.

Sometimes they went night-clubbing; the Duchess was an excellent ballroom dancer and loved a few hours at Ciro's or the Mayfair Club. They went incognito to the cinema at Marble Arch.

Gradually the Duchess was being initiated into the RFTU – the Royal Family Trade Union – with its rules of duty, high standards and the need to behave unflinchingly well in public.

But soon the young couple found White Lodge 'rather exhausting'. Sometimes they travelled into London twice a day on engagements and then went out again in the evening. The Duchess felt that really it was 'altogether too far from London' and did not give them enough privacy.

Her first public engagement was on the last day of June 1923, when she arrived with the Duke, the King and Queen Mary at an RAF pageant in Hendon. She wore a cloche hat and a neatly pretty outfit, but she was rather shy and, like the Princess of Wales in her early days with Prince Charles, kept looking down. But there was always that slightly mischievous smile and often a moment shared with the King as they walked along together. His new daughter-in-law engagingly asked him about de Havilland Nines as they zipped above their monarch at the remarkable speed of 150 miles an hour. In front, the redoubtable Queen Mary stalked along in her long coat and high toque. The King was his courtly self. He later confided in the Archbishop of Canterbury that he secretly rather enjoyed the Duchess's 'slight unpunctuality', because, he said, 'if she weren't late, she would be perfect.'

One of her first engagements out of the country was to Northern Ireland, the start of a deep affection for Belfast. The Duke told his father, 'Elizabeth has been marvellous . . . she knows exactly what to do and say to all the people we meet.'

They went to Belgrade, travelling across Europe by train to be godparents to Peter, son of King Alexander and Queen Marie of Yugoslavia. The baby yelled as it was carried, naked, three times round the altar, and the unfortunate godparent was quite non-plussed. 'You can imagine what I felt like, carrying the baby on a cushion. It screamed most of the time, which drowned the singing and the service altogether.' On these occasions the Duke's stutter was not too noticeable: a quick, ready smile from his wife was their mutual telegram. It gave him confidence to speak without too much hesitation.

She subtly began to change the order of things.

To this day, the Queen Mother does not like it when men stay too long over their port and cigars, while the women are left chattering in the drawing-room, feeling rather flat when the mood of the evening has been broken. At a dinner party shortly after her marriage, she said to the man sitting on her left, 'Now, we are only three women and you are only three men, so don't stay too long over the brandy and leave us to gossip among ourselves. We've got lots to talk about . . .'

Once, at the Castle of Mey, the Queen Mother's home in

Caithness, while some of the men were still in the dining-room they heard voices. Outside in the windswept meadow was their royal hostess, leading the women singing 'Why are we waiting . . . ?'

One of the most carefree times the Yorks were to enjoy was a glamorous five-month trip to Africa on their own. The Duchess had just recovered from bronchitis – she was to be plagued with chest infections, often laid low at times of stress or tension. It was old-fashioned, stylish travel. They boarded the *Mulbera*, a P and O liner, at Marseilles in December 1924. The Duke was dumped in the ship's swimming pool in keeping with tradition as they crossed the Equator. A member of the crew remembered 'the little Duchess laughing as one after the other was barbered and tumbled into the ship's pool'.

From the moment they reached Mombasa they hardly ever wore anything more formal than safari clothes, the Duchess like a *Vogue* model in her cream silk suits and pith helmets. They slept in tents and around them the wildebeeste hoovered up the grass until the sun rose early in a scarlet African dawn. The Queen Mother still adores Africa and finds it hard to believe that it has changed so much, remembering, as she does, Kenya, Uganda and Rhodesia in a context of beating tom-toms as natives performed war dances in grass skirts, carrying lighted candles for the monarchy – with no thought then of independence from the Empire.

She proved a remarkably good shot with her Rigby .275 game rifle. This skill at such a vigorous and predatory sport seemed at odds with a girl usually seen in pastel chiffons, large-eyed and demure under a cloche hat. But it was just another aristocratic accomplishment. Her early days learning to stalk deer with her father and brothers made her a competent markswoman, which endeared her even more to her father-in-law. For the driven birds so much loved by King George, the women were not expected to join the guns, but Queen Mary always did, and what daughter-in-law would stay behind unless she had good reason?

The Yorks' trip to Africa was a real 'white hunter' safari. They bagged two rhinoceros, a lion and lioness, dik-dak, two buffaloes, an impala and a few oryx. They sailed along the White Nile in a paddle steamer called *Samuel Baker* and then on to Khartoum. Sometimes it was scorchingly hot and the mosquitoes bit; often it rained. 'Ah,' she sighed, looking at newsreels of the trip later, 'all over the world under the umbrella.'

Home again in the spring of 1925, the Yorks were refreshed,

buoyantly well and very happy. It had been a real 'getting to know you' trip. Together they could now face public life with confidence; their worries were few. A different house would be welcome, and they longed for a baby. Royal couples are often beset by the ritual of the atmosphere they live in. It can be difficult to adjust in the early days of marriage, no matter how much in love they are. It is hard even to have a row without a private secretary, valet or chauffeur overhearing, however much they try to make themselves invisible.

The Duchess was pregnant. 'We always wanted a child to make our happiness complete,' the Duke wrote to Queen Mary. Now the couple had every reason to move from White Lodge without hurting Queen Mary's feelings. Their new home was to be 145 Piccadilly, but builders were tearing it apart and the Duke was on the verge of renting another house at 40 Grosvenor Square. The King and Queen did not take the hint, but wise, motherly Lady Strathmore offered her daughter the family home at 17 Bruton Street, the house from which she had married into the royal family. White Lodge would later echo with the sound of squeaky pumps at the bar when it became the Royal Ballet School.

During her pregnancy the Duchess was cosseted by her husband and the whole royal family. She saw good friends and had feminine lunch parties. The layette was made by a friend of Queen Mary's, Hannah Gubbay, and a nanny was arranged. 'Alla' Knight was wheedled away from Lady Elphinstone, the Duchess's older married sister Mary, who was reminded slyly, 'Well, I had her first'.

It was not an easy birth. The baby was born by Caesarean section at 2.40 A.M. on Wednesday, 21 April 1926 and called Elizabeth. The Duchess breastfed her baby and felt 'tremendous joy'. Her husband was thrilled with his daughter, but had been worried about his wife. He wrote gratefully: 'I am so proud of Elizabeth at this moment after all that she has gone through during the last few days, and so thankful that everything happened as it should, and so successfully.'

The King and Queen had been woken at four in the morning with the news. 'Our darling Elizabeth has a daughter, such a relief and joy.'

The Duke was tired out. An eminent medical team had been installed in the house for the birth: Sir Henry Simpson, surgeon; Walter Jagger, Consultant at the Samaritan Hospital for Women. But, much worse for the fretting father-to-be, was the archaic rule that the Home Secretary had to be present at the birth of a royal child.

The Home Secretary, Sir William Joynson Hicks, had been at the house during the long and tense day of waiting. Later, when the Duchess was expecting her second baby, she remarked: 'If there have to be gentlemen waiting outside my bedroom door, I hope it's someone we know . . .' Harry Boyd, the Ceremonial Secretary at the Home Office, was rather more welcome as he was distantly related to the Duchess's sister-in-law, Lady Glamis.

When Princess Elizabeth was born she became third in succession to the throne, Prince Henry, Duke of Gloucester, moving down to fourth place. The Duke of York was amazed at the interest in his baby, saying proudly that his only claim to fame was that he was the father of Princess Elizabeth.

The King and Queen left Windsor Castle as soon as they could and called on mother and baby. As they entered Bruton Street, a liveried footman, carrying a spectacular spray of purple lilac and a smaller sheaf of pale pink carnations, followed respectfully behind. The bell on the front door later broke down — there had been so many enthusiastic callers. The baby had to be smuggled out by a back door when Alla wheeled her out for an airing round Berkeley Square or through the crocus paths in St James's Park.

The future Queen of England, Elizabeth II, was christened in a robe of creamy Brussels lace on 29 May in the private chapel at Buckingham Palace. Although the General Strike had just ended, Jordan water from the Holy Land was delivered to Bruton Street in time. The baby cried loudly through the ceremony at the gold lily font, silenced only by a liberal dollop of dill water.

She was a source of great delight not only to her parents but to her grumpy grandfather, whom later she would call 'Grandpa England' as she tugged at his beard. One minute the King would be bawling out the Prince of Wales for his involvement with the wrong sort of women; the next he would be on his knees playing horse and groom with his first grandchild.

But even at that age, after a romp with the King, the tiny girl who had been making him chuckle managed a 'perfectly sweet little curtsy' before going off to her nursery. Sir Owen Morshead, librarian to George V, remembered seeing an officer commanding the guard stride humorously across to the royal pram and shout: 'Permission to march off, please Ma'am?' At two years old the snugly mittened hand of Princess Elizabeth gave her assent. The baby was a perfect distraction for the King, who was seriously worried about his eldest son, and Queen Mary often defused his bad moods with a cry of 'Ah, here comes the bambino'. They relaxed more with their grandchild than they ever could with their own children.

The Duke and Duchess of York became increasingly popular with the King, their happiness and model behaviour only increasing George V's rage and feeling of impotence at the antics of his insouciant eldest son. At the time, David seemed to admire his sister-in-law for bringing an effervescence and fresh spirit into the royal family. But later, stung by her contempt for Mrs Simpson, he was to refer to her cruelly as 'that fat Scotch cook'. In the 1920s, however, he admitted that his brother Bertie had 'one matchless blessing enjoyed by so many of you and not by me – a happy home with his wife and children'.

David found the company in royal circles more and more dreary and was beginning to tire of royal tours abroad. He complained to a sympathetic woman guest at Windsor that he felt very low at the thought of going off to Australia for such a long time; that the endless ceremonial did weary him; and that the only thing he really liked were children's functions . . . though he had to draw the line at kissing them. Soon he would tire of the company of Mrs Freda Dudley Ward and the entertaining, stylish Thelma Furness. No woman seemed to hold his interest for long. When he sailed into New York, a young woman seen leaving his cabin made an unfortunate remark: 'He wasn't much good,' she confided. 'But it's not every night that one sleeps with the future King of England.'

There were ugly scenes between the Prince of Wales and his father, all the more galling as the King now so openly admired his second son and his wife. 'The more I see of your charming little wife, the more I like her.' He also saw qualities in Bertie which a loving marriage had helped to bloom. Even his stutter was now on the verge of becoming a thing of the past, much to the relief of the Duchess who had suffered almost as many agonies as her husband.

Lionel Logue, an Australian speech consultant, first met the Duke in October 1926. He gave this rather touching description of the Duke, walking into his consulting room in Knightsbridge: 'a slim, quiet man with tired eyes'. The meeting had been at the 'ingenuous insistence' of the Duchess. Often she went with her husband and later there would be a lot of laughter as they struggled over the speech exercises – athletics for the tongue – set by Logue: sentences like 'Let's go gathering healthy heather with the gay brigade of grand dragoons . . .' and, 'She sifted seven thick-stalked thistles through a strong thick sieve.'

Logue was persistent and the Duke was determined. It won him a new confidence. For so many years he had been burdened with the implied feeling that there is something inherently wrong with anyone suffering from a speech defect. The Duke of York, who often needed to put people at their ease, could now cope with visitors to the palace. The exercises gave his speech a slow, measured pace which was to be particularly effective in broadcasts and on other moving occasions during the war.

(During her 30 years on the throne, his daughter has been experiencing a different speech problem. According to the linguistics specialist Professor John Honey, the Queen's cut-glass pronunciation in the early years of her reign gave her an exaggeratedly upper-crust image. Research has shown this to be a disadvantage in a public figure. But Professor Honey believes that the Queen has been very well advised, so that by 1983 she had modulated her accent to that of 'standard BBC newsreader English'. She had become 'a model for anyone who sets out to be successful in public life. It is now truly the Queen's English.')

Enjoying their baby and the triumphant hope that the Duke of York would soon be able to speak without any impediment, the young couple were suddenly told that they would be going to Australia and New Zealand. 'But why us?' they asked the King. He gave them some excuse about the Prince of Wales having been in Australia too recently to go again. They did not argue with the King: they would go. But they were not allowed to take their baby with them.

Their daughter Elizabeth was only seven and a half months old when they sailed from Portsmouth on HMS *Renown* on 27 January 1927. Having to leave her baby was almost too much for the Duchess. She had grown up in such a warm family atmosphere that this cold parting from a child seemed utterly heartless. But that is the royal way and Duchesses had to learn that babies were not only for keeping and enjoying but also to be parted from and inquired about from capable nannies.

'The baby was so sweet, playing with the buttons on Bertie's uniform that it quite broke me up,' the Duchess wept. Her wretchedness was made worse as the Princess in her innocence was too young to know that her father would be going away for six months.

So great was the Duchess's distress that the Duke told the chauffeur to circle Grosvenor Gardens twice so that his wife could dry her tears, and he could, perhaps for the first time in his life, question the demands of monarchy. Yet typical of that rigorous training was Queen Elizabeth's reaction years later – as Queen – when she heard the commentary about her parting with her baby in a newsreel about *Renown*. When she remarked: 'She was beautiful,' everybody thought she meant her baby but no, she meant the ship. No personal emotions are allowed an airing, even half a century later. While the Duke and Duchess were away, coded messages about Princess Elizabeth and her new teeth were sent to them at least once a week. They had left behind a coral necklace as a Christmas present for her.

The tour was a success far beyond all hopes. At home the Duke had been diffident and in the shadow of his articulate and glamorous brother. But as a pair the Duke and Duchess of York had an engaging magic; they looked good together, he always a little solemn while she smiled her way into the crowds. The Duchess in her pretty clothes and with her soft manner and caring, low-pitched voice, was a complete change from Queen Mary. Despite the baby's being left at home they were smothered in teddy bears, fur rabbits, koalas and dolls to take back for her.

The royal suite on board the battleship was fitted with blazing log fires, good to write letters by before a banquet, and to read messages from Queen Mary describing her grandchild as 'too sweet, stumping around . . .'

Every evening the Duke and Duchess would rehearse his speech for the next day. Then the Duchess would sit serenely on the platform smiling, but not too openly in case it diminished his image of poise. The Duke would deliver his speech slowly, but everyone listened and cheered.

In New Zealand, the royal couple heard from the Prime Minister, Joseph Coates, that he had been told by a communist in the crowd that he was relinquishing his belief in Marxism – because, to his amazement, the Duke and Duchess were human. One of his children had waved and, 'I'm blessed if the Duchess didn't wave back and smile right into my face, not two yards away. I've done with this bloody communism,' he said. 'I'll never say a word against them again.'

A crowd of 50,000 cheered when the Duke in naval uniform took a golden key and unlocked the doors of Australia's Parliament in Canberra. The Duchess, in flattering grey chiffon trimmed with fur, listened to the soaring voice of Dame Nellie Melba singing the National Anthem, and then her husband made one of the best speeches of his life as he opened the Parliament building on the King's behalf.

But, in New Zealand, the pressure and exhaustion of the tour took its toll. The Duchess got severe tonsilitis. Convinced that nobody would want to see him on his own the Duke was touched when the crowds thought differently and cheered him enthusiastically.

They sailed home with three tons of toys. There was a fire on board *Renown*, which meant further tantalizing delays. But, again, the Duchess defused the anxiety on board and laughed afterwards when the captain wondered whether she had suspected that the flames had nearly reached the oil tanks. 'Ma'am, did you realize how bad it was?' The Duchess laughed, 'Yes, indeed, every hour someone said there was nothing to worry about so I knew there was real trouble.' Everyone was falling in love with the Duchess – on both sides of the world.

When *Renown* docked at Gibraltar on the way home the Garrison Band played 'Now thank we all our God'. To parents, children never seem quite grown up, and when the Duke and Duchess arrived back at Portsmouth having proved themselves superbly, the King warned his son: 'When you kiss Mama, take your hat off,' as if Bertie was in the habit of lounging around with his naval cap over one eye. One wonders what the old King would have made of Prince Andrew's jumping up and down with a rose in his mouth in front of his mother, the Queen, when he returned from the Falklands in April 1982.

There was a quick congratulatory peck on the cheek for his sister-in-law from the Prince of Wales. At Buckingham Palace, the Duchess scooped her 14-month-old baby into her arms and took Elizabeth with her on to the balcony for the first time in her life – and the King seemed to clear his throat rather a lot.

6

Hints of Unease

The Duke and Duchess of York were basking in a new aura of achievement in the summer of 1927. They had won the hearts of the people, and the regard of that stern taskmaster, the King. The Duke could now report to Lionel Logue that he found it much easier to speak to his father. From Balmoral, Bertie wrote about the relief of even getting his father to understand him. 'Up here I have been talking a lot with the King, and I have had no trouble at all. Also, I can make him listen and I don't have to repeat everything over again.' He had conquered his stammer, which he once called 'the curse which God has put on me'.

One of the Prince of Wales's ex-women friends, Mrs Freda Dudley Ward, also watched with a perceptive eye the gradual change in the King's attitude to his second son, at the cost of the eldest, David. But if George V saw Bertie through different eyes now, he was totally disarmed by his daughter-in-law. It seemed that after his marriage Bertie gradually became the King's favourite, able to do no wrong in his father's eyes. Not that Bertie was likely to do anything outrageous anyway. He was dutiful, caring, conscientious and besotted by the airy grace and sweetness of his young wife. When Bertie got into one of his nervous rages, she had a magical way of defusing the 'gnash'. If her husband was fuming about being kept waiting for a minute or so, his wife would say 'now Bertie' and gently take his pulse, counting 'tick, tick, tick, one-two-three'. Private secretaries and equerries would sigh with relief as they watched a smile creeping to the Duke's eyes and then his mouth. But he did fret over the years about his wife's unpunctuality since he was as meticulous about time as George V.

His first taste of a real home life was when the couple moved into their home at 145 Piccadilly. The Queen Mother says as she drives past now: 'Poor Piccadilly got a direct hit in the war, you know,' and adds almost incredulously: 'Did we really live there?' But the Duke and Duchess of York enjoyed a blissful nine and a half years there before their abrupt and unwanted move to the cold grandeur of Buckingham Palace.

No. 145 was a pleasant four-storey house, built of Portland stone, which stood on the right of Apsley House, the Duke of Wellington's London home at Hyde Park Corner. The Duke's house is still there, but the Park Lane dual carriageway runs over the site of No. 145.

The Duchess loved flowers, so there were always blue hydrangeas or daffodils in the window boxes.

At the beginning of the New Year the Duchess got bronchitis again and had to miss the wedding of Crown Prince Umberto of Italy. When Bertie returned from the excitable party in Rome, where he had felt very lost without his wife, she broke the news to him that she was pregnant again. The Duke was delighted and looked at her with an air of pride.

There were still dinner parties and evenings at the theatre. Virginia Woolf, less caustic than usual, spotted the Duchess of York in the royal box enjoying Edgar Wallace's *The Calendar* at Christmas 1929, with Carol Reed as a juvenile actor. She saw the Duchess as 'a simple, chattering, sweet-hearted, round-faced young woman in pink: her wrists twinkling with diamonds, and her dress held on the shoulder with diamonds'.

The chattering was probably the Duchess confiding in Queen Mary, who was also in the royal box, about plans for the new baby. It was a pregnancy without strain. There were leisurely visits to art galleries and days spent at the old house, The Bury, with her sister-in-law Rachel, who was also pregnant. Rachel's baby, a daughter, Lavinia, was born on 2 May, her father David Bowes-Lyon's birthday, and was to be like a twin for Princess Margaret.

Those were flippant days of flappers in clinging, but flouncy, frocks of Nottingham lace, dyed to exciting new lilacs and pinks, dancing the Charleston. At the same time there were hints of unease: the aftermath of the General Strike at home and the Wall Street stock market crash in America.

The Duke and Duchess of York felt certain that their second child would be a son. The Duchess wanted her baby to be born at Glamis, where the Yorks always went for the month of August. The King agreed to a confinement in Scotland: the gynaecologist, Leon Reynolds, and the Home Officials found it was no great hardship to be in Forfar for the late summer months of fishing and shooting.

As the baby would be in line of succession to the throne the Home Secretary, J. R. Clynes, and the Ceremonial Secretary at the Home Office, Harry Boyd, went by train to Glamis to await the imminent birth, due on 5 August. By the 10th and 11th the two solemn men in their sombre suits had attended two false alarms, when the local doctor had thought the baby was due 'any minute'.

Earnest and diligent, they began to get on the nerves of the easy-going Strathmores. Mr Boyd produced a book for the Duchess, underlined in red, telling of the secretive birth of the son of James II when it was rumoured that another baby was sneaked into the bedroom in a warming pan in place of the prince who was whisked out for a lifetime in a croft. Harry Boyd said he was anxious not to let anything happen in an 'irregular hole-and-corner way', which was offensive to the upright Strathmores. He was becoming a bit of a pest. When Lady Airlie took him off their hands everyone was relieved.

August 21 1930 had been a pleasant day with croquet on the lawn, but, as Boyd and Clynes were dressing for dinner, there was a phone call at 8.30 warning them that the baby was on the way. They were rushed by car from Airlie Castle to Glamis – reciting poetry out loud for the eight-mile dash.

For the Duchess of York, who was intensely private and hated any discussion of illness, the nearby presence of Mr Boyd at the birth at 9.20 P.M. was distasteful. But the Duke, when he became King, abolished the custom, sparing his daughter the intrusion of White-hall at a most intimate moment.

Princess Elizabeth was four. She had been hoping for a brother from the moment she had heard about her nearness to the throne. She looked at her new-born sister, Princess Margaret Rose, in her cot and announced: 'I shall call her Bud . . . you see, she isn't really a rose yet.' The Duke and Duchess wanted to call their second daughter Ann, but the King would not allow it.

Family friends say to this day that, to the King, 'Lilibet was his pride, and Margaret his joy'. Margaret made him laugh helplessly; even Queen Mary thought her deliciously outrageous, so frightfully *espiègle*, she would say, using a modish French word for what royal nannies called plain 'unmanageable'. Elizabeth, earnest and atten-tive, was a very lively child with darting movements. There was a competition stirring amongst enlightened mothers at this time, each claiming to be the first to abandon the barrier of the green baize door that traditionally separated children from adult life. It was something like the trendy habit today of vying for the most authentic working class origins: 'We were so poor we had to clean the house with our tongues', or, as Neil Kinnock, Leader of the Labour Party, lyrically imagines: 'We were so poor in South Wales my mother had to tie slices of bread on our feet for shoes; in the winter it was toast. Mind you, not everyone was poor as that, I did once see a mine manager's daughter wearing croissants.'

There is no doubt that at 145 Piccadilly the nursery door was only shut to keep draughts out. The Duke of York heard the constant sound of laughter and romping as he tried to write a speech in the mornings. The two princesses, their shiny rag-rolled hair in spiky curls, wearing button shoes, pleated skirts and round-neck Fair Isle sweaters would jump on to their mother's four-poster bed, or play with the glass bowls of powder on the kidney-shaped dressing table. The corgis would climb on to the bed, too. Occasionally, 'Mummy', as the Queen and Princess Margaret still call their mother, would slip into the kitchen to make her daughters their favourite real Scottish scones, enjoyed twenty minutes later, still warm from the oven, by children and dogs.

Princess Elizabeth and Princess Margaret were taught by their mother how to cope with ceremonial and meeting people – in a painless way. 'Now, I'm Grannie . . .' or 'Now I'm the Archbishop of Canterbury . . .' meant that the two princesses, in flower-trimmed straw bonnets and pale blue coats with velvet collars, were never frightened when a large bishop in flowing robes loomed down to shake their hands. They were self-possessed at an early age.

They had lessons at home, and their mother talked to them in French; in the evenings they had enthusiastic singsongs round the piano.

The Duke asked the King if there might be a chance of having a house at Windsor for weekends and was given Royal Lodge. That house, like a toy thirties castle painted outside in a delicate shade of strawberry mousse, was where the family had the most privacy and fun. The Duke stitched a dozen chair-covers in *petit-point* for Royal Lodge. There are classic pictures of the two princesses peering out of the 15-foot-high model Welsh cottage given to them by the people of Wales in 1932 – 'all the generations have loved this little house', the Queen Mother has always said.

In the garden corgis snappishly hurried through the ornate azaleas and purple rhododendrons planted by the Duke of York. Gardening was his relaxation and he loved his family nickname, 'The Foreman'. Today, the garden at Royal Lodge reminds the Queen Mother of her husband. 'It had been a sort of jungle. The King made all the garden himself . . .' The Duke of Edinburgh has memories, too, of one of his first meetings with his future father-in-law after the war, when the King emerged, swearing, from the leathery leaves of his favourite rhododendron bush wearing a rabbit-skin cap.

In the spring of 1935, a month before King George V's Silver Jubilee Celebrations, Bertie wrote a charming letter in the language of rhododendrons to his hostess which spoke volumes for his devotion to his wife and his flowers.

It was a great disappointment to me that my wife was unable to come too. I am glad to tell you that she is much better, though I found her looking Microleucrum [small and white]. It was nice of you to say that I deputized well for her on Saturday, but I feel that she could have done everything much better, as she has the Agastum [charming] way of Charidotes [giving joy].

The rest of the letter went on with horticultural references; he felt, for example, 'quite Lasipodum [woolly-footed] with walking round so many lovely gardens' at Lochinch Castle.

But while the Duke and Duchess of York were happy and contained, the King and the heir to the throne were becoming more and more estranged.

By 1934, Mrs Ward, the Prince of Wales's long-term companion and confidante, had been ousted in favour of an American divorcee, Mrs Ernest Simpson. Her Christian name, Wallis, was to crackle on the Duke's lips in the flat speaking tone he had inherited from his father. Mrs Ward was dismissed in a brutal way. When she tried to speak to the Prince of Wales a stumbling telephone operator had to tell her that no calls from her were to be put through to the Prince of Wales. It is like the legendary stories of newspaper executives first hearing about their sacking from the liftman.

David, failing 'to settle down', had managed to get Wallis Simpson presented at Buckingham Palace, confident that her glossy, severe, groomed style would go down well. But afterwards the King was furious that he – and particularly Queen Mary – had been forced to meet 'that woman'. He was to confide in Baldwin: 'After I am dead, the boy will ruin himself in twelve months.' George V had been seriously ill, but his temper was still vigorous.

Bertie had been the first to wed, now two of his brothers were also marrying. The engagement of the King's best-looking son, George, Duke of Kent, to Princess Marina of Greece and Denmark cheered him enormously. He was no flirt but he loved the company of elegant pretty women who had something to say for themselves. 'Marina', he said, 'has not a cent.' Marina was the youngest daughter of Prince Nicholas and Grand Duchess Helena of Russia and was a first cousin of Prince Philip. Cultivated and with a fine-boned Slavic beauty, she brought a feeling for music and the arts to the royal family. She had been originally suggested as a bride for the Prince of Wales, but Prince George fell in love with her as soon as she arrived in England.

Queen Mary put it succinctly: 'No bread-and-butter miss would be of any help to my son, but that girl is sophisticated as well as charming . . . theirs will be a happy marriage.'

The Kent wedding was an excuse for London to be festive in the November gloom. Garlands stretched high in a cross, with crowns in the middle, all along Bond Street, and all the exclusive clubs were celebrating.

Princess Marina arrived at Buckingham Palace to prepare for her marriage on 29 November 1934, and to everyone she was 'most gracious and chatty'. Lord Wigram found the Palace suddenly filled with exotic creatures, speaking in that captivating broken English which was less familiar in Britain then. He told his wife how a few days before the wedding he had come upon 'two beautiful ladies sitting on a sofa'. Two other Greek princesses, undoubtedly, he had thought. He made them a bow, a very correct one, and was rather piqued by their lack of response. He felt a footman touch his arm, saying: 'Beg pardon, Sir Clive, them two sitting on the sofa are only fitters from Molyneux . . .' Royal servants can be terrible snobs.

A child of that marriage, Princess Alexandra, is one of the Queen Mother's favourite nieces. Alexandra and her husband, Angus Ogilvy, often stay with 'Aunt Elizabeth' in Scotland and the princess, with her bitter-sweet smile, has to plead, 'Oh, please, we mustn't have any more cream', when the Queen Mother tries to fatten her up.

It is sometimes said that the young in the royal family do not go and see the Queen Mother enough at Clarence House because they are too caught up with their own lives. The Duke of Kent and his wife, the ailing Duchess, have had their own family problems, and Prince Michael, who is such a good mimic, and his statuesque wife, Marie Christine, are often abroad.

In the family there is bickering and tittering just like in any other. It is said that the Queen thinks Princess Michael far too grand, calls her 'Our Val' – after Wagner's terrifying Valkyries – and does mock curtsies to her.

The Duke of Kent, like his brother Bertie, had married a woman who was artistic and musical. In 1935, Prince Henry, Duke of Gloucester, who always looked rather forbidding in later years, married Lady Alice Montagu Douglas-Scott, daughter of the Duke of Buccleuch. The Duchess of York took the princesses to Norman Hartnell for their dresses, which were pure Kate Greenaway, with rosebud sprigs all over. The King, who liked to interfere in everything, ordered the dresses to be shortened. 'I want to see their pretty little knees,' he said. Naturally, the Duchess of York pandered to him.

There were two Gloucester children: Prince William, who was killed in a plane crash in 1972, and Prince Richard, his younger brother, an architect, who has been Duke of Gloucester since his father's death in 1974.

Although their father looked rather blimpish he had all the nervousness of his brother Bertie. Once, in Egypt, he was taken by diplomats for an evening's entertainment in Cairo, where the best belly dancer in the country gyrated enthusiastically. Afterwards, the Duke was taken backstage by the supercilious young men accompanying him, longing to hear what he would say to the perspiring girl, dressed in a thong. After the preliminary introductions, all the Duke could stutter was, 'Ever been to Tidworth then . . . ?' The girl looked puzzled, not being familiar with this Wiltshire military base, and suppressed snickers quite creased the diplomats and courtiers. The old Duke was not a great lover of opera and once, when the diva disappeared behind a tree for a sob, said loudly in the royal box: 'Is that it now, has she gone? Can we all go home?'

With four of his five children married, the King began to fret even more about his eldest son. The Prince of Wales was now 40, and constantly seen in the company of Mrs Simpson, with her spiky wit and regal ambition.

7

I Miss Him Dreadfully

In the summer of 1935 you could buy a country house in North Devon 'with glorious view extending to Dartmoor', two cottages and two fields included, for £3,000; a tweed jacket and plus-fours from Kenneth Durward in Conduit Street for six guineas; a bottle of 'finest dry sherry' for six shillings; and a Light Twelve Four Austin Saloon for £218, with another £9 for tax.

On 6 May 1935 a gentle, warm day, the King and his 'darling May' drove to St Paul's for a service in celebration of his Silver Jubilee. The crowds were delighted, cheering the two little upright figures, and prompting the King to admit – but only in the secrecy of his diary – 'I'd no idea they felt like that about me. I am beginning to think they must really like me for myself.'

Queen Mary was swathed in festive white fur and the King beamed inwardly at the sea of faces under the bunting. That day in his bluff way he had a glimpse through the invisible barrier separating a monarch from his people, as a congregation of 4,406 in St Paul's Cathedral prayed that he might enjoy many more years on the throne.

In the royal maroon and gold state landau were the smiling Duke and Duchess of York, she in powder blue, and their two 'tiny pink children' in rose bonnets.

Later, on the balcony at Buckingham Palace, Queen Mary was very emotional but kept bowing her head rapidly, looking a little like a figure in a Chaplin film. The thousands who had not been at St Paul's danced and cheered their appreciation for the King's life until nightfall. It was spontaneous, urban-proud and jolly.

The King broadcast to them that evening and, moved by this genuine celebration, he sounded just like his eldest son as he thanked his 'very dear people . . . from the depths of our hearts for all the loyalty and, may I say so, the love, with which this day and always you have surrounded us.' His surprise at the delighted crowds was exactly like the Queen's on her Silver Jubilee in 1977 and the Queen Mother's when she first sees children waiting to give her flowers on her birthday. Those closest to her will tell you that she is always touched that anyone outside the family should remember her birthday.

A single flower in tinfoil, a sleepy baby, a sticky finger reaching out to pull the flower off a royal hat or a 'good on yer' from a Smithfield porter in overalls, speeds to the hearts of the Queen and her family – perhaps because they are usually surrounded by smoothly articulate courtiers. This quality in the royal family to be genuinely surprised and grateful when the people turn out to say 'thank you' shows an integrity and lack of complacency in our monarchy.

George V loved it all. Once, driving through the outskirts of London with the Duchess of York and Princess Elizabeth, he teased his granddaughter, 'I suppose you think those flags are hung out for you? Let me tell you, they're all for me.' He had promised his people that he would dedicate himself to them 'for all the years that may still be given to me'. But, once the momentum of the celebrations eased, the King's health began to fail.

He was tired, ill and worn by anxiety about the Prince of Wales. He had barked at his son: 'You dress like a cad. You act like a cad. You are a cad. Get out!' The qualities he saw in the Duchess of York, and the way she was influencing his second son made him say that summer: 'I pray to God that my eldest son will never marry and that nothing will come between Bertie and Lilibet and the throne.'

In December, Elizabeth of York went down with pneumonia. On Christmas Day she was not well enough to get up and ate something light from a tray. Her husband stayed with her at Royal Lodge, enjoying the rare treat during a royal family Christmas of having a little private time alone together.

Then Queen Mary telephoned to say that the King was not well and, 'please', would Bertie help her with the house party? It was typical that royal tradition had to be observed: guests stayed at Sandringham while the King, in his sickroom, was being his lovable but impossible self, telling his doctor, Sir Frederic Willans, what he thought of his prescriptions. 'Willans, I'm not having any more of your blasted muck.'

Everyone in the family was concerned about the King; he seemed to be so tired, though occasionally he was his old rumbustious self.

It would be unfair to the residents of a seaside town in Sussex not to mention the King's view of the sedate resort where he had often convalesced. There are two versions of his classic 'Bugger Bognor' remark. One is that he gave the salty reply at the suggestion of some fawning attendant: 'Your Majesty will soon be at Bognor again.' But Kenneth Rose, in his book *George V*, says that once, when the King was due to leave Bognor, a deputation of leading citizens came to Craigweil, the royal holiday house, to ask if their town could be known as Bognor Regis. They were received by the King's Private Secretary, Lord Stamfordham, who invited them to wait while he consulted the monarch in another room. The sovereign's response was the celebrated obscenity, which Stamfordham then deftly translated: 'His Majesty,' he said, 'would be graciously pleased to grant their request.'

Straw hats resting on the elderly white heads of old gentlemen in creamy coffee-coloured linen jackets might have lifted off in shock had they heard the unmentionable fate predicted for their prim haven of retirement.

The King always got great pleasure from the company of his granddaughter, Lilibet. Next to her mother she was the person who could lift his spirits most. One Christmas, Lady Airlie had given her a present of a housemaid's uniform, and George V had hugely enjoyed her earnest imitation of below-stairs' duties. As small children, the two princesses were often apprehensive if they were told that Queen Mary wanted to see them. 'We always felt that we were going to be hauled over the coals for something we had done. But we never were.' Both the Queen and Princess Margaret still remember the 'hollow, empty feeling' in the pit of their stomachs whenever she sent for them.

As a young girl, Princess Elizabeth confided in a friend that she sometimes found her grandfather irascible. The friend said he had a grandfather like that, but he always chivvied him back. The Princess solemnly told him: 'That is not something you do to the King of England.'

To the family, who had little idea how ill the King really was, his decline came suddenly. The bowls of Christmas roses, the holly and opened Christmas presents lying around the house at Sandringham had a poignancy as they reluctantly accepted that the old man was dying, his heart getting weaker and his recognition of them growing more faint.

On the morning of his death, 20 January 1936, the inflexibility of monarchy brought six Privy Counsellors to his bedside. The King, his face drawn, wearing his oriental dressing gown of yellow, blue and green and sitting in an armchair, managed to give them 'a delightful smile of recognition'. But, eventually, he had to concede: 'Gentlemen, I am unable to concentrate.' The Counsellors filed out, close to tears.

Later in the day he asked his Private Secretary, Lord Wigram, 'How is the Empire?' but then had to admit, 'I feel very tired', unable to hear the answer to that huge question. That night the world learnt that the King's life was drawing peacefully to its close. By 11.55 P.M. he was dead, and a 'heartbroken' Queen Mary remembered in her grief to kiss the hand of her eldest son, the new King Edward VIII. 'The sunset of his death has tinged the whole world's sky,' she wrote in her diary.

The Duchess of York ignored doctor's orders and left her sickbed the next day to be with her husband and Queen Mary at the big house at Sandringham.

And those who were most sad thought of the 71-year-old King not so much as the King Emperor in his star and ribbon of the Garter, but for his moments of tenderness: his love for his wife; his sense of humour; his affection for his parrot, Charlotte, and his kindliness to the woman who was nervous when a hairpin dropped in her soup from what was obviously shiny and recently washed hair. 'Did you come here expecting to eat winkles?' he teased. His daughter-in-law, Elizabeth, on whom he doted, mourned: 'He was so kind and dependable . . . and always ready to listen and give advice on one's silly little affairs, and when he was in the mood, he could be deliciously funny too.'

A country cortège of tenants, gamekeepers, estate workers and gardeners walked alongside the coffin to Wolferton station for the journey to London and the state funeral. Jock, the King's white shooting pony, was led by a groom. After the King's funeral, the Duchess of York said simply: 'I miss him dreadfully. In all the twelve years of having me as a daughter-in-law he never spoke one unkind or abrupt word to me.'

8

Had a Good Crossing

'It is quite simple,' a friend of the royal family explains, 'the Queen Mother believes that Mrs Simpson shortened her husband's life and she has never been able to forgive her. The interesting thing is that she never openly blames her brother-in-law, the Duke of Windsor.' Her attitude has been that of a wronged wife who feels vindictive about the 'other woman' for luring her husband away.

Some argue that Mrs Simpson could not help it if she was attractive to Edward VIII. She made him laugh, pleased him and unfortunately had had two husbands, but that is no crime. He liked her astringency, her enamelled glamour and New World confidence.

Wallis Simpson, they say, never wanted the Abdication and was ready to flee. Living in chilly castles, being pleasant to courtiers who despised her and visiting the Women's Institute were not exciting prospects for this sophisticate. If she could not marry the King she could flit off to the Caribbean, or round the world in the private planes of rich admirers who liked her crackly voice, sharp wit and undeniable chic.

Mrs Simpson was at the cinema the evening George V died. Some of the thoughts which ran through her head when the bulletin flashed on the screen were uncanny in their accuracy. 'I was sure I had a big hurt coming. My head was spinning. But something kept telling me it's going to end now. You're going to know heartbreak . . . Was I going to revert to plain Mrs Simpson, a discarded woman? Nobody believes that David had never asked me to marry him . . . I often felt that he thought a woman was only to be enjoyed, not to be taken seriously. Ernest warned me that I was just the froth on his champagne.' But her second husband Ernest Simpson was proved utterly wrong in his hopeful prediction.

Edward seemed hysterically upset by George V's death, which was surprising in view of the uneasy father–son relationship. Cynical courtiers supposed that the grief of Edward VIII was in anticipation of all the horrendous difficulties ahead. If there had been a chance of marrying Mrs Simpson in George V's lifetime, now, as the King, it was going to be virtually impossible. An equerry, Major Verney, described his revolt as against 'the deadening inevitability of his destiny'.

Edward had cajoled George V into meeting Mrs Simpson on the silky grounds that it would improve Anglo-American relations. The King was furious and felt he had been hoodwinked. He sent for all papers and files on the lady, whom Queen Mary christened 'The Adventuress'. She had met her in the convivial atmosphere of Prince George's wedding. 'I want to introduce a great friend of mine,' David told his mother, and Queen Mary found herself shaking hands with the woman who was to come between her and her son like 'a coiled malevolence'.

From the beginning, Edward was different from his brothers and sisters. He was blond and confident – they tended to be dark and diffident. He was flippant and full of charm, which he could switch on with an ease that was worryingly facile. Edward VIII humorously made fun of himself and his ability with people when he described a meeting with Anne Morrow Lindberg, wife of the American aviator. Anne had been shy, 'but', said the King, 'with my well-known charm I put her at ease . . .'

He was bored easily, even by his own charm. At times there was a narcissistic shallowness which made him appear insensitive. A month after the King's death he was playing the bagpipes after dinner. He liked to put on a rakish beret with lots of ribbons and his Balmoral dress kilt. He would lead the musicians round the table as the bagpipes squeezed out some lament or tribute to the 'Bonnie Prince' who had also had an unfortunate parting from his country.

More than anything else, the beautiful jewels which the Prince of Wales gave Mrs Simpson have remained an irritant to the royal family. Suitable ambassadors have been sent to see the Duchess of Windsor in Paris. The names of all sorts of royal princesses, hardworking and without a hint of nastiness about their reputations, have been put forward as possessing ideal throats and skins for the valuable necklaces and earrings bestowed on Mrs Simpson, but without success.

'Princess Alexandra and the Duchess of Kent are loyal, hardworking girls, both of them, and they haven't many jewels. Unless you've made other plans, you might remember them,' proposed Lady Monckton, widow of Sir Walter Monckton, one of the truest and best friends the Windsors ever had. But the Duchess later said: 'Everything is going to Prince Charles. He wrote me a beautiful letter after the Duke's funeral.'

In contrast with her brother-in-law, after George V's death the Duchess of York became even more aware of the duty and responsibility which rested on her husband's shoulders, and she often appeared a little solemn in public. She seemed less resilient and complained to one of the royal doctors, Lord Dawson, that every little thing now seemed to affect her. Deep in her heart, with that canny intuition of someone receptive and caring, she felt uneasy about Mrs Simpson. But there were loyal excuses: 'I think I am now suffering from the effects of the family break-up – which always happens when the head of a family goes.'

But still the Duke and Duchess of York enjoyed their two daughters and their homes in London and Windsor. They dismissed what they feared most and were busy with even more engagements.

They saw less of Edward now that he was King. Once he had loved to pop into 145 Piccadilly, reading to the princesses and being teased by his sister-in-law as he set off wearily on another royal tour. 'You old Empire builder,' she would laugh.

One weekend, Edward said he would like to call on his brother and his wife because he wanted to show off a new American station wagon. In reality, Wallis Simpson was the exhibit. The Duke and Duchess would normally not have come across a woman like Wallis. Their friends were solid aristocrats with a feeling for the land and owning vast quantities of England's heritage – exactly the sort of people the King found boring. Mrs Simpson was considered by people like the Strathmores to be extremely vulgar. In royal circles she was regarded as 'common' because she wore too much make-up, frequently dressed in bright red and was loud.

The class structure may have changed in Britain now, but not that much. Koo Stark, the young articulate American actress who appeared in few frisky films without her clothes on, at least was single and available when she met the Queen's second son. Prince Andrew was captivated by her invitingly 'sassy' style. But the shutters came down on the romance at Buckingham Palace in a fairly ruthless way soon afterwards, although the Queen, who had met Miss Stark, was reported to have said, 'What a very nice girl.' Her views on Katie Rabett, the model and girlfriend of Prince Andrew, who posed in the nude, are less well known.

Mrs Simpson did not go down well with the Duchess of York, who to this day makes jokes at her expense, doing her excellent imitation of an American accent. Mrs Simpson found she was at the receiving end of that 'justly famous charm' and suspected that underneath the fluffy whipped-cream exterior there was a layer of rock-hard caramel. Proud of their garden at Royal Lodge, the Duke and Duchess winced when the King's American friend told them some trees should be moved to give a better view.

Mrs Simpson was thought far too proprietorial with the King. This was not something which would be approved of in aristocratic circles. The Duke and Duchess of York considered it bad form. Even Princess Elizabeth, then nine years old and rather used to having her glamorous uncle's attention, wanted to know: 'Who is she?' and then was quickly taken out of the room for tea, her unerring instinct causing the adults a tingle of embarrassment.

But Mrs Simpson knew how she appeared to the little Scottish aristocrat and, later, liked to refer to her rather feebly as the 'Dowdy Duchess' or, on bad days, as 'that fourteen-carat beauty'. When she realized she would never be HRH she called her 'the monster of Glamis'.

Harold Nicolson, who was struck more by the Duchess's personality than her glamour, recalls how in Lord Londonderry's house he met

. . . a dear little woman in black sitting on the sofa, and she said to me, 'We have not met since Berlin.' I sat down beside her and chattered away all friendly, thinking meanwhile, Berlin, Berlin? How odd. Obviously she is English, yet I do not remember her at all. Yet there is something about her which is vaguely familiar. While thus thinking, another woman came in and curtsied low to her and I realized it was the Duchess of York. Did I show by the tremor of an eyelid that I had not recognized her from the first? I did not. I steered my conversation onwards in the same course as before but with different sails: the dear old jib of comradeship was lowered and very gently, the spinnaker of 'Yes, Ma'am' was hoisted in its place. I do not believe she can have noticed the transition. She is charm personified.

Winston Churchill, who had an American mother, thought the Simpson romance one of the great loves of history and warned a luncheon party: 'Make no mistake, he cannot live without her.' Earlier he tried to draw out the Duchess of York at a dinner party given by the King which, of course, included Mrs Simpson, bringing up the romance between George IV and Mrs Fitzherbert. But the Duchess, in that way of hers, put her head on one side and sweetly reminded everyone at the table, 'but that was a very long time ago . . .' Later, when she and her husband talked over the evening, the resentment at being forced to attend a dinner party with Mrs Simpson, and to have her name alongside theirs in the Court Circular, brought home the remorseless momentum of the King's unpalatable love.

There was a romantic cruise on board the *Nahlin* along the coast of Yugoslavia. The large white yacht – belonging to Lady Yule and chartered by the King easily held the party of twelve mostly newly-made friends of Mrs Simpson. But a group of loyal friends, including Lady Diana Cooper, saw how much the King was influenced by Mrs Simpson and were distinctly shocked when he was sent scurrying to fetch a nail file for her. In royal circles where the rules of etiquette were so stringent, Mrs Simpson's behaviour made them shudder. A retired lady-in-waiting, explaining the importance of tact, knowing when to be silent, the need to be subdued when a laugh would be harsh, and generally to be subservient to the royal family, was appalled by Mrs Simpson, who would run a red-painted fingernail along a mantelpiece in search of dust. In HM's presence ladies-in-waiting used their fingertips to stifle a sneeze, pressing the index finger to the upper lip just below the nose. Now specks of dust were being discovered at Balmoral and the below-stairs staff were shocked. Often the staff in royal service are highly critical of the people around their employers, and quick to see solecisms which suggest middle- or lower-class backgrounds.

But Edward VIII thought Wallis's housekeeping ways delightful. He had wanted changes in the royal homes, anyway. When his father was dying he rather insensitively, and with indecent haste, ordered the clocks at Sandringham to be put back to the correct time. It had been one of the late King's Lewis Carroll eccentricities to keep the clocks in Norfolk thirty minutes ahead of Greenwich Mean Time. To make matters worse, Mrs Simpson was now using the bedroom at Balmoral where Queen Mary slept, and this seemed to confirm 'the adventuress' as châtelaine. The Duchess of York was disgusted to find herself being received by 'that American woman', who kept pressing guests to have double-decker toasted burger sandwiches in the small hours of the morning.

In October 1983, the Queen Mother went to Aberdeen University to receive an Honorary Degree of Doctor of Law and to open the university's £1-million library. The chapel was packed, but a retired head teacher, Charles Bisset, managed to squeeze into a corner near the organ loft. As the Queen Mother sat with a rapt smile on her face, looking at the invited guests as if they should be the ones receiving the honour, Bisset said: 'We have a great affection for the Queen Mother here. Aberdeen always remembers how Edward VIII was meant to open our new hospital buildings but cried off because of Court mourning, sending the Yorks instead. Then he was seen that very day in Aberdeen, meeting Mrs Simpson at the railway station.' He whispered, 'I was one of the students who greeted the Duchess of York when she came here with the Duke, and we have never forgotten it.' Mrs Simpson described it later in her book *The Heart Has Its Reasons* as another of those 'unfortunate coincidences'.

The Trustees of the Royal Infirmary in Aberdeen were deeply offended, the whole of Scotland outraged. This slap in the face to her home country could not have been more vexing for the Duchess of York. She and her husband knew that the King, far from being in mourning, was at the station hiding his face behind a large scarf and making Wallis laugh as she stepped off the London train.

Edward VIII at that time seemed so unaware it was as if he were in a trance, and to Queen Mary he was remote and cold. He had embarked on a love affair; his family did not approve, and he retreated into an impenetrable shell, intimidating anyone who might air kindly-meant criticism. The royal family was not a talking household; deepest feelings of anger, fear or love were never raised at the dining table. The Duke of Windsor later said: 'There was never a word about what was gnawing their souls.' To this day, one does not talk about sex, politics or religion in a royal house-party, which takes a lot of fun out of conversation. Lord Harlech, a great favourite with the Queen Mother and Princess Margaret, says that every so often conversation veers off on exciting and provocative lines; but there must always be a sudden halt to avoid putting members of the royal family in a position where they might have to express a view – and that is something which must never be sought.

On the other hand, there is more talking within the royal family today. The Queen is not a cosy person, but she is a perceptive mother and Prince Philip is an outspoken father. Queen Mary was inwardly sensitive, but repressed and so terribly shy she could not say what was in her heart to her children. To her good friend, Lady Airlie, she confided, 'I have not liked to talk to David about this affair with Mrs Simpson. And, because he is the most obstinate of all my sons, to oppose him over doing anything is only to make him more likely to do it.' Pretending to be busy with her embroidery, she said complacently, 'At present David is infatuated, but my great hope is that violent infatuations usually wear off.'

The Duke of Kent, who had earned family approval with Marina, his beautiful and cultivated wife, exploded, 'David is besotted. One can't get a word of sense out of him.'

The King and Wallis were entertained by all the hostesses of the day, who competed desperately for their presence, although Lady Colefax learned to regret her hunger for the company of royalty. She organized an evening when Arthur Rubinstein would play for her guests, the King and Lady Diana Cooper, Harold Nicolson, the Duchess of Buccleuch, Sir Kenneth Clark, then Director of the National Gallery, and the Princesse de Polignac. Things began to get slightly out of hand after dinner: the men, following the King's example, stayed over their port and brandy until well after eleven. There was nothing Lady Colefax could do. Rubinstein despised 'society' performances and had only agreed to play to indulge Sybil Colefax.

Eventually, when the men arrived in the drawing-room, as Lady Colefax and Diana Cooper sprawled on the floor trying to look relaxed, the great pianist began to play Chopin. But the King talked throughout the three pieces and, when he was silent, looked desperately bored and indifferent.

The American-born hostess Emerald Cunard grew very excited because she had often entertained the King when he was Prince of Wales and had egged on the romance with her countrywoman. In her flights of fancy she saw herself at the court of Queen Wallis as Mistress of the Robes – the grandest title, and one taken seriously today by the formidably correct Duchess of Grafton, a good friend of the Queen and the Queen Mother.

The King's behaviour was not only indiscreet, it was offensive. Mrs Simpson obtained her divorce on 27 October 1936 on the grounds of her husband, Ernest Simpson's, adultery with the woman he later married. But as far as the royal family was concerned, and the Government, the Archbishop of Canterbury and, above all, the Duke and Duchess of York, this formal release of Mrs Simpson from her marriage did not alter anything for the 42-year-old King. Mrs Simpson was no more eligible now as Queen Consort than a dancer at the Folies Bergère.

In November, the Duchess of York had her annual 'flu. She resented this weakness in her health and believed in the nourishing value of an 11 o'clock egg flip made with sherry and port. As soon as she was strong enough she went to Scotland. Mrs Simpson fled to Cannes.

The Duchess waved, but was economical with her smiles and seemed rather preoccupied in Edinburgh, where she was given the Freedom of the City. The Duke was also desperately unhappy and uneasy in Scotland, expecting to be rushed back to London at any moment, like 'the proverbial sheep', he thought, 'being led to the slaughter'. He knew intuitively that his brother was determined to marry and that there was nothing now to protect him from 'that fierce light', the tradition of royal duty 'which beats upon the throne'. He admitted feeling sick.

When the Yorks returned from Scotland on the night of 2 December they saw at Euston, before any courtier could get to them, the newspaper billboards with huge black lettering: The King has decided to put personal happiness before duty; he would marry. The details of what they feared most were being worked on in the capital by the King and the Prime Minister, Stanley Baldwin.

'My heart dropped,' the Duchess said later. In the car she turned to her husband and saw the distress of this highly-strung man. All the signals were there, in particular the nerve working in his left cheek, as he bit his lip. From that moment, seeds of resentment against 'that woman' were sown in the Duchess's heart. They grew into tendrils of uncharacteristic bitterness, wound round an otherwise soft and loving nature and still in place after half a century.

Back home at 145 Piccadilly, the Duchess went straight to bed with particularly bad 'flu again, the body registering psychological stress and collapse.

For the Duchess those last few days of the Abdication crisis were 'like sitting on the edge of a volcano'. When her brother-in-law ceased to be King in the eyes of Parliament, the small household staff were gently told: 'I am afraid there are going to be great changes in our lives – we must take what is coming to us and make the best of it.'

On 10 December 1936, Edward VIII signed the Instrument of Abdication and, at 2 A.M., after 327 days on the throne, left England for ever, 'to marry the woman I love'. His cousin, Lord Louis Mountbatten, was shocked by his high spirits: 'Gay as a lark . . . it was absolutely incredible . . .' In the great downstairs bedroom at Fort Belvedere a vast double bed was covered with telegrams and cables and he was having his corns done before catching the ferry to France. This springy attitude on the surface appeared shallow and uncaring, but possibly the hysterically good mood was a reaction to the tension of the previous weeks when often he had seemed so debilitated, wearied by calls from Wallis Simpson and various members of the Establishment. His was not a reflective personality and, like a spoilt child, he enjoyed the moment without the maturity to work out the waves ahead.

'This can't be happening to me,' the Duke of York turned disbelievingly to Mountbatten as he heard a servant call him 'Your Majesty'. When he returned to London from Windsor he went to see his mother and, on what the world has thought of as an unsympathetic shoulder, he rested his head and wept. Anger raced to take the place of heartbreak. Queen Mary could not help but take sides. 'The person who needs most sympathy is my second son. He is the one making the sacrifice.'

He was seen returning home to Piccadilly, running indoors from his car in the way you do when there is good news. But his face was 'deathly serious'.

To make matters worse, there was a lack of confidence in the Duke of York as King. The Duke himself had said to Mountbatten: 'This is terrible, Dickie. I never wanted this to happen. I'm quite unprepared for it. David has been trained for it all his life, whereas I've never seen a State paper. I'm a naval officer. It's the only thing I know about.' There had been a feeling that perhaps the Duke's speech impediment would mean he could not be a dynamic enough personality to be King.

The Duke of Kent looked more prepossessing, but this hardly made him eligible for anointing with the holy oil. He had dabbled in drugs and was not thought of as reliable, and neither was Prince Henry, Duke of Gloucester, totally bound into a military mould. So the throne went to Bertie.

But the uneasy sentiments of the Prime Minister, Stanley Baldwin, and others in the New Year of 1937, were to prove unfounded. The British public, with its basic core of common sense and an instinct about what is right for the country, made up its own mind.

The speculation had been galling for Queen Mary and worse for the Duchess of York. Now at least it was settled. Bertie was King, and Queen Mary hurried round to her daughter-in-law. The new Queen was still wrapped up in bed, which was rather fortunate because visitors were often not sure whether she was coping with a runny nose or tears. But when the old lady left her bedroom after an hour and a half with her daughter-in-law the old Queen was in no doubt: 'Tears were streaming down her face'.

Queen Mary spoke about her 'dear daughter-in-law' to the people. 'I need not speak to you of the distress which fills a mother's heart when I think of my dear son who has deemed it his duty to lay down his charge. I commend to you his brother, someone who so unexpectedly takes his place.' Elizabeth prayed fervently that her husband 'would be granted not a lighter load but a stronger back'.

'Had a good crossing. Hope Elizabeth better. Best love and best of luck to you both,' was the brief telegram from the Duke of Windsor when he arrived in France. It was an airy message, almost saying, 'Byee – have a super reign!'

The stability of the monarchy rested now with a slight young man who said he only knew about being a sailor. He had seen his brother revert from King to Duke in just a matter of hours: 'D and I said goodbye. We kissed, parted as freemasons and he bows to me as his King.'

The Queen was still angry about Mrs Simpson, and she had been hurt by the unworthy vacillation over the choice of which brother was to succeed Edward VIII. A different person began to emerge from the 'sweet little Duchess' who had taken to her bed a week before.

What she had dreaded most when refusing to marry the King's son had happened now. But this gentle woman was to be the symbol of modern royalty. Before her the royal ladies played a very minor role. Queen Alexandra was very decorative and adored for her sweet personality. Queen Mary was downright withdrawn. They did their duty in a dull way, opening bazaars, visiting hospitals and sometimes cheering up the Forces. It was thoroughly admirable, but lacklustre. Until 1936, royal women were congenitally shy in public, a disease which seems to be hereditary in the royal family, although perhaps less so now.

The Queen Mother's voice is hardly ever heard, but she has persuaded everybody that she loves them all. There was perhaps an inherent lack of shyness about the new Queen; being the second youngest of a large family probably taught her a great deal. She was married to a man who was vulnerable; she had to protect him and learn to do what he could not.

The new Queen was to come out of the Abdication splendidly as her husband's support. But to this day, she resents the implication that she was the strong one of the two.

She would never have married a weakling, and she never under-estimated his strength: but she had not wanted to be royal. The present Princess of Wales, coping at first with the accurate beams of the spotlight homing in on her marriage, her tears, her shopping expeditions, won sympathy by cleverly letting slip on a royal tour: 'When something awful is written about me I get this awful feeling inside and don't want to go out for days.' In 1936, newspapers had to be more restrained.

Friends of the Duke and Duchess of Windsor cannot forget the bitter hostility to Mrs Simpson, arguing that one can be reasonably angry for so long and then the time comes to forgive. In September 1939, the Windsors offered their services to the war effort, but the Queen said: 'I will not receive her.' A friend, Mrs John Gilmour, mother of Sir Ian Gilmour, Tory 'wet', asked, 'May I make this known?' Lowering her voice, the Queen replied: 'You certainly may.' In his play *Crown Matrimonial*, which opened in 1972, Royce Ryton represented the Duchess of York in a petulant light; people were shocked to see her depicted as shrieking and weeping when she knew the Abdication was inevitable.

What moved the King most was that when he returned to 145 Piccadilly for the first time after his Accession, on 12 December, his daughters curtsied to him in the hall. Then, at a family lunch, he teased them: 'Now, if someone comes through on the telephone who should I say I am?' The princesses laughed and the light moment helped lift all their spirits.

George VI, whose slow way of speaking seemed to give extra meaning to his words, told the nation: 'With my wife and helpmate by my side I take up the heavy task which lies before me.'

David Bowes-Lyon, the brother who was more like a twin to the Duchess of York, told a friend that the day his sister became Queen a door clanged shut behind her, and 'nothing would ever be the same again'.

9

Nobody Minded the Rain

There was a flatness and uncertainty about the early part of 1937. The monarchy had been shaken badly but those closest to the King found he had a new decisiveness. For years, even when representing his father George V on tours abroad, he had complained that he felt overshadowed in the family: 'rather like a human buff slip marked "pass on to you for action please"'. Those in the royal household who took comfort in recalling this and thought George VI's was going to be an easy-going reign, found they were working now for a King and Queen with exactingly high standards, for themselves and their household.

The Coronation was still to be on 12 May 1937, the day originally fixed for Edward VIII. Same day – different King. The trouble was that although the Duke of Windsor was in France with Mrs Simpson, he could not quite realize that he no longer reigned. He made interminable telephone calls to counsel his younger brother about the issues of the day. He was also very keen to see that Wallis was given the title Her Royal Highness.

'What a damnable wedding present,' the Duke was to huff and rage when the King decided firmly that there would be no title for Wallis. As an HRH there would have been a certain obligation to receive her, paying her the courtesy of her title. For the new Queen and her mother-in-law the prospect was intolerable. The Duke of Windsor immediately realized the implications of the King's decision and, sadly for him, made the rash statement: 'No HRH for Wallis, no homecoming for me.'

It was a show of strength in the new King, the way he handled these requests from France, particularly since he had always adored his older brother and looked up to him. But those who knew them both had always thought Bertie's the steadier, more determined and much finer character. Now it was evident.

The King settled an allowance of an estimated £60,000 a year on his brother in exile. A capital sum of about £1 million was thought fair compensation for Edward VIII's life tenancy of Balmoral and Sandringham, which had now passed to the new King. While it seemed a lot of money then, the settlement probably explains the

Duke of Windsor's reputation for meanness in later years. He was, said one of the royal family, 'a man of great overwhelming charm, but frightfully mean'. Apart from his training to be King, he had no particular skills.

This would not happen today, largely due to Prince Philip's influence and an insistence that the royal sons should be proficient in as many disciplines as possible. The Queen loves her little joke about Britain becoming a republic. 'We'll go quietly,' she says solemnly. Her two elder sons could become airline pilots, or, perhaps, effective executives.

A friend tried to plead Mrs Simpson's case with the Queen, pointing out that she had done much to stop the Duke drinking too much, and that he looked a lot better. Yes, maybe that was true, the Queen replied. 'But', she asked, 'who has the pouches under his eyes now?'

One evening, about a month after the Abdication, the King was asked to telephone his brother, who was on holiday in Austria. The King, who was busy, returned the call but was told by the Schloss operator that the Duke was half-way through a pleasant dinner; he would have to call later. That did it. The Queen was outraged and enlisted Queen Mary's help. Together they put pressure on the King, who agreed now that the calls must end. He had found them truly irritating.

Sir Walter Monckton told the Duke of Windsor that telephone calls to Buckingham Palace must end. Monckton understood the Queen's attitude. 'Naturally, she thought that she must be on her guard because the Duke of Windsor is an attractive, vital creature who could become a rallying point for a subversive pro-Windsor party.'

The Queen found the constant telephone conversations insidious. The couple had not yet been crowned and felt unsure of themselves. 'How will the country take us?' they asked themselves, 'horribly aware that they lacked the superficial appeal of Edward VIII – or so they thought. They seemed to forget that they were a personable couple and that the two princesses, Elizabeth and Margaret, in their pretty clothes, added a bonus to the image of a happy family, something the Duke of Windsor would never have provided, for he and the Duchess remained childless.

One of the King's happier moments of authority was being able to give his wife the Order of the Garter in the first week of his reign, on his 41st birthday. Elizabeth immediately sent a letter by hand to

Queen Mary, even though she was coming to lunch that day, to tell her about her delight in receiving the highest and oldest Order her husband could confer. 'Bertie discovered that Papa gave it to you on his birthday and the coincidence was so charming that he has now followed suit and given it to me on his birthday.'

Queen Mary was delighted and touched by this thoughtful gesture by a tactful daughter-in-law. She warmed to the apparent helplessness of Elizabeth's early days on the throne and confided to a close friend: 'I plan to compile a little book on everything a Queen ought to know and give it to my daughter-in-law.' They had become close through the Abdication. Queen Mary was plagued with a feeling of inadequacy and guilt about her eldest son. Perhaps if she had been a warmer mother he might have been more mature and less capricious? It would have helped if Edward had felt able to talk to his mother.

Spirits began to lift as preparations were made for the Coronation. For the Queen there was even the beginning of a return to normal life – if you can call a move to Buckingham Palace an ordinary experience. She would bring touches to the Palace which would make it 'lived in'; the family moved from their happy, homely 145 Piccadilly on 15 February 1937.

The King indulged his daughters, telling them that, of course, they could have a 'medieval' tunnel from the bleak, forbidding Palace to 'home' in Piccadilly. It was important that the princesses should feel that life was not going to change dramatically and that 'Mummy and Papa' were still the same. The King continued to tease them and was always pretending that he wanted to send them to Eton.

The corgis went to the Palace; so, too, did the Queen's four-poster bed, her piano and her gramophone records. The Palace was sombre and glumly Victorian, neglected during Edward VIII's short reign, when the King had spent as much time at Fort Belvedere as he possibly could. The Fort, six miles from Windsor, is like a child's idea of a castle. For Edward VIII it meant freedom and the only home he really ever enjoyed in England. He persuaded his father to let him have it when it fell vacant in 1929. 'Why do you want the queer old place?' the King asked. 'Those damn weekends, I suppose.' He let him have the derelict folly, which with the help of his women friends was tastefully redesigned and the gardens were filled with delphiniums and Sweet Williams.

But there was not only Buckingham Palace to worry about, there were also Windsor and Sandringham and Balmoral. The new

Queen spent her own money on some furniture because the State apartments at Windsor Castle looked so drab. Early on, she had developed a taste for twentieth-century art, knowing people like Epstein, the sculptor. Royal homes were soon to have paintings by John Piper, Matthew Smith, Augustus John and Wilson Steer alongside portraits of surprised-looking Hanoverian ancestors. Sir Kenneth Clark was an ideal mentor, and also friends like Osbert Sitwell and Sir John Betjeman influenced the Queen's view. Captain Ririd Myddleton became Assistant Master of the Household. He was a friend of the Queen's brother, David Bowes-Lyon, from Eton days and was a clever choice. Together they could plan changes in confidence. Any hint of criticism about the old order would never escape his lips in the household dining-room.

The royal family has never felt a great warmth towards Buckingham Palace: even today it is their office. 'We live over the shop' the Queen will tell foreign visitors. What her mother missed most when she moved from Piccadilly to The Mall was not having the time, or really being able, to go into the kitchen. Nowadays, the royal apartments have tiny kitchens attached where the Queen likes to make toast and scrambled eggs. But in 1937 the Palace kitchens were grim, though ideal for preparing the 18,832 meals to be eaten during the Coronation week.

As the first British Queen Consort since Tudor times she had a great deal to do, and kept reminding herself of one of her mother's favourite sayings: 'One must hasten slowly.' As Queen Consort, apart from sharing the same protective privileges as her husband the King, e.g. not paying income tax and not having to make her will public, the powers are limited and intangible. But the Queen was to have an influence unprecedented for any consort in history. She started in the Palace itself. She would nip 'downstairs' to congratulate the chef or have a final word with the housekeeper. Often, before a banquet and just before she put on her tiara, she would look into the dining-room to make sure the Sèvres and gold cutlery were correct or, sometimes, rearrange the flowers.

Dressed in her clinging light wool dresses with bows and ruched skirts, the Queen cheered the staff in those drab winter months. She would hold her head on one side and wonder if something could be done, even if it was asking the impossible. The grumpiest old butlers and pages found the Palace a happier, lighter place; even their gout seemed less painful when they heard the Queen laughing in the corridor.

Those who had sneered about the 'unsophisticated' Duke and Duchess of York, and secretly mourned the wit and lightweight charm of Edward VIII, quickly tried to get closer to the new King and Queen. Their antennae were correct. Harold Nicolson, with the eye of the diplomat yet never missing fine, almost feminine, subtleties, was captivated. 'I cannot tell you how superb she was,' he said. 'What astonished me is how the King has changed. He is now like his brother. He was so gay and she so calm.'

At a dinner party at Windsor Nicolson thought nothing could exceed the 'charm and dignity' of the new Queen of England. 'I cannot help feeling what a mess poor Mrs Simpson would have made of such an occasion. It demonstrated to us more than anything else how wholly impossible that marriage would have been.' The Queen's sense of humour has warmed many a royal engagement; Nicolson remembered how she had teased him, 'very charmingly, about my pink face and my pink views'.

Diana Cooper, one of the great beauties of the time, had transferred her witty allegiance rather dextrously from Edward VIII and the Fort Belvedere set to the new King and Queen. We have her to thank for some vivid pictures of the *Nahlin* cruise, when she was a guest on board: 'The King appeared with an old shrimping net on his shoulder, looking like a child of eight. He ordered out a dinghy and set about catching a jellyfish while we all leant over the ship's side shrieking, "There's a big one, Sir".' Now, with her husband Duff Cooper, who was Secretary of State for War, she was delighted to go to Windsor, and reported, 'Everything at Windsor Castle was still Victorian, the "good" coal fire, piano, well-stocked writing tables, tapless baths lidded in mahogany, a throttlingly stuffy bedroom and, everywhere, innumerable oil paintings, plaques, miniatures, wax profiles and bronzes of the old royal family.' The Coopers thought Queen Elizabeth 'simply spellbinding'.

They had been told by the King's Private Secretary, Alex Hardinge, to expect the royal 'goodnight' at 10.30, but this was not the Queen's style. When first married, the Yorks liked to eat at about nine, and Queen Mary sometimes clucked grandmotherly disapproval of such late hours for the princesses. So, late in the evening, Duff Cooper was sent for by the Queen, much to the chagrin of Lady Diana, left on her own in a guest turret. The Queen looked, he said later, 'too ravishing in a gloss of satin – a lily and rose in one' as they drank tea and talked until it was nearly midnight. She spoke frankly of monarchy as 'the intolerable honour'. But,

relaxed, with her feet on the sofa, she managed to talk about the
burden of kingship without once mentioning the Abdication or the
names of Edward VIII or Mrs Simpson. Duff Cooper was impressed.

Whether the Queen was entertaining her guests in Windsor
Castle or walking round a flour mill or shipyard, she always did the
rounds with a faint smile, giving the impression that if she were not
Queen of England she could relax and enjoy the engagement even
more.

The King still found time for old friends. He had a new confidence
and his restoration of stability at Court brought him appreciation.
'The little King' was the maternal nickname the talkative Mrs
Grace Vanderbilt gave to him. She had known him since he was a
baby, and had always been devoted to the King's sons – those 'dear
boys'. There was a rather endearing exchange between the two
when, shortly after he came to the throne, the new King went to
Claridges in London to call on her. He told her she was 'very
naughty' to have smuggled her dog into the country, hiding the
pooch from the Customs men. 'I could have you locked up for the
rest of your life,' he told her sternly. 'Well,' she said, flirtatiously,
'why don't you, Your Majesty?'

The King and Queen had spent the Christmas of 1936–7 at
Sandringham, as guests still of Queen Mary until the Coronation. It
was a chance for the family to have some peace together, to walk the
marshy land, through the woods and coverts as the woodcock,
pheasant and partridge soared into the wintry sky, safe until the
King with his left-handed skill bagged them at the New Year shoot.

After the traumas earlier that month there was something comforting about Christmas in Norfolk, the corgis trotting round the
corners and snoozing in front of the log fires; pink ribbon marking off
each pile of presents – jade paper cutters, silver cruets, little
diamond brooches, enamel or decorated rose bowls, small pink satin
eggs; and Queen Mary watching the family opening their presents
with cries of 'too sweet,' 'too generous'.

The King asked his mother if she would like to be at their
Coronation, a sensitive invitation which was accepted. This would
be the first time a Queen Dowager would see the crowning of her
successor in the Abbey. She had lost two stone in weight during the
crisis and prayed daily for her sons, particularly Edward, hoping
that Mrs Simpson 'would make him happy'. 'It is no ordinary love
he has for her,' the old lady astutely remarked.

David Bowes-Lyon and his wife spent New Year with the King

and Queen. It was like a trip back into the warmth of family life at Glamis. The first issue of the Court Circular for the Coronation year was devoted to the announcement that the 'Hon D. and Mrs Bowes-Lyon had left Sandringham', perhaps typical of the new Queen's sense of priorities. In 1961 Sir David, who became President of the Royal Horticultural Society, officially dropped the hyphen between Bowes and Lyon.

But not even the security of a family reunion could take away the dread of the Coronation ahead. The Queen broke down and cried out: 'I can't go through with it. I can't be crowned.' But last-minute nerves eased during a weekend with the two princesses at Royal Lodge. Then they drove back to London and the Archbishop of Canterbury went to the Palace that Sunday evening to talk about the spiritual joy of the ceremony. This time he found the right words and did much to heal the damage done by his clumsy oration at the time of the Abdication. In the way of some churchmen, Dr Lang had early taken upon himself the task of illuminating the nation about the new King's speech defect. Well meaning, perhaps, but it merely drew attention to George VI's inability to pronounce his 'r's' very well. Mercifully, he said, the new King had been able to bring the momentary hesitation in his speech under full control. And 'to those who hear it need cause no sort of embarrassment for it causes none to him who speaks'. There was fierce embarrassment at 145 Piccadilly as the King and Queen listened to this unfortunate and insensitive ramble. They were mortified.

But Dr Lang was forgiven. The King was no longer the shy, diffident man the Archbishop remembered. George VI joked, 'According to the papers, I am supposed to be unable to speak without stammering, to have fits and to die in two years. All in all I seem to be a crock.' But laughter is the best cure for nerves, and luckily he and the Queen, who were closer than ever now, found it all very amusing.

Deeply spiritual, the Queen found that when the Archbishop talked to her about the Coronation she felt at peace. He noticed when all three knelt for his personal blessing in a sitting-room at the Palace that evening that 'there were tears in their eyes when we rose from our knees. From that moment I knew what would be in their hearts when they came to their anointing and crowning.'

There was a lunch party next day, just for the royal family. There was, for 'Bertie and E our gift of a gold tea set'. For Elizabeth there was also a beautiful tortoiseshell and diamond fan with ostrich feathers which had once belonged to 'Mama Alix', as the family called Queen Alexandra. For the King there was a dark blue enamel snuffbox with miniatures of his parents on the lid. That night the King and Queen gave a banquet for 450 guests. Most of the guests were in the ballroom, but the Queen was hostess to a smaller, more intimate gathering in a supper room; she was full of sparkle, showing no signs of strain or hoarseness.

Tuesday was set aside for the last-minute touches to the Coronation clothes. The Queen's dress was white satin with a square neck and all the symbols of the British Empire, the lotus, mimosa, fern, maple, leek, rose, shamrock and thistle, embroidered in diamanté. Some women would have shirked high heels under the scrutiny of some 7,700 people in Westminster Abbey, but her femininity ruled and high-heeled white satin shoes were made to match, with oak leaves of England and the thistle of Scotland stitched in gold. Her robe was purple velvet lined with white satin. The Coronation robes had been made by Mme Handley Seymour, the Court dressmaker who was really a bit behind the times, but the Queen would not dream of hurting her feelings even though she might have preferred one of the smart new couturiers like Norman Hartnell.

On the wet Wednesday morning of the Coronation, none of the royal family could sleep. The King and Queen had been woken early – at 3 A.M. – by the testing of loud-speakers on Constitution Hill. 'One of them might have been in our room,' George VI grumbled. In her room, Princess Elizabeth had crept out of bed at 5 A.M. to look once again at her dress of white lace and silver, with gold bows dotted down the front. She curled up on the window-seat and watched the Royal Marines lining the rosy-surfaced Mall; her maid, 'Bobo' MacDonald, gently put an eiderdown round her shoulders.

The King could eat no breakfast; the hours of waiting since dawn had been quite nerve-racking. He had been practising breathing exercises for weeks so that he could get the responses right. Now he confessed to a 'sinking feeling inside'. The Palace staff were the first to glimpse the King and Queen in their robes and gave them shy smiles of support.

At 10 A.M. the King and Queen stepped into the pretty gold State Coach, with its trumpeting cherubs and gods and goddesses holding up the crown in panels circled with clusters of gilded leaves. But it made a queasy start to the day. It was old and rickety, bobbing along to Westminster Abbey on uneven, iron-shod wheels. Later the Queen made sure that it was thoroughly overhauled in the Royal

Mews so that no other member of the family would have this miserable journey again. As the King got out at Westminster he looked as if he might faint.

At the Abbey, the Queen's procession was just about to go up the nave when one of the chaplains did pass out. For what seemed an eternity, this robed figure lay in a heap, halting the procession; the King took some pleasure in pointing out that the recumbent figure was a Presbyterian. Eventually, the offending prelate, sweltering in his long woollen scarlet cloak held at the neck with red and white cord, was hauled away.

The procession started again and the Queen looked calm, with a hint of a smile. Lord Mersey breathed a sigh of relief. You could positively feel the waves of 'widespread affection and admiration' for her, he said. Her composure won all hearts. Her prettiness had been enough when she was Duchess of York, but now other qualities were revealed, which made people say a prayer of thanks for the Abdication. The slight shoulders of this 37-year-old Scottish aristocrat's daughter could stand the intensity of that 'fierce light' which beats upon the throne.

Now the King was able to move forward a little nearer to his Coronation. His face was white and he moved as if in a trance, that tell-tale muscle in his cheek working overtime. He noticed that his white surplice was being offered inside out. George V would have had a thrombosis at such sloppiness, and his son shared his meticulous eye for detail. But worse was to follow.

We have to thank the King for his detailed note of the day. The royal family have always been earnest diarists, finding diaries a good way of relieving stress. That night he recalled that when

. . . the great moment came, neither bishop could find the words, so the Archbishop held his book down for me to read, but, horror of horrors, his thumb covered the words of the Oath. My Lord Great Chamberlain was supposed to dress me but I found his hand fumbled and shook so I had to fix the belt of the sword myself.

Queen Mary raised her lorgnette and looked at her son. Princess Margaret had been remarkably well behaved during the long hours in the Abbey, only occasionally rustling her prayer book or standing on tiptoes to watch her father. He was kneeling at the scarlet faldstool with an intense seriousness. The Archbishop anointed his head with oil from the golden ampulla. The King, his robes glittering, moved to the Coronation chair. For a second the Archbishop held the St Edward Crown up high above him before resting it on the head of the withdrawn figure. 'God Save the King!' the Westminster boys shouted; bells rang out; the fanfare sounded; and the peers put on their coronets with smiles that said, 'Thank God'. As one, the guests in the Abbey rose to their feet to sing the National Anthem for their new King and Queen.

Lady Strathmore, in mushroom-coloured lamé with a feather design in rhinestones, was standing beside Princess Marina. For all the decorum drilled into her over the years she could not keep herself from leaning forward anxiously as her daughter was crowned.

Slowly, the Queen rose, the crown with the Koh-i-Noor diamond on her head, the sceptre and ivory rod in her hands, and began the long walk from the altar along the nave. From that moment, she always said, she never felt the same again, seeming to gain a new understanding and optimism.

Diana, Princess of Wales, has ahead a steady, long haul to the Coronation, but for Queen Elizabeth there had been just five months to prepare for an experience she can still only share with her daughter, the Queen. They both believe in the mystical quality of the monarchy and see it as a God-given destiny. For the Princess of Wales, in moments of slight panic at the thought of her Coronation, there is reassurance from the Queen Mother that the placing of a crown on her fair hair will give her strength.

The newly crowned King and Queen, their crimson trains spread out behind them, walked slowly out of the Abbey past curtsying peeresses, bowing lords and European crowned heads and then Canadian, Australian and South African friends.

Outside in the streets of London, the people took this unassuming couple to their hearts, and, driving back to the Palace, it did not seem to matter any more that the gold coach rattled. The King and Queen waved and smiled and nobody minded the rain which by now was bucketing down. When they arrived at the Palace the young Duke of Norfolk was being congratulated on his arrangements; the lavatory facilities in the Abbey were pronounced 'excellent' and the special underground train which had carried hundreds of peers and members of Parliament between High Street Kensington and Westminster was a success.

The King, however, did not congratulate the bishop who had pinned him to the ground, standing on his robes at the dreadfully sacred moment when the crown was placed on his head. 'I had to tell him to get off it pretty smartly as I nearly fell down.'

By the end of the day the Queen had completely lost her voice, so it was only with the brilliance of her eyes that she could thank the King for his perfect gift to her that evening. He had pinned on her dress the glittering Badge and Star of diamonds, sapphires and emeralds, investing her as the only Lady of the Thistle there has ever been. He had designed the emblem specially and it crystallized his love for her. It was his thank-you and a gift to Scotland, too.

The King thanked the people, also, that evening. He had, as Harold Nicolson had noticed, a 'really beautiful voice'. Speaking slowly, George VI described 12 May 1937 quite simply as 'this day of inspiration which the Queen and I will always keep in our hearts'.

10

Fun Time

The Queen Mother will allow her couturier to cajole her into anything new just so long as it is in blue, has a crossover bodice and a flutter of feathers. She adores lilac, hates dark colours, resists sensible overcoats and shares with her younger daughter a distaste for crêpe. Mother and daughter make this harmless crinkly fabric sound like a German expletive; 'Krrrep,' the Queen Mother will say, 'Margaret hates it.'

Time and again the Queen Mother will arrive at Buckingham Palace in a stunning confection and the Queen will give a quizzical look – 'But I haven't seen that before, Mummy,' and her mother will hold out her arms placatingly: 'Well, darling, I suppose it is rather new.' And another outfit will be crammed into the wardrobes at Clarence House, where you could hardly get a silver cake slice to separate the dresses, except between the bodices of tea cosy crinolines and evening dresses with great cabbage roses and silver bugle beads. In this vast cupboard every dress she has ever had in her life stands indestructible. Some have been in her wardrobe for half a century; some are white and virginal with little square necklines, the sort of dress Jeanette MacDonald might have worn sitting on a swing in a Metro-Goldwyn-Mayer film. There is the dress the Queen Mother never really took to; to make it more sophisticated gold stitching was added. The seamstress was thanked sweetly but the Queen Mother never put it on her back again.

One of the grandest is in white tulle with white flowers appliquéd in silver; her favourite is a pink semi-crinoline tulle, its embroidery lovingly restored. There are the masses of shoes to match. Unlike the Queen, the Queen Mother will be adventurous and have shoes dyed – the royal cobbler, Edward Rayne, finds this quite revolutionary in royal circles. For years the touching wish for a little extra height meant that she teetered round on impossibly high heels; even the soles of her shoes were rather thick, to exaggerate her height of 5 feet 2 inches. But after the injury to her leg at the time of Prince Charles's wedding there was the resigned acceptance of a lower heel.

Clothes are the Queen Mother's weakness. Her style is all her own, totally feminine and captivating. The man responsible for the grand-occasion dresses and the look about her that people adore was Sir Norman Hartnell. She has never bought clothes abroad. As a young wife in London, 'the Duchess of York dressed to perfection,' the diarist Chips Channon wrote. Later, Lady Churchill described her as 'very sweet and *soignée*, like a plump turtle dove'.

There is a model of the Queen Mother in the Hartnell salon which has scarcely changed over the years, a compliment to her figure, even though she loves good food. Sometimes the stand will carry a satin evening dress – with a mock Garter across the front – or it might have a simple plaid skirt for Scotland. Usually there are about three fittings.

As the Duchess of York she first went to Norman Hartnell in 1935. It was an exciting time in fashion for a woman for whom the garçon look, with no waist or admission of curves, had little appeal. She loved the waisted look with a sash, and a draped neckline. Norman Hartnell was enraptured by his new client. On that first occasion she brought the princesses to his salon, the Duchess wore silver grey georgette and the solemn princesses were in silver-buttoned blue jackets and with forget-me-nots on their straw hats. It was the start for all four of a delightful liaison – Hartnell designing creations for the Queen and her daughters through their lives, wedding dresses and the Queen's coronation robes in 1953.

Hartnell excelled at bringing out the best in upper-class English women of the time, combining in perfect good taste delicate pale blues, eau-de-nils and rose pinks with pearls and fresh complexions. There was the aura of a Winterhalter painting in his graceful 'picture dresses' and embroidered crinolines. Like her daughters, the Queen Mother is not eager for innovation. In the thirties she had found a style which suited her, which the King loved – and she has stayed with it ever since. She has always loved lady-like afternoon dresses and never fell for the fun accessories of the time favoured by Schiaparelli, with buttons in the shape of lemons and even lamb cutlets! But then the Queen Mother hardly needed a novelty button on her crossover bodice where pearls and diamonds could sit so appealingly, so 'becomingly' – a favourite word.

Hartnell never really enjoyed making practical day clothes anyway; he thought 'who's for tennis?' dresses an awful bore; nobody could be a more perfect client for him than the Queen Mother, sharing as she does his love for satin and silk, with pearls, sequins, aquamarine and topaz added wherever a space of material allowed. Occasionally she visited his salon in Bruton Street, with its

Waterford chandeliers – and Hartnell himself with shocking pink ties and glasses of champagne – but usually he went to Buckingham Palace and, later, Clarence House. The Queen Mother liked his 'unassuming manner' and he was never complacent – shaking like a leaf before he did his deep bow. But, within minutes, the couturier would be standing back wondering if he'd got the design quite right. 'Oh, Mr Hartnell, by the time we've put a little "mmmmmmm" here, it will be very nice,' and the anxiety would disappear and they would both beam at the improvement made by adding a fistful of diamonds.

In the halcyon pre-war days Norman Hartnell made his name with the clothes he designed for the young Duchess of York, both loving all those floating panels, lumps of fur at the bottom of hems; rhinestones, pearls and black osprey, white fox; frilled organdie matching parasols. She was never a dedicated slimmer, nor did she envy the self-consciously fashionable slim-hipped shape of women like Edwina Mountbatten.

'Why should I not be known for my style of dressing?' the Queen Mother rightly asks. She has never had a lean clothes-horse figure. It is womanly, curvy, and now a softer grandmotherly outline. She is small-boned and a hundred per cent feminine. Today, though a size 14 on her hips, she has a remarkably slim waist and, if anything, has recently lost a little weight.

So, whatever the fashion, the Queen Mother has stayed steadfastly with her draped bodices and palest pastels, sailing through the eras of elegance, extravagance and austerity. Norman Hartnell, known to the Queen and her mother as 'Dear Mr Hartnell', was rewarded in 1977, when he became a Knight Commander of the Royal Victorian Order. When illness forced him to retire two years later, he handed over his sketch pad to John Tullis, with warnings that on no account was he to try to change the Queen Mother. The Master, long cigarette holder in hand, briefed Tullis: 'Dear boy, she is tiny – a very little lady.' But both men knew that although quite small, there has always been about the Queen Mother an aura of the *grande dame*.

The first time John Tullis met the Queen Mother in London he had three commandments set firmly in his head. One: keep to the crossover bodice and never stray to square or strappy necklines. Two: unlimited choice of colour, as long as it ranged from yellow to peach, pink to blue and lilac. Three: beware the tight sleeve. The Queen Mother likes to wave warmly – and sleeves are easily torn.

But, as Tullis says today, now living in South Africa designing tapestries: 'Why should I try to change the Queen Mother? She has always looked sensational with a style all her own. She is a lady of great distinction and always looks ravishing.' He swooped on an early sketch of the dress she wore to St Paul's on her 80th birthday, with all the favourite features in pale mauve-blue silk georgette. 'Without doubt,' he thought, 'she will go down in history as the Queen of the crossover bodice.'

When he went to Clarence House, as soon as the Queen Mother walked in, he found 'she was always enchanting. We would look at sketches together, but the Queen Mother would never say "what a perfectly hideous design". She would smile and, closing the book, turn to me and say, "Mr Tullis, that is a lovely idea, but why don't we wait until the next time . . ."'

John Tullis is a cousin of Captain Edward Molyneux, a British couturier who had the distinction of being accepted in Paris. It was in France that Tullis learned his art of understated elegance, designing for some of society's smartest – and toughest – women. The world of fashion then was a funny mix of extravagance and penny-pinching. In the post-war days, a celebrated aristocratic London beauty with a passion for clothes was appalled, on a cross-Channel ferry, to see the staff of a Mayfair couturier she patronized all drinking champagne on the way to the collections in Paris. 'No wonder the clothes are so expensive,' she sniffed disapprovingly as the bubbles flowed, 'if you can all afford to drink champagne.' The leading *vendeuse* spoke up while the fitters pretended to be looking into their bags of pins and thimbles: 'All I can say, my lady, is that if we relied on you paying your bills, we would be drinking water . . .'

An intuitive knack of knowing what is right for her – the more fur and feathers the better – makes the Queen Mother decisive to the point of insistence about her image. Other women dither and waver about colours. Another pale blue outfit – 'well, you see, that is what is expected of me,' the Queen Mother will tell you, wryly remembering the day in the north of England when she overheard a Lancashire woman say to her friend, aghast, – 'Eeh, but she is in yellow, love – in't that strange?' repeated in a convincing Northern accent.

For the Queen Mother, appointments with her couturier are 'fun time'. 'How nice it is to see you again,' she will say, turning to greet them as they arrive with designs and swatches of fabric. There is usually a team of about three, the designer, the fitter and the *vendeuse*. 'Miss Evelyn', the *vendeuse*, wears a darkly discreet outfit, and the fitter 'Miss Margaret', trim in a tweed coat, black shoes and lots of red lipstick, has her hair gathered up and lacquered. In the good old days there was a fitter for evening clothes and another for day dresses. For years the Queen Mother knew 'Miss Emiliene'; then there was 'Miss Isabel' and 'Miss Elsa'; and now it is 'Miss Margaret' who jumps in the taxi at 2.40 P.M. in Conduit Street, outside the Norman Hartnell salon.

There is a touching devotion to the Queen Mother at Hartnell. Evelyn Elliott was rather ill in 1979 with peritonitis and has really given up work. Her husband has recently retired from the building trade and they have two adopted daughters. But the Queen Mother hates change, so rather than tell her that she has retired, the 56-year-old *vendeuse* travels from her home in Kent to go to Clarence House. 'Miss Margaret' happily copes with day and evening clothes – rather than send someone else to Clarence House, a new face for the Queen Mother. But it works both ways. The salon has had changing fortunes, gone are the days of *haute couture*; and the Queen Mother remains the salon's chief client. Her bills are always paid on the dot. Quite often Princess Margaret will ask the fitters searching questions about the salon where she was taken as a little girl with her sister to have frilly pink party dresses made. They say at Hartnell that Princess Margaret might easily have been a model if only she had not been so tiny – a life of 'ifs' . . .

At Clarence House there is a friendly 'Hello' for the Hartnell team. They go through the hall and up to the private apartments, passing extravagantly pretty ostrich feathers, with a tiny light on top of each one, on the staircase. In the ante-room they are offered coffee or sherry.

Sometimes there is a wait for fifteen minutes – and always, even if it has been only five minutes, the Queen Mother will apologize. 'So sorry, I had a lunch party which went on and on.'

Her innate good manners bring one or two smiles. Who would want to be back in the salon squeezing a tycoon's wife into a *jeune fille* red taffeta evening dress or unpicking the hem of the black dress of a frumpy old dowager yet again when they could be waiting in the Queen Mother's sitting-room, anticipating her appreciative purrs as new outfits are unfolded from the white tissue paper?

There is some light chatter about holidays in Scotland. 'So windy, but wonderful,' the Queen Mother will say if she has just come back from her Castle of Mey. Then there will be a waving of her finger as the corgis grunt and snuffle through the georgette and chiffon. 'Oh,

Geordie, not on the tulle,' as their mistress indulgently shoes them away.

'Oh, Evelyn, do come and look at the magnolia blossom on the lawn.' 'Your Majesty, may I suggest your roses need pruning?' 'I know, but I do love them like this,' the Queen Mother will reply, looking at the roses all blossomy and fullblown. In the right season the sitting-room is filled with blue and pink hydrangeas. But, as with her daughter the Queen, racing comes first. Amongst the French furniture there is a television set and if there is a race meeting on fitters, *vendeuses*, maids, dressers and designer all stop what they are doing to watch.

The hems of her evening dresses are torn again and again when 'Ma'am darling' dances the Gay Gordons into the small hours. She resists having her clothes dry-cleaned. 'They always seem to be different afterwards.'

These days, evening dresses are much less extravagant, with fewer sequins. Her instinct for the mood of the moment makes her acutely aware of economic pressures. But she adores embroidery. 'I do love those little paillettes,' she'll say of the delicate concave sequins, a glittery hallmark of Hartnell. For the Queen's coronation dress Miss Edith Auley Read did 3,000 hours of hand embroidery – even the Christmas cards from the Master were hand embroidered – all five hundred posted to expensively dressed women the world over.

It is sometimes said that the royal family cannot know much about real life. But the Queen Mother subtly draws out the people who work for her. 'What does your husband think about . . . ?' she will ask, and it can be anything from 'Mr Wedgwood Benn's plan to turn all Rolls-Royces into dustcarts' to clothes worn by young people. One fitter who complained about the latest pop music expected her to agree.

'Oh, Madame Isabel, after all when we were young – remember doing the Black Bottom? Well, what must we have looked like?' and she gave a spirited few steps with her hands in the air.

Often the radio is on during a fitting and *vendeuse* and Queen Mother will laugh their heads off at some recipe that is either hilarious or disgusting. When Miss Evelyn's father died the Queen Mother wrote to her. 'It was such a lovely letter saying, "I know that nothing will bring your father back . . ."; it was such a comfort.' When one of the fitters was ill the Queen Mother asked, 'What can I do? I should love to send a posy of flowers; do you think she would like that?' – but the suggestion must always be from the Queen Mother.

The distance is always there. The Queen Mother may say, 'Oh, come and listen to the band.' She loves hearing the Grenadier Guards playing after the Changing of the Guard. But it would be fatal to overstep the mark. The royal family has a deeply instilled feeling of being different and apart – they do not really like those who try to ingratiate themselves by pretending to be equal. It can be a delicate balancing act.

The joy of dealing with the Queen Mother is her delicate way of rejecting an idea without ruffling feelings. The Princess of Wales has intuitively the same diplomatic skill. The milliner John Boyd, an unassuming Scot who has made the Princess some of her prettiest hats, says that she might show a moment's hesitation – 'What do you think, Mr Boyd?' and he knows immediately that the hat is not a favourite. Whereas Princess Anne will say, in her father's forthright way: 'Mr Boyd what do you think you are at?' and Princess Margaret will also be much more outspoken. 'I see Mummy was wearing that blue coat again,' she will say, her eyes rolling if she thinks it is unflattering.

Occasionally the couturiers have suggested that perhaps the Queen Mother would like a more fashionable tailored outfit, the sort you see in the pages of *Vogue* worn by a model looking bored in the desert in Arizona or some other location far from 'cosy' Clarence House . . . or countrified Birkhall. Too subtle and gentle to say an out and out 'no', the Queen Mother will tip her head and her eyes will dart from side to side: 'Don't you think that would look wonderful on the Duchess of . . . ?' she will say, referring to some aristocratic beanpole. A small hand on her bosom and the argument is won.

She has indulged a pleading *vendeuse* but on one such occasion, as Evelyn Elliott remembers,

. . . the laugh was on me. I once made her a suit in black and white and it was so smart. As soon as the Queen Mother tried it on I said: 'Your Majesty, that does look so elegant.' Well, she bore with me – just smiled and said softly, 'Now apropros something becoming . . .' She turned with grace and picked up a piece of 'perfectly charming' blue silk, wondering if it 'might make an afternoon dress?'

Clothes for the Queen Mother have to be 'fun'. It is amazing how much pale blue creeps into outdoor warm country outfits for tramping the heather in Scotland. There is always a matching scarf and a pretty hat.

The Queen speaks to her mother several times a day, and there is a lot of laughter and consultations about what they are going to wear on engagements together. In the morning Miss Betty Leek, the Queen Mother's personal maid for the last eight years, will lay out a selection of dresses – about three – for her to choose. Shoes, handbag, gloves and the chiffon scarf will be matching. As her other maid, Miss Angela Benjamin, quietly carries the rejects back to the wardrobe, the Queen Mother may say: 'Oh, I have such a busy day, but do stay and talk to me . . .'

She steadfastly refuses to have any heavy clothes. The nearest to an evening coat will be a chiffon caped effect. Anyway, the weight of the diamond clips drags the shoulders down. Thrifty and full of Strathmore sense about money, the Queen Mother will sometimes find dresses she had ten years ago and send them back to Hartnell 'just to put in some little sleeves'. No woman likes that upper arm showing when it starts to get jowly like a basset hound. Even a repair will get a 'thank-you' – 'I shall enjoy wearing that again . . .' But frugality goes only so far. It was a real put-down when a pushy actor, who had already been a bit too forward, received the startling reply to his compliment on her dress. 'I made it myself,' she said cuttingly.

Joy Quested Nowell, walking in the rain to Clarence House, is strikingly fashionable with a brown Greta Garbo hat pulled over her eyes, a shawl round her shoulders, and she is carrying a black and white striped hatbox. She is the milliner who creates those great oystershell and cartwheel hats for the Queen Mother. She worked with the designer, Rudolf, for many years.

When Rudolf, a gentle mid-European, died of cancer three years ago, Joy Quested Nowell assumed that the hats for the Queen Mother would now be ordered from some rival house. But once again that enduring loyalty which is part of the Queen Mother's make-up led to a phone call to the salon in Curzon Street. It is now closed and rather sad, with pieces of silk and osprey and ostrich feathers scattered about. As it was also Miss Quested Nowell's home, she thought the telephone call was from a friend. It was an invitation to Clarence House; the Queen Mother would like some hats, please. The Royal Warrant was transferred. The osprey feathers would be needed again.

The Queen Mother adores hats. Nowadays, it is like searching for the Holy Grail trying to get pure silk veiling and feathers dyed the right shade of the favourite royal lavenders and blues. Joy Quested

Nowell goes to Paris where there is one old-fashioned and dedicated supplier left who can do the job. Her hats are always off the face; sometimes an old shape will be re-covered if it is particularly good.

Until the Princess of Wales came on the scene, it seemed that the Queen Mother was the milliners' only champion. Even at a private family weekend at 'The Bury' with her sister-in-law and nephew, the Queen Mother, eating a green iced-lolly with one of the children, will wear a feathery hat as her grand-nieces and nephews drag her off for a walk to the intriguing wood of her childhood.

She sees a great deal from her car as it whisks out of the red-stoned yard at Clarence House and likes window shopping. 'I saw some lovely hats the other day – they really were so becoming.' But the milliner knows this is just a hankering, and not a criticism.

As a young wife she wore cloche hats – close fitting and perfect for her features in the 1920s. Now the Queen Mother looks back on them with an amused, 'Did we really use to wear those funny hats . . . ?'

When Rudolf was in hospital only Miss Quested Nowell knew how ill he was. She went to Clarence House for a fitting and, to her horror, she found her eyes suddenly brimming and was unable to speak when the Queen Mother asked, 'How is Rudolf?' 'I burst into tears, it was dreadful. The Queen Mother stepped forward and put her arms around me and said, "It's good to talk."'

On the Queen Mother's 80th birthday, the sitting room at Clarence House was filled with presents from the royal family, all lovingly and ingeniously arranged by her Steward, William Tallon. One of them was a box with blue and white ribbons and, when they unfurled it from the tissue paper, there stood a small Meissen figure of the goddess of music. With it was a scroll: 'I come from Prague.' It told the story of Rudolf's escape from Czechoslovakia when the Russians had marched in. He had been away in Paris and London and had left a wife and family and a thriving, exclusive millinery salon in Prague. Years later, a good friend managed to get on a workers' cruise ship sailing from Odensk to England and he smuggled out, up his sleeve, one of the few of Rudolf's precious possessions he had been able to salvage. Now, dying in hospital, Rudolf thought the small figure would be the only present he could give to the Queen Mother. When she saw the little goddess and read the scroll, she was very moved. At one A.M. she sat down and wrote Rudolf one of her marvellous letters. That

Meissen goddess from Prague stands amongst the Fabergé *objets* in the Queen Mother's sitting-room at Clarence House.

Hats are as important to her as blue and lilac and high-heeled shoes. A man once complimented the Queen Mother on her hat, saying, 'It looks lovely from the back, Ma'am.' Her prompt reply was, 'I suppose I'll now have to walk backwards.'

11

Lumps in Our Throats

The Queen could not resist asking Ramsay MacDonald in May 1937, 'Am I doing all right?' He gave an expansive sweep of his arm; 'Oh, you . . .' and, for once, words failed him. He had just resigned as Lord President of the Council and Stanley Baldwin, who was returning as Prime Minister, recommended him for a peerage. MacDonald went to see the King and had refused his offer of an Earldom. Then he went to the Queen to tell her he thought her husband had come on magnificently. When she asked how she was doing, the Queen was not seeking compliments: but she knew she would get an honest answer from the former Labour Prime Minister.

'I can hardly now believe we have been called to this tremendous task. The curious thing is that we are not afraid. I feel that God has helped me,' the Queen felt able to write to the Archbishop of Canterbury. The worst had happened, but the dread had vanished. And the King and Queen were more than ever 'so particularly together, leaning so much on each other'. There had been a blossoming in the acceptance of their destiny.

But, like a mosquito, there was intermittent buzzing from the Duke of Windsor in the South of France. He was bitterly disappointed that not one of his family, not even his mother, would be at his wedding at the Château de Candé 12 miles from Tours. His love affair was no aberration, though in the past he had been incapable of staying in love with the same woman for longer than a few months. Now he would marry Mrs Simpson on his father's birthday, 3 June, 1937.

The London barber, Charles Topper, went to France to trim the bridegroom's hair for the ceremony. The bride wore a long blue satin dress with a short nipped-in jacket and a stunning diamond and sapphire bracelet that was a wedding present from the Duke.

Later, the Duchess had the pleasure of seeing Lady Diana Cooper curtseying to her at a cocktail party in Paris. When they were upbraided afterwards by their friends they dissembled, pretending they had only done it 'to please the Duke, not for any formal reason'. After the war when Duff Cooper was ambassador to France the Duke and Duchess of Windsor knew they had supportive friends at the Embassy.

From Buckingham Palace, the King announced that he would visit Wales. His Ministers had wanted him to abandon the idea, but he was adamant. 'Where my brother went I will go too.' He chose the route Edward VIII had taken when he had glamorously flitted in and out of derelict towns like Mountain Ash and Neath. George VI spent his Coronation year conscientiously visiting all parts of the country and did a tour of the mining villages of South Wales. Although it was Edward VIII who, shocked by the despair and unemployment during the Depression, said, 'Something must be done', it was his brother Bertie who had earned the title 'Industrial Prince'. As Prince Albert, he became popular in Wales for his efforts to ease the lot of the miners. He worked tirelessly as President of the Industrial Welfare Society and loved it when his brothers called him The Foreman. He was no stranger to the Rhondda Valley where the Miners' Trade Union leader Frank Hodges challenged him to a game of golf on a miners' course – the Ton Pentre Welfare Scheme Golf Course. The miners won and a dog ran off with the royal ball at the last hole.

A State visit to France was planned for 28 June, but was delayed by the illness of Lady Strathmore in London. She had lived long enough to see her daughter a credit to her and those caring precepts, which had been put to such good use. The King and Queen were at her bedside in the mansion block in Portman Square when she died after a massive heart attack. Sympathetically, President Lebrun of France telephoned the Palace that he expected the royal couple to cancel their visit.

But the Queen had heard so much talk in the royal family about Queen Victoria's long-enforced mourning at the cost of the people that she decided she must go to France. Imaginatively, Norman Hartnell suggested to the King that, as white was a colour of mourning, perhaps the Queen would not have to wear black or purple after all.

Today, the young Princess of Wales is often criticized for the amount of money she spends on her clothes, but they are a vital prop. Nobody is waiting to hear her views on nuclear physics, the future of the yen or the Stock Exchange's electronic recording of share transfers. The Princess cheers people up, her clothes catch the eye of the grumpiest, lifting the spirits. Her wardrobe is almost as important as Prince Charles's speeches, and the approach as professional.

When Hartnell visited the Palace before the trip to France, the

King took him into the Long Gallery to see the royal paintings, the Empress Eugénie crinolines and the billowy Winterhalter dresses, and asked the couturier if he thought he could capture some of their 'picturesque grace'. He took a keen interest in his wife's clothes and loved her in stately crinolines.

He liked perfection and once noticed that the pleats of a piper's kilt were pressed the wrong way round.

Hartnell's instructions were clear and, as the Queen was the sort of woman who dressed to please her husband, he designed a collection of long, frothy, waisted dresses. They were original and feminine and the French thought the choice of white *formidable*. When they sailed for France on board HMS *Enchantress* 30 white dresses were carried aboard by the Royal Baggage Master.

At a banquet in the Elysée Palace the Queen wore a white satin dress held by a cluster of white camellias; a romantic dress of Valenciennes lace was sprinkled with silver; a sweeping hat with white osprey topped a dress that trailed the green lawns at a garden party. When she opened a parasol of transparent lace and tulle at a ballet by the lake on the Île Enchantée, Parisians went wild.

It had been a gamble. The Queen, who was pretty enough and had the personality to wear these nostalgic clothes, had interpreted her husband's slightly old-fashioned romantic dream of her. Perhaps the most ironic compliment came from Hitler, who watched her success in France and described Queen Elizabeth as 'the most dangerous woman in Europe'.

'We have taken the Queen to our hearts. She rules over two nations,' cried the French. 'France is a monarchy again.'

Each night's flourish outdid the last. Lady Diana Cooper thought one of the best was the occasion when the Queen 'shining with stars and diadem and the Légion d'Honneur' walked up a marble staircase, never once looking down, escorted by two footmen carrying twenty branched candelabra of white candles.

The French danced in the streets all night and the Queen was smiling and confident. The King basked in the admiration for his wife; he was beginning almost to enjoy State visits.

Cecil Beaton later thought the Queen 'an enchanting, almost fairy-story figure in her sparkles and spangles' when she posed in one of the King's favourite crinolines under a parasol on the steps of Buckingham Palace.

It was a subtle move to invite Cecil Beaton, a sensitive and artistic photographer, to make the best of her image, for the Queen felt that photographs of her had really not been flattering. She is aware of her roundness and hates it; Lord Snowdon and Norman Parkinson have taken some of the best shots of her. Poor Cecil Beaton had his pictures returned to him once, but those were the days before 'neutral density' and clever soft lighting. 'It is so distressing to me that I always photograph so badly,' she confessed shortly after she became Queen. 'It is difficult to know when not to smile.' Image was important, and Beaton vowed when he went to the Palace for the first time that his photographs should give some hint of 'her incandescent complexion, brilliant, thrush-like eyes and radiant smile'.

Previously, the court photographer was allowed ten to fifteen minutes to capture a royal wedding or christening. He would work nervously under a black velvet cloth and go away hoping something would come out of the stiff solemn group, looking like startled dolls in the ground glass of his camera. It was very different from the press photographers nowadays, who shout in their excitement, not meaning to sound rude: 'Look this way, Ma'am' . . . 'Just one more' . . . or . . . 'What a cracker!' as the Queen Mother smiles back at them.

She has never shared the royal family's distaste for photographers and is their favourite royal. You never see a bad photograph of her because, as the photographer Michael McKeown explains: 'If it is not flattering, we throw it away.' Her timing is immaculate. She never poses for a minute too long and once, spotting a photographer being manhandled by security men, intervened with, 'Please don't; he is a friend of mine.'

The royal family is fiercely protective of its privacy, and in the fifties a great chasm grew up between the monarchy and the people. The Queen was criticized for being old-fashioned; the whole image of the royal family was dull and still coloured by the grumpy remoteness of George V's court. His Private Secretary, Lord Wigram, often tried to persuade the old King to go to a football match; and even today the royal family become involved only in sports they like, the upper-class pursuits of the fox and the stag and, in the summer, polo. The Queen Mother, however, is good at snooker. The journalist Peter Grosvenor says, 'She plays a mean Southpaw.' She was the first honorary lady member of the Press Club, of which Grosvenor is Vice-President. Her royalty comes through marriage and experience, and although dignified and stately she somehow produces a warmth which makes Smithfield porters kiss her hand and burst into song. 'Glorious' is the adjective used about her most often by her friends.

Today photographers are seen as 'occupational hazards' by the royal family. The Palace machinery is astute enough to know that a royal tour abroad without the accompanying 'clickniks' would mean pedestrian coverage at home. Television is more acceptable; the camera is not quite so intrusive, but the sound men irritate Prince Philip and the Princess of Wales. 'You are a pest!' the Princess snapped at one of them on a tour in Canada. The Queen Mother also hates 'What is that thing called? The boom, yes that's it,' finding it intrusive when she is trying to have a private conversation.

In 1984, the Queen was furious when newspaper pictures showed her grandson, Master Peter Phillips, whirling a dead pheasant over his head at Sandringham watched by the grinning marksman, his father Captain Mark Phillips. You almost felt that the Queen Mother might get a rocket from her daughter when they returned to the house, for instead of glaring at the photographers as the Queen had done, astride her horse with her 'Miss Piggy' face under her headscarf, the Queen Mother just looked helpless, as if to say, 'I know you poor boys have a job to do,' and could not stop herself wishing them a 'Happy New Year' and giving the twiddly wave of her fingers normally reserved for her great-grandchildren.

Norman Parkinson was once asked, 'You be the model, please Mr Parkinson, and I shall take a picture of you,' as the Queen Mother got him to pose in the rose garden at Clarence House.

In the public eye, the Queen Mother has a talent which is possibly shared by the Princess of Wales. She manages to give a warm feeling of euphoria before she has shaken a single outstretched hand. Once, when she was telling Prince Charles how important it is to wave, she explained: 'This is how you do it, it is like opening a huge jar of sweets.' Nobody taught the young Duchess of York these lessons; she learned instinctively. Queen Mary was far too inhibited to explain how you make contact with 'ordinary people'. But, helped by a genuine interest in people, a quick responsiveness and a sense of humour, her daughter-in-law has always known the exact magic moment when to wave, when to smile, when to look back and when to say the most reluctant goodbye.

When Cecil Beaton went to the Palace for the first of many visits the atmosphere was still very formal.

. . . the page announces the imminent arrival of the sitter [he remembered]. At the far end of a long corridor a very small figure, possibly wearing a crinoline is approaching. As the swish of her dress material becomes louder, I go towards the advancing figure and make my bow.

Beaton was helped by the Queen to choose between the soft light of the Blue or Yellow Drawing-room, or the Music Room. She posed on the Gothic staircase at Windsor and among the marble columns beneath the garlanded and gilded cherubs on the ornate ceilings. She took small steps along the Savonnerie carpet to pose by a tall window hung with crimson silk, where photographer and subject could hear the slap of the rifle butt salutes and the growling voices of the guards below. They did not talk much at the Palace then about 'promotion' or 'image-making' – but those pictures were a triumph.

The King and Queen were not complacent, but there was a warm feeling that things were not going too badly. The King kept saying, 'Must get the country to settle down.' Occasionally, the Queen would worry about her husband's tiredness. He was still anxious before a speech and she would say, resentfully, 'If only Wallis had not blown in from Baltimore.'

And soon Princess Elizabeth had to be taught 'the ropes' of monarchy. The King was a thoughtful and excellent teacher. It was all fairly new to him, too. He liked the company of his serious eldest daughter and they would tramp across the marshes at Sandringham together. They would be up early, while the Queen and Princess Margaret slept on until at least eight. Father and future Queen would have an early morning cup of tea in the dark, pull on wellingtons and set out wildfowling, or she would watch him shoot and listen to the wind in the rushes.

The Duke and Duchess of Windsor visited Hitler in the autumn of 1937, much to the King's embarrassment. Hitler thought that Frau Wallis would have made a good queen. He was already being pursued by one of the Mitford girls, who was seen at a party of the Anglo-German Fellowship with a plate of sausage on her knees. The Duke of Windsor saluted the Führer twice in Germany in public and years later, long after the Second World War, seemed unrepentant. 'I never thought Hitler was such a bad chap.' Either he was being naive or provocative.

The highly successful State visit to France had been undertaken in the hope of maintaining stability and peace. But even then Hitler was on the rampage. There was a growing fear in Europe and across the Atlantic that the Führer would not be content with taking Czechoslovakia but dreamt of a whole continent run by the Nazis.

Now it became imperative to nurture friendship with North America, though the King hated being away during that uneasy spring of 1939. The idea came from the Prime Minister of Canada, MacKenzie King, and President Roosevelt smartly suggested that the royal couple should visit him afterwards.

The children saw them off. They had been invited along too, but their parents thought the trip would be too exhausting. As the King and Queen boarded the white ship, the *Empress of Australia*, there was a great deal of snuffling from Princess Margaret, who was only nine. Her sister tried to cheer her up, telling her handkerchiefs were *only* for waving.

The *Empress* hit heavy seas and fog and avoided icebergs. The Queen, who had remained irrepressibly cheerful, wrote to Queen Mary about the three and a half days when the *Empress* hardly moved.

The fog was so thick that it was like a white cloud round the ship, and the foghorn blew incessantly. Its melancholy blasts were echoed back by the icebergs like the twang of a piece of wire . . . incredibly eerie . . . The poor captain was nearly demented because some kind cheerful people kept reminding him that it was about here that the *Titanic* was struck and just about the same date.

When someone suggested that the delay must have been terrible, Queen Elizabeth replied: 'Yes, it was. You see, we lost two days of the tour.' The King took lots of photographs of the Queen on deck looking like a smiling pixie in her hooded coat.

In Quebec, the King spoke French and the Queen was described as *vraiment charmante*. They went to Toronto, Calgary, through Kicking Horse Pass to Vancouver and by steamer to that most English of islands, Victoria, which is loyal to the Crown to this day. They had a breath of fresh air at a log cabin at one of the highest spots in the Rockies. They struck Lord Tweedsmuir, the author John Buchan wearing his other hat as Governor-General of Canada, as a delightful pair.

Lord Tweedsmuir saw that the Queen had an intuitive knack for the spontaneous gesture. He remembered when she laid the foundation stone at the new Judicative Building in Ottawa. 'I heard the masons talking and realized some of them were Scots, and she made me take her and the King up to them. She spent ten minutes in Scottish reminiscences in full view of seventy thousand people, who went mad!'

In America, the Roosevelts had secretly been expecting a rather dull young couple, lacking the glamour of Edward VIII. But solidarity had to be shown in the face of war. The invitation had originally been in the belief that Britain, Europe and America might all be engaged in a life and death struggle.

Without formality, President Roosevelt shook the King's hand with a cheery, 'How are you? I am glad to see you.' Joseph Kennedy, father of the future President, thought it the most important handclasp in modern times.

From that moment, the two men got on. The President, assured, wise and a good talker, liked the King immediately. They had common interests, and the King enjoyed his company.

When the King and Queen arrived at the White House, the President's daunting old mother, Mrs Sara Delano Roosevelt, insisted that a good English tea should be served even though it was eight in the evening. The President explained: 'My mother doesn't approve of cocktails.' The King replied with a smile: 'Neither does my mother.' And both men had a large drink.

The President's English butler had left in a huff because the black staff were going to be allowed to wait at the royal table. 'Wait' is hardly the word. There was a series of comic mishaps which were pure slapstick – just the kind of thing the royal family loves. The Queen always finds it great fun if there is a hitch because, for just a moment, she feels she is seeing people as they really are, flummoxed, bad-tempered or simply in a panic.

One butler from the South lost his footing, slid in on his backside and the whole tray of drinks scattered to the floor. During dinner, a serving table collapsed and priceless plates broke into smithereens. 'I hope none of my dishes was among them,' the President's daughter-in-law said, half-seriously, half-joking. Everybody was in high spirits and there are whimsical stories about a black servant shaking his head and telling his friends throwing out the broken dishes about 'that honeychile, Mrs Queen'.

The heat was sapping. Washington humidity found its way through the Queen's parasols and several times she had to sit down and rest. Mrs Roosevelt thought she was perfection, 'never a hair out of place' in the sweltering 97° atmosphere. Her crinolines were a sensation and reminded some senators of the Southern belles they had left behind. 'My, you're a great Queen picker,' one of them said as they slapped the King on the back. The King grinned at the thought of an MP being so forward in London. It hardly helped his digestion, as he suppressed his laughter and ate traditional American dishes of clam cocktail, boned capon and ice-cream.

It was the first stay of a reigning British King and Queen on American soil.

There was serious talking with Roosevelt and the King played his part in ensuring the support of the United States should Britain be at war. Later, the King sat back on the royal train after dinner as it trundled through the Rockies and felt confident enough to say: 'It's in the bag,' using a shooting metaphor as if the President were a pheasant.

The tour of America and Canada lasted for seven weeks. The travelling was exhausting, but perhaps a little more leisurely than a similar journey today. In 1927, when as Duke and Duchess of York they sailed to Auckland in New Zealand the voyage took six weeks. Later, the Queen Mother was to jet to New Zealand in as many hours as it had taken her days at sea on her first visit.

Modern jets mean that the visiting royals may be expected to fulfil a couple of engagements on the day of arrival, make a speech and then travel 500 miles more to a far-flung sheep station. But as the Queen and Prince Philip, and Diana and Charles, go round the world, the Queen Mother has been almost everywhere before them.

On the voyage home, the King and Queen talked and laughed about the visit. Many a moment had been saved by their mutual sense of humour. Once the Queen was jostled in a crowd the police could not hold back and the King became anxious and furious. 'What a happy crowd,' his wife said, not in the least ruffled.

When the *Empress* neared Southampton on 22 June 1939, the two Princesses, travelling across the Solent in the destroyer *Kempenfelt* were brought on board. Even in the excitement of the reunion, they remembered to thank the captain and the crew who had clubbed together to buy them two nightdress cases shaped like giant pandas.

Something had happened to the British people while the King and Queen had been away. They had been entranced by reports of their sovereigns at barbecues, eating hot dogs, water melon and doughnuts and drinking beer; and at the way the Roosevelts had developed a parental attitude towards this 'very, very delightful' royal couple. Now the King and Queen were home and it was as though their absence and their stunning success across the Atlantic made the people realize the strength of the new monarchy.

The crowds went mad as the royal boat train came into Waterloo. They lined the streets, and MPs stood in Parliament Square. The Speaker could have shouted 'Order, order . . .' but they had, as Harold Nicolson recorded, 'lost all dignity, and yelled and yelled. The King wore a happy schoolboy grin. The Queen was superb. She really does manage to convey to each individual in the crowd that he or she has had a personal greeting. We returned to the House with lumps in our throats.'

Outside the Palace, Londoners sang 'The Lambeth Walk' and 'Under the Spreading Chestnut Tree' as a welcome home. It was as if they wanted the King and Queen to know they now had more than the goodwill shown towards them at the beginning of the reign. Now, they were proud – and they were damned if they would go home before midnight. The King and Queen had a disjointed dinner and at 8.40 P.M. were persuaded to come out on the balcony again. The King, in his modest way, thought the tour had seemed a success and that maybe, in the eyes of the people, 'this has made us'.

It had been a liberating experience. In the same way Australia and New Zealand, in 1982, proved a turning point for the Princess of Wales in both her marriage and her approach to public life; the freedom, the sun, the more relaxed style of the people gave Diana a chance to enjoy her royal role as she gained confidence in the freshness of a new world.

Now this unassuming couple who had come to the throne barely three years earlier in circumstances 'without parallel in this country' felt quietly pleased. They went to Balmoral for the family holiday, had picnics by the Dee; the Queen fished and they sang in the evenings.

At the end of one summer afternoon, when Cecil Beaton was taking pictures near the lake in the gardens of Buckingham Palace, she said: 'You watch, Mr Beaton. In a little while the sky will become rose colour. I often feel that Piccadilly is on fire at night.' Her words were almost prophetic, for war was declared on 3 September 1939.

The King's Christmas message that year was to be historic. George VI had not felt that his people needed to hear him speaking to them on the wireless every year but now, with war declared, he was persuaded to broadcast, largely because of the uncertainty in Europe.

The Queen supervises the princesses' French homework at Windsor Castle during the war. The King's walking-stick is by the empty chair while Princess Elizabeth looks earnestly at an illustrated dictionary

'Around the world under the umbrella' is one of the Queen Mother's favourite
expressions

Left Wherever she is, the Queen Mother tries to make time for a little fishing. Deep in
the Waikato River near Auckland, New Zealand, the royal angler is about to land a 2lb
rainbow trout

A celebration photograph of the Queen Mother on her 80th birthday with the Queen and Princess Margaret, who looks tanned after a holiday in the West Indies

Right The Queen tried hard to stay in the background during the celebrations for the Queen Mother's 80th birthday, not wanting to steal any of her mother's limelight. Mother and daughter in St Paul's Cathedral 1980 at the service of thanksgiving for the Queen Mother's life

The robes of the Order of the Garter seem almost designed with the Queen Mother in mind. Prince Charles escorts his grandmother in the procession to the annual Garter service at Windsor

Right The Queen Mother with the cast of the music-hall show, *Underneath the Arches* in March 1983

Peace at the Castle of Mey, the place which helped the Queen Mother to overcome
her grief and loneliness after the King's death in 1952 and restored her to public life

Someone had sent the King a copy of a book of poems by Marie Louise Haskins, published in 1908 under the title *The Desert*. Both the King and Queen found one particular passage intensely moving. When he was wrestling with his script, she persuaded him to use it to end his broadcast:

A new year is at hand. We cannot tell what it will bring. If it brings peace, how thankful we shall all be. If it brings us continued struggle we shall remain undaunted.

In the meantime, I feel that we may all find a message of encouragement in the lines which, in my closing words, I would like to say to you: 'I said to the man who stood at the Gate of the Year, "Give me a light that I may tread safely into the unknown." And he replied, "Go out into the darkness, and put your hand into the Hand of God. That shall be to you better than light, and safer than a known way."'

Today, the Queen Mother remembers how proud she was, listening to the broadcast in another sitting-room, as she heard her husband's hesitant but firm voice reading what has become known as The King's Prayer.

12

We Stay with Our People

If there were still those who thought the Queen a 'sweet' little thing at the beginning of the war, by the end of it that slightly patronizing description would not do. 'Sweet' hardly applied to a woman who chased rats out of the bomb-blasted Palace, or coped with an intruder in the same magnificently cool way as her daughter did in 1982, and who had learnt to handle a .38 revolver and a .303 rifle.

Lord Halifax, the Foreign Secretary, who was allowed to take a short cut through the grounds of Buckingham Palace, was once practically scared out of his black jacket and striped trousers by the sound of rifle shots. It was the Queen practising rapid fire; 'I shall not go down like the others,' she told him. She had been horrified by the plight of European royals like the Grand Duke of Luxembourg and Queen Wilhelmina of the Netherlands, who arrived in Britain with nothing more than a tin hat and a handbag, driven out by the Nazis and given shelter at Buckingham Palace.

The Queen always liked the Foreign Secretary and sent him a nice note once about Hitler's book:

November 15 1939

My dear Lord Halifax,
I send you *Mein Kampf*, but do not advise you to read it through, or you might go mad, and that would be a great pity.
Even a skip through gives one a good idea of his mentality, ignorance, and obvious sincerity.

At the very first rumbling of war the Queen was with the two Princesses at their house near Ballater, Birkhall, but she refused to stay there in safety. George VI was in London. 'If things turn out badly I must be with the King,' the Queen told her lady-in-waiting, Mrs Geoffrey Bowlby, as she left Scotland by the first available train.

A soldier in the Cameronians, who still treasures a handwritten note from the Queen, remembers vividly her 'into battle look' when she visited Westminster Children's Hospital in Vincent Square on one of the last delicate days of 'phoney' war in 1939.

The King and Queen remained in London: 'We stay with our

people' the Queen said. In 1939, before the bombing really began, it was thought that the King and Queen might send the princesses abroad. Parents were sending children away with their nannies at a rapid rate of knots to the safety of Canada and America. The Queen listened to the arguments and was touched by the invitations from the Dominions. But, as she wrote: 'So kind, but no, there was no question of the royal family taking up their kind offer because the children could not go without me, I could not possibly leave the King and the King would never go.'

There was nevertheless a real fear that she might be killed. Hitler had marked the Queen when she scattered poppies at a war cemetery in Paris in the summer of 1938, and there was a 'Kami-kaze' determination by many of the German Luftwaffe to score a direct hit on the Palace.

First, an unexploded bomb fell near the King's study, but it was defused. Then, on 13 September 1940, the King described how he and the Queen '. . . heard an aircraft make a zooming noise above us and saw two bombs falling past on the opposite side of the Palace and then heard two resounding crashes as the bombs fell in the quadrangle about 30 yards away . . . We all wondered why we weren't dead.' The German pilot must have been surprised, too: he had taken a huge risk, flying straight up The Mall underneath the camouflage of cloud to drop a stick of six bombs. Nobody was killed, but the Palace was damaged extensively. When the King and Queen went down to see if the staff were all right, a policeman said, rather foolishly, 'A magnificent piece of bombing, Ma'am'. He then had the wit to add, 'If you'll pardon my saying so.'

The Queen replied: 'I'm glad we've been bombed. It makes me feel I can look the East End in the face.'

When the Queen went to visit the East End she deliberately wore light and pretty clothes: no sombre black and no green. Norman Hartnell designed discreet outfits in inoffensive gentle pastel blues, greys and lilacs. She took great trouble with her appearance because, she felt: 'If the poor people came to see me they would put on their best clothes.'

'Some clothes do not like me,' she explained, and decided against wearing a uniform of any kind. It was not a frivolous decision; she knew that a mannish uniform on her would not cheer anybody up. Again and again, during the war, she was seen stepping nimbly over rubble in high heels; the men with the shovels would see her smile and one Cockney sang out: 'Ain't she just bloody luvverly?'

In 1941, she visited the decimated city of Sheffield. Lord Harlech, the Midlands Commissioner, described how, when her car stopped, 'the Queen nips out into the snow and goes straight into the middle of the crowd and starts talking to them. First they would just gape; then they all started talking at once. "Hi, Your Majesty! Look here!"'

Distressed Londoners, scrabbling through the debris, would suddenly look up and see the Queen standing beside them. One woman was trying to get her terrified dog to come out from under a pile of dusty rubble. 'Perhaps I can try,' the Queen suggested. 'I am rather good with dogs.' A mother with an injured arm was trying to dress her baby. 'Let me help,' the Queen said as she darted forward, leaving officials open-mouthed.

On another occasion in the East End someone digging in the ruins shouted, 'Thank God for a good King!' The King, deeply touched, replied: 'Thank God for a good people.' Now, they were cheering his wife too.

'The destruction is so awful, the people so wonderful, they deserve a better world,' the Queen wrote to Queen Mary, who was staying at Badminton, the home of the Duke of Beaufort, where she kept busy by savagely attacking the ivy.

The Queen ran sewing parties twice a week in the Blue Drawing-room at Buckingham Palace. There was always that calm and reassuring air about her and she was proud of 'the fortitude of women'. Her dark hair was flat to her head with little Marcel waves; her voice on the radio had a squeakiness like the present Queen's in early broadcasts. But gradually her voice mellowed.

She talked about 'the men at the front' and their wistful thoughts of home. For someone who really does not like the sound of her own voice, she did a lot of broadcasts in the war – always appealing to women. 'The King and I know what it is to be parted from your children.' Their own two girls were at Windsor for the duration of the war.

She went to lunchtime concerts at the National Gallery and to recitals by the pianist Myra Hess. Sometimes, the emotion of the music made her feel that the suffering endured by the people was 'almost too much to bear'.

The Queen scoured the Palace vaults for furniture for victims of bomb damage; every day she worked, carrying her compulsory gas-mask; and every evening at six she telephoned the princesses.

She enjoyed a threepenny lunch with other people's children

evacuated from London. She ate jam tarts and drank water from a bakelite mug: 'This is all very good,' she told one of the 264 excited children around her in the calm of the countryside.

Her life was a strange contrast to that of her brother-in-law, the Duke of Windsor. He and his wife had sailed from Portugal to the Bahamas where he took up his position as Governor. It was hot, but the Duke in heavy khaki service-dress wore suede shoes. He perspired so much that he had trouble signing the oaths of allegiance and office.

People in London, too, were finding it desperately hot that summer, as German bombers repeatedly assaulted the city every night.

Balmoral was shut down for the six years of war; so was Sandringham, but the lawns and golf course were used for food production. The pink walls of Royal Lodge were changed to the muddy camouflage of war.

Both King Haakon of Norway, also driven out by the Germans, and Queen Wilhelmina of the Netherlands thought the King and Queen very 'lackadaisical' about their security. The King felt perhaps they were right, but explained that they had a good alarm system at the Palace should German paratroopers land in the gardens. But not for the last time was the Sovereign's press of a Palace bell to go unheard. The King pressed an alarm signal, and then pressed again, but nothing happened. He got into one of his 'gnashes', but the Queen thought it was funny and the two foreign royals enjoyed a look of 'We told you so.'

The Palace was hit by nine bombs altogether: water poured through the roof; ceilings collapsed; blasts shattered all the windows; the Palace chapel was destroyed; and rats were rampant in the grounds. 'Everyone had great fun pursuing them,' the Queen said.

The King and Queen tried to get to Windsor every night to be with their daughters and, besides, it was safer. One evening the Queen was dressing for dinner when a deserter got into her bedroom. He hid behind a curtain and then reached out and grabbed her ankle. 'For a moment my heart stood absolutely still,' the Queen told her family, and then, with that intuitive knack, she asked him to tell her about himself. He had been unhinged by the death of his whole family in an air-raid, and had got a job with a building firm doing work at the Castle. He had reached the Queen's room by pretending he was replacing a light bulb. As he talked, the

Queen moved gently towards the bell, waiting until a servant came. 'Poor man, I was so sorry for him,' she said afterwards. At night the whole royal family would troop down to shelters. By day the princesses put up pictures of Mother Goose and Humpty Dumpty where valuable royal portraits had hung before being moved to the vaults for safe keeping. 'Do you like my ancestors?' the King used to ask.

In 1941, the Queen's nephew, Patrick, Master of Glamis, was killed in action and another nephew, Andrew Elphinstone, was taken prisoner of war. Then, in August 1942, the King's youngest brother, George, Duke of Kent, was killed when his RAF plane crashed in Scotland on the way to Iceland. He had taken off, in a strong east wind and mist and driving rain, from the Cromarty Firth in a Sunderland flying boat. After only half an hour, the great lumbering plane hurtled into the top of a mountain at Morven, turned over and slid down the mountainside.

He left behind a young wife, the graceful Marina; a son, Prince Edward, now Duke of Kent; a daughter, Princess Alexandra, who is married to Angus Ogilvy; and a baby son, Prince Michael, born seven weeks earlier. One of Queen Mary's favourites, he always understood her love for artistic things better than anyone else. She had doted on this best-looking and youngest of her sons and sent him parcels on the quiet when he was serving abroad. She once scribbled to one of the King's equerries: 'Be an angel and find out for me from the Admiralty whether any ship is likely to go to Malta before Christmas as I have two or three largish parcels for Prince George.'

The King said after the funeral at St George's Chapel, Windsor, 'I have attended very many family funerals in the Chapel, but none has moved me in the same way . . . Everybody there I knew well but I did not dare look at any of them for fear of breaking down.'

In October, the King and Queen had to put up Eleanor Roosevelt. The Palace was very spartan and icy cold; the wind whistled through the broken windows. The American President's wife now realized how bleak things were in Britain, and was filled with admiration for the King and Queen. The food was frugal – dried eggs and parsnip jam – but it was served on gold and silver plate. Churchill had become very close to the King and Queen during the war years; to the extent that the King would write to him as 'Dear Winston'. The Queen would organize 'sawdust' sand-wiches for working lunches with 'Winnie' as they called him, but the conference would often be interrupted to take cover in an air-raid shelter. Once President Roosevelt's personal representative, Harry Hopkins, was at one of these self-service lunchtime conferences when the air-raid warning went off. In the shelter, he was moved by the Queen's feeling of debt to the people. 'She told me that she found it extremely difficult to find words to express her feeling towards the people of Britain in these days. She thought their actions were magnificent.'

The Queen was filled with dread when her husband insisted that he must go to North Africa to see the troops. In the war the King was the rock the Queen leaned on; she sustained him, but he was the strength. She knew she could not argue once he had made up his mind. Flying was unpredictable and the royal family were understandably frightened of wartime travelling.

But George VI was determined. The flight was delayed by fog and the Queen experienced 'every sort of horror and walked up and down my room staring at the telephone'. The King travelled 6,700 miles in desert heat, but every minute of it was worth it when he met 3,000 British troops on a beach. The Queen regretted her anxiety when she saw this eye-witness account of how her husband was received:

As he walked out on the verandah of his villa, first one man, then another, recognized him.

And as if called by one voice, the thousands of men, most of them semi-nude, many of them still dripping with water, raced up the beach like a human wave.

Then, as if the wave had suddenly frozen, they stood silently below the verandah, a solid mass of tanned and dripping men.

There was one of those strange silences one sometimes gets among a huge crowd.

A voice started 'God Save the King'. In a moment the National Anthem was taken up everywhere. It swelled deep-throatedly from a mass of soldiers.

As the last notes of the Anthem died out, the King suddenly turned, stepped down from the verandah. He stood there, surrounded by hundreds of men, talking to them, asking them about their experiences.

Then the men broke into song again, this time with 'For He's a Jolly Good Fellow'.

In 1944 Princess Elizabeth was 18, and old enough to take part in the war effort. She had wanted to join the Auxiliary Territorial Service to 'do as other girls of my age do'. She became 2nd Subaltern

Elizabeth Windsor, with a two-ounce chocolate ration and an intimate knowledge of the workings of the carburettor. The Queen thought it would be good experience for her daughter 'to compete against other brains'. Like any loving parents the King and Queen visited the Training Centre in Surrey. The King pretended he could not understand what Subaltern No 230873, as the Princess was known, was doing with her head under the bonnet of a utility van. The Queen and Princess Margaret did not think much of Elizabeth's dungarees, but knew how much it all meant to her as she talked of nothing but D and M (driving and maintenance) at Windsor Castle. The course ended on 16 April 1945. Three weeks later the war in Europe was over.

By now the King and Queen were mentally and physically exhausted. During the war the King had worn artificial tan on his face so that he would appear well to his people. The Queen had often burst into tears during those war years – but she had laughed too.

On one visit to Lancashire a council put on a spectacularly lavish meal which she sat through growing more and more embarrassed. Finally she turned to the mayor and said: 'You know, at Buckingham Palace we're very careful to observe the rationing regulations.' He said to the Queen: 'Oh, well then, Your Majesty, you'll be glad of a proper do.'

Princess Elizabeth, in uniform, stood with her parents on the floodlit balcony of Buckingham Palace on the evening of 8 May 1945, VE Day. Then she left with her sister, Princess Margaret, and ran into the crowds who were shouting 'We want the King, we want the Queen.' The King said to his wife as he saw the princesses go: 'Poor darlings, they've never had any fun yet . . .' The crowds missed the two princesses completely, having eyes only for the two people on the balcony: the King looking terribly drawn but allowing himself that slow smile, and the smiling Queen who would pay a high price for this famous victory.

They were called out on to the balcony eight times. Their children in the crowds below were waving at them; Princess Margaret said later: 'Everybody was knocking everybody else's hats off, so we knocked off a few too.'

Vera Lynn, the 'Forces' Sweetheart', who still sings famous songs like 'The White Cliffs of Dover', remains a youthful-looking lithe blonde who likes to wear blue tracksuits in her garden in the country and thinks it very appealing that the Queen Mother identifies with her as someone of her own age. 'Ah, Vera,' the Queen Mother says dreamily when she hears a wartime song, 'this is our era, our period.' 'Well, not quite the same age, just a teeny bit of difference,' Vera laughs.

She has been included in all sorts of parties given by the Queen Mother. Her husband, Harry, found himself telling his royal hostess once, 'Ma'am, we've been married now for 42 years . . .' The Queen Mother smiled and pretended to be busy persuading two young Bowes Lyon boys to take off their tweed jackets because it was such a sweltering day. But, just as she was walking away, she said: 'Isn't it nice,' then, over her shoulder, 'when it works?'

Vera was invited to an eve-of-peace party at Windsor Castle. 'We felt very privileged when we were told the war was over – but we had to keep quiet. I remember to this day a picture, like a photographic print, I have of the King and Queen and the two princesses. Margaret ducked her head, and the King was rather jumpy.' Vera had a mink wrap with her, and Tommy Trinder, the comedian, was 'larking about', handing it from one person to another as if it was alive, while they stood at the buffet. Suddenly, the King said crossly: 'Will you please put that down.' Tommy Trinder quickly told him a joke which made him laugh and forgive 'those silly showbusiness people'.

Ever since, the Queen Mother and the singer have met at least once a year at 'Lest We Forget' reunions, Burma Star get-togethers and Battle of Britain singsongs. Afterwards, Vera and her husband will often receive an out-of-the-blue invitation from Clarence House. 'The Queen Mother has personally asked if you would like to join her for the afternoon performance of the Royal Tournament in her box . . .' She is a great favourite.

'I think it is because the Queen Mother remembers the war years with her husband, going down to the air-raid shelters. Her eyes get very misty if I sing "We'll Meet Again".'

13

A Bargain Was Struck

Whenever the King was complimented on one of his speeches, he would look across the room and his eyes would light up when he spotted his wife. 'She helps me,' he would say with a nod.

But the Queen's two sisters, Lady Rose Granville and Lady Jean Elphinstone, noticed after the war how 'the King was a rock' to their sister and how much she relied on him. This had always been the balance of their marriage, but because the King seemed a slight figure, a shy man with an inability to deliver speeches in that flat positive way of his father and Edward VIII, it was assumed that he was not strong. His dependence on the Queen was obvious, but not that of his wife on him.

The King had suffered most those five years. He had lost weight, his fair hair was streaked with grey and there was an uncomfortable tautness about him which gave people a shiver. He never did recover from the trauma of war and said simply: 'I feel burnt out.' Beside him his bubbly Queen had maturity and a stoic faith which would keep for her an eternal set of values. Whatever happened later in her life, she would be able to cope that much better because of the suffering she had seen in two world wars. Her compassion was practical. A couple who lived at Windsor had lost everything in the war. But, far from being dispirited, the wife was pleased to be wearing one of the Queen's couture dresses and her husband was in one of the King's suits.

Everybody hoped that the King would soon be fit again, wandering round the gardens at Royal Lodge with his wife, enjoying the camellias and rhododendrons blossoming in rainbow clumps of pink, white and flame. He smoked incessantly. They were to have only six and a half more years together.

George VI was a doting father and wanted to enjoy his daughters' company, which he had missed during the war. Princess Elizabeth had fallen heavily for a young naval officer. Prince Philip, with his pale good looks, acerbic wit and a little too much self-confidence, made an impression on this serious girl, sophisticated in constitutional matters but not worldly wise. Her mother had all the reticence of the Edwardians about the facts of life, so the two princesses must have been fairly innocent.

Prince Philip was a great-great-grandson of Queen Victoria; his mother, the rather saintly Princess Andrew, who became a nun, was a sister of Lord Mountbatten. The King did not consider these credentials quite enough for the husband of his beloved Lilibet, though Mountbatten pressed for the marriage.

The King thought that because of the war his eldest daughter was inexperienced. The usual eligible young men had not been around to take her to night clubs, race meetings and house parties; so he arranged dances at Windsor and Sandringham for her. She was patient, but often daydreaming, a look of quiet sensuality taking her miles away where Philip was earning eight guineas a week as a sub-lieutenant.

The King and Queen's friends tended to be serious men who had served in the Navy or aristocrats who loved hunting and shooting, so Sir Philip Sassoon was unusual, a stylish and flamboyant host. His mother was a Rothschild and his father's family rich Parsees from Bombay. He entertained the King and Queen with just the right amount of sybaritic informality at his home in Kent. There was a swimming pool of bright blue, flamingos and scented lilies on the lake, and the guests were a mixture of people like George Bernard Shaw, Osbert Sitwell, a great friend of the Queen's, and Lord Boothby, arguing over tea.

The King enjoyed golf, and if his partner was wise he did not win too many holes. In the evening, after a dip in a marble bath, the Duke and Duchess went down to the deep blue lapis-lazuli dining-room with its Glyn Philpot frieze of white cows driven by negroes. After brilliant fireworks over the lake, Richard Tauber sang to the guests relaxing on the terrace.

But none of these friends were producing young men who could interest Elizabeth for longer than a few waltzes. The Queen just hoped that the King and his eldest daughter would see eye to eye.

The atmosphere in the royal homes had become easier. Some of Queen Mary's cronies were shocked by the sound of the radio, 'worked' incessantly by Princess Elizabeth, by the young guardsmen jiving with the girls and the jigsaw puzzles cluttering the card tables in the hall.

Meanwhile the Queen had the Gainsboroughs cleaned and commissioned new work from Edward Seago and John Piper, the entertaining artist who did such dramatic watercolours of Windsor.

John Piper, who works to the music of Poulenc and Walton in his studio at Fawley Bottom near Henley, was introduced to the Queen by Sir Kenneth Clark. He worked in solitary gloom at Windsor Castle during the war and his paintings were to be an 'artistic' record, should the Castle be destroyed. When the King saw the paintings he asked, 'Why is it, Mr Piper, that it always seems to be raining when you do a sketch of Windsor?' pretending he did not understand the artist's brooding backgrounds. 'You've been very unlucky in the weather,' he went on. The Queen Mother cherishes the paintings and keeps them at Clarence House. Piper says, 'They were tattily framed because of the war and the Queen Mother asked who I would recommend to reframe them. I suggested the best framer I knew, Alfred Hecht. Afterwards she complained, "He's frightfully expensive," but she was pleased.' Over the years Piper has become a great admirer of the Queen Mother and he is quick to tell you that she is not all 'racing and roses' and thinks her 'frightfully jolly – a generous, warm countryhouse girl'.

The royal artistic adviser was Ben Nicholson, who really did not enjoy going to Windsor, finding it far too formal. He was a Bohemian and lived in scruffy clothes. It was suggested once that it was time another portrait of the Queen was commissioned but he airily advised a photograph instead – 'so much better'. He remembers having to take part in games at Windsor after dinner and being dismayed when, hunting the villain in a game of 'Murder', he found himself under a piano in the dark and poking his finger into a soft cushion which turned out to be the Queen's bosom.

Queen Mary suggested to her son and his wife that the famous royal portraits in the long gallery were *soi-disant*; if she had her way she would banish them and put up some tapestries in their place.

Other distractions were race meetings, a delight shared by Princess Elizabeth and George VI, the best horseman in the family. On the Queen's 45th birthday the family went to Ascot and one of the King's horses, Rising Light, won in a stunning finish by a few inches.

The King and Queen also got an immense amount of fun out of their dogs. Before the war, Queen Maud of Norway brought in a rare Shih Tzu puppy for the then Duchess of York. These furry creatures from China, of impeccable pedigree from ancestors called Ah Tishoo and Ming, and with honey or black and white markings, suited the Duchess perfectly. She thought her dog, Choo Choo, had a face like a chrysanthemum. When she became Queen she reluctantly handed over this delicate oriental dog to her brother, David, in the country. But she kept her sturdy army of corgis.

There were endless parties for Princess Elizabeth; sometimes the Queen would tell the band leader Maurice Winnick not to stop playing until five in the morning. The Queen, dressed in a lime silk dress and tiara, and the King, wearing black suede shoes, laid on a dance for the staff with a cabaret provided by Florence Desmond, Frankie Howerd and Jimmy Edwards; later the Queen danced with a senior footman, Freddie Mayes, the man who wound all the antique clocks at the Palace.

The King could still get into one of his 'gnashes' over an imagined slight. Once, when the Queen was in her sitting-room looking at some new sketches by Hartnell for her summer wardrobe, the King caught sight of one of these, a model's head and shoulders lightly pencilled in, and barked: 'Is this meant to be the Queen?' – immediately imagining a lack of respect. 'Oh, no, darling, I only wish I was as beautiful as that,' the Queen soothed.

There was always a posse of young ensigns from the Household Brigade around the princesses, 'The Bodyguard', as Queen Mary called them. One of them, Peter Letcher, remembers that the Queen quickly made things fun when they were invited to Windsor Castle. 'She was always so warm and motherly.'

But Lady Airlie noticed at one dinner how strained the King had become. He hardly ate anything and went straight back to the Red Boxes after dinner. Everyone else stayed up, with the Queen leading the dancing. Old Queen Mary, then 79, and Lady Airlie, 90, danced the hokey-cokey.

There was lots of gaiety, lots of fun but Princess Elizabeth, in her determined way, told her parents that she would like to marry and soon. The King asked her to wait until after the important royal tour to South Africa, writing privately to his mother, 'We both think her too young for marriage.' The Queen was sympathetic but did not interfere. She was happy in her own marriage, proud of her daughters and never a demanding or possessive mother.

A bargain was struck. Princess Elizabeth would go to South Africa with her parents and her sister, and, afterwards, the engagement could be announced. Everyone was happy. Long before the tour, in February 1946, the Queen whisked her daughters off to Hartnell for a feast of frivolity and to encourage her eldest daughter who was not very interested in clothes.

On the tour, the Queen and her daughters wore pretty draped

frocks in beige and cream and big matching hats; the princesses stuck to fairly sensible shoes while their mother teetered in impossibly high heels. At one point, as they were about to climb up some rocky path, Princess Elizabeth said briskly: 'Typical of Mummy' and, removing her own shoes, handed them to the Queen and padded behind in stockinged feet. At least, someone said, they are not attempting an assault on Table Mountain.

The royal party travelled in the White Train, which stopped several times a day in places well named, like Hicksdorp. The King was tetchy in the heat and waited with shoulders hunched at the door of the train, gazing into a sea of excited Bantu faces. James Cameron remembered the Queen's charm at work when the royal couple stepped down at uninspiring places.

'"Oh, Bertie, do you see, this is Hicksdorp! You know we've always so wanted to see Hicksdorp! Those people there with the bouquets, they must be the local councillors. How kind! And those people at the far, far end of the platform, behind that little fence – I expect they are the Bantu choir. How kind! We must wave, Bertie."'

They spent 36 nights on the train and, as one of the entourage put it, 'We would be woken at half past six the next morning when a large, black gentleman would come with a wet broom and start cleaning the windows.' The Queen put up with any little irritability on the King's part. He was often a little testy, much more ill even then than anyone realized. 'Oh, come on, for God's sake let's get going,' he'd grumble, and the Queen would give a winsome smile, disentangle herself from the group she was talking to and join her husband again. She was rightly preoccupied by his health.

Princess Elizabeth celebrated her 21st birthday in South Africa and made her dedication speech, offering her life, 'whether it be long or short', to the service of her country.

In Oudtshoorn, they went to an ostrich farm. The King was expected to snip a tail feather off one of the unsuspecting ostriches, but the large bird squawked as the King accidentally took a quarter of an inch from its behind. The Queen, smiling, came forward and took the scissors and delicately snipped a piece of feather, and the wretched ostrich, its head still in a sack, stopped quivering.

'We do a lot of gardening at home: the King is good at digging and weeding and it is I who concentrate on the secateurs,' she glossed over his nervous clumsiness.

Princess Elizabeth was lovesick and self-absorbed, pining for Prince Philip's refreshing company. She really only cheered up on the way home, on board *Vanguard*, being chased round the deck by young officers, happy at last that the King had consented to her marrying.

The tour had been a triumph but the King lost over a stone in weight and came back to a frozen Britain, locked in the bleak winter of 1946–7.

Prince Philip became a British subject on 28 February 1947 and on 10 July the engagement was announced. They married on 20 November 1947, the bride wearing a white dress dotted with thousands of raised pearls and a wedding ring of Welsh gold, made from the same nugget which had produced her mother's ring. The King wrote a moving note soon after the wedding to his daughter.

He explained why he had wanted her to come to South Africa. 'Our family, us four, the royal family, must remain together, with additions, of course, at suitable moments. I was rather anxious that you had thought I was being very hard-hearted about it. Your leaving has left a great blank in our lives, but I can see that you are sublimely happy with Philip.'

The Queen saw her daughter go off on honeymoon, wrapped up in an open landau, a corgi at her feet and a cheeky, appealing young husband by her side. Thirty-four years later, at her grandson's wedding, she would turn to Prince Philip with great affection and say, 'remember yours,' and Prince Philip laughed as they waited together for the bride to join Prince Charles at the steps of the altar in St Paul's Cathedral.

In April 1948, the King and Queen celebrated their silver wedding. When their daughter had her first baby, Prince Charles, born at 9.14 P.M. on 14 November in Buckingham Palace, they rushed, in evening dress, to see Princess Elizabeth and their first grandchild and heir to the throne.

The Queen hugged Prince Philip and they had a glass of champagne.

14

A Great and Noble King

The King had been far from well. He had been suffering from cramps in his legs which doctors diagnosed as arteriosclerosis early in November 1948. They asked him to cancel the proposed tour of Australia and New Zealand, and warned that if he refused to rest there was a danger that his leg might have to be amputated.

This was a most stressful time for the Queen. During Princess Elizabeth's final months of pregnancy, she flitted between her husband's room in the Palace and her daughter, cheering each of them with delicious morsels of gossip about the other. He seemed to respond to treatment and the doctors thought that surgery could be avoided.

But, in the following spring, doctors decided that after all the King should have surgery to give free circulation to his right leg. With heart-rending disappointment, George VI said: 'So, all our treatment has been a waste of time?' Now that the operation was inevitable, doctors thought he might be coaxed into the Royal Masonic, but he replied with shades of George V, 'I have never heard of a King going to a hospital before.'

Professor James Learmouth operated. The patient promised to lead a quieter life.

The King and Queen both liked Learmouth. During his convalescence the King produced a sword which had been hidden under his pillow and, with a flourish, told the surgeon: 'You used a knife on me, now I'm going to use this one on you.' It was a warm moment as Learmouth rose from bended knee a Knight.

The Queen's hardest task then was to persuade the King to slow down. 'He may pay more heed to you, Ma'am, than to his doctors,' had been the advice.

There were compromises. The King insisted on going to the Trooping the Colour ceremony, but he made history by sitting in an open carriage watching his daughter take the salute in his place. In the late summer it was easier to get him to relax. At Balmoral, the King and Queen went on picnics in their old clothes, happy and surrounded by the family. He found an ingenious way to shoot while not upsetting his doctors by standing or walking too much.

He designed a harness with a long trace fixed to a pony, which hauled him up steep hills. But there was the rotation of royal ritual and the King drove himself to keep engagements. In 1951 there was the Festival of Britain and he made a speech from the steps of St Paul's which, in his mother's view, was very impressive and 'very good'. She thought the South Bank buildings awful: 'Really extra-ordinary.'

In May 1951, the Queen went alone to Northern Ireland. When she telephoned the King at Balmoral, she was filled with foreboding. He had overtaxed his strength and had what he described as 'flu. With a sinking feeling she returned to London immediately, cancelling all her engagements. The doctors said the King must rest for three months and that they would also like to do a few tests. The King returned to London, telling friends, 'Now they think there's something wrong with me blowers.'

The tests confirmed that the King had lung cancer. Doctors operated, and one of them, Sir Harold Graham Hodgson, had to break the news to the Queen that the surgery was six months too late. The King could not be expected to live longer than eighteen months. Now, for the Queen, came the hardest test of all – to be with her husband, loving and cheerful as ever, while keeping secret the specialists' prognosis. One of the doctors remembered how, even then, she spread balsam, 'Friar's Balsam,' he said, 'if you'll forgive the medical expression.'

The Queen's bravery in those months was stunning. The King seemed stronger. Princess Elizabeth took off for her tour of Canada in October feeling more optimistic about her father. His health did seem to have improved enormously. But, in her luggage, was a draft Accession Declaration.

George VI enjoyed his daughter's success in Canada and the United States, and chuckled over President Truman's compliments about Princess Elizabeth: 'We have reason to be proud of our daughters,' he said. 'You have the better of me because you have two!'

At Christmas the King seemed a little better and appreciated the decorated trees at Wolferton, the station near Sandringham where he had stepped off the train with his bride-to-be almost 28 years before. After Christmas, he wanted to shoot and the doctors could not argue with him. 'You have had your fun,' he said. 'Now I am going to have mine.' He wore a special electrically-heated waist-coat, specially heated gloves and boots – and shot well. The doctors were so pleased with him that by 29 January the whole family celebrated by going to see the musical *South Pacific* at the Drury Lane Theatre. The next day Princess Elizabeth and Prince Philip were off to Australia, stopping in Kenya on the way.

The King had guessed how ill he was. He was always a slight man but now you could pick him up in two hands. One of the doctors remembered his thinness, 'that big jaw, those bright eyes and the quietness of his courage'. Even when he was very ill his dry sense of humour sustained the family. Princess Elizabeth always remembered to curtsey even when she came to see her father in bed.

There was a look about his face which in recollection still disturbs those who saw him standing on the tarmac watching the Argonaut aircraft carrying his daughter and her husband away. There was a bitter wind; the King wore no hat and others around him chatted and shivered. Princess Margaret looked unhappy, but the Queen kept up cheerful pleasantries while King George, his hands dug deep in his pockets, watched until the plane disappeared into grey cloud.

A photograph of that parting, the King so pale and with shoulders hunched, following the flight path of his daughter's plane, proved to be historic. It had been taken in a routine way by a news agency photographer on duty at London Airport, but soon it was to flash around the world: the last picture of George VI and the last time the people would see their monarch in public.

As they drove back, the Queen cheered him up with talk about his favourite Keepers' Day Shoot with the tenants, the police and the farmers on the estate at Sandringham. They had tea with Queen Mary and talked to her about their own trip in March to South Africa, where they planned to stay at a private house while the King recovered his strength.

The morning of 5 February 1952 was bright with a sparkling blue sky over the tall forests of Sandringham. The air made the skin tingle and put the King in good spirits for the shoot. The Queen felt he was so much better that she could get away for a few hours to look at some paintings by the local artist, Edward Seago. She needed a break, and, besides, her trips with Princess Margaret made the King feel that life was carrying on normally.

'Ted' Seago had invited the Queen and her daughter to lunch at his home by the river at Ludham. Mother and daughter loved going to his studio and coming away with the paintings and sketches they had commissioned. It was such a clear day, Seago had imaginatively laid on a motor launch, *Sandra*, to take them to Barton Hall for tea.

It swathed through the dark waters past ploughed fields and forests, such a 'lovely cruise on the river', the Queen Mother always remembered. Thirty miles away, the King was enjoying an excellent day's shooting with Lord Fermoy, whose widow is Ruth, Lady Fermoy. He chatted with his tenants and, at the end of the day, the bag of hare, rabbit and wood pigeon was 480 – the King having shot nine hares and a pigeon. He said to his friends: 'A good day's sport, gentlemen. I will expect you here at nine o'clock on Thursday.'

When the Queen got back to Sandringham she went to the nursery to say goodnight to her two grandchildren, Charles and Anne – and the King had been to the kennels to make sure a thorn was removed from a golden retriever's paw. After dinner, they listened to news of Princess Elizabeth's tour of Kenya on the radio and felt proud of their daughter. Princess Margaret played the piano and, after a while, the King said cheerfully that he would have an early night, saying, 'I'll see you in the morning.'

By 10.30 the King was in bed. He read for over an hour, drinking hot chocolate. He stood at the window of his room, fiddling with the latch, before turning out the light at midnight. It was not until 7.15 A.M. the following day, when his valet, James MacDonald, knocked on the door of his room and entered as usual, that he found the King dead. He had suffered a coronary thrombosis in the early hours of the morning.

The Queen's maid, Gwen Suckling, had brought tea to her room as usual and drawn back the curtains. It was the task of Sir Harold Campbell, Equerry in Charge, who had been with the royal family for 30 years, to tell the Queen that her husband was dead.

'I must go to him,' the Queen said, and told the staff that a vigil must be kept outside the King's open door. 'The King must not be left.' Typically, her next thought was for her daughter, and she tried to comfort Princess Margaret. No longer Queen, she went to see her grandchildren, and those around her were amazed by such strength. 'I must start somewhere,' she explained. All Sir Harold could say was: 'I never knew a woman could be so brave.'

It was 11.45 A.M. – 2.45 P.M. in Africa – when Prince Philip took his young wife for a walk by the banks of the Sagana River, and broke the news to her that the King was dead.

The new Queen, when she had recovered her composure, went to see her staff. To them, she looked so young and vulnerable, standing before them in her beige cotton dress and white shoes. Bobo MacDonald, her devoted maid, was told to unpack the black outfit which the Queen would change into on the flight home. The royal couple drove to Nanyuki on the Equator. The streets were filled with silent crowds, the Kenyans like a chorus in a tragic opera, murmuring as their Queen drove past, her eyes fixed, '*Shauri mbaya kabisa*,' 'the very worst has happened,' and the whisper was taken up along the dusty red earth track.

After the 500-mile hop to Entebbe, the Queen and Prince Philip stood huddled in raincoats at the airport, unable to board the Atalanta because of sudden, fierce tropical storms, 50-mile-an-hour gales and driving rain.

In New York, the Duke of Windsor, in his apartment at the Waldorf Towers, was profoundly shocked by the news of the King's death. He announced he would go to his brother's funeral – alone. He marched in procession at the funeral and stood as part of the royal family once again in St George's Chapel, Windsor. There was a meeting with his mother, but the coldness towards him by the rest of the family was not hidden. He flew back to America with an even greater feeling of alienation.

Quietly, on the evening before the King was buried at Windsor, the Queen Mother slipped out of the Palace to say her own private goodbye. Earlier in the day, her daughters had been to Westminster Hall, the Queen, looking young and slight, curtsied to her father's coffin. Just before midnight the widowed Queen Elizabeth, in black, stood in the shadows by the East Door keeping her own vigil, the diamonds in the brooch on her lapel shining in the gloomy light. She wore nothing on her head and, sometimes, took her eyes away from the purple-draped catafalque to look at the flowers. There were posies of primroses from country children scattered on the grey carpet near the coffin with its sentries of tall candles. The air was heavy with hyacinth, the spring bulb whose sweetness can be a reminder of sickrooms.

Nearly two hours later, the Queen Mother whispered to the Lord Great Chamberlain, the Marquess of Cholmondeley. The great oak door opened and she was gone. The next day, the eyes of the world would be on her. Great moments of royal happiness, and of grief, have to be shared.

Early on Friday, 15 February 1952, a drab sleety day, a naval party in white gaiters drew the King's coffin in a dull green gun carriage with its gleaming brass, to the door of Westminster Hall. The ratings gripped their ropes in one hand, doffed their caps with the other and bowed their heads on their chests.

The Queen had sent her father flowers: 'To darling Papa, from your sorrowing Lilibet', a message from the daughter who had paid him the most moving tribute, 'He never faltered.' One of the wreaths was of white lilac and carnations in the shape of a George Cross; in purple flowers were the words 'For Gallantry'.

The gold, red and azure Royal Standard dressed the coffin: on top was the Imperial State Crown on a royal purple velvet cushion; the gold Orb; the Sceptre; the insignia of the Order of the Garter; and Queen Elizabeth's white flowers – for 'my dear husband, a great and noble King'.

The bareheaded Grenadier Guards had carried the coffin on their shoulders to the gun carriage. Big Ben tolled 56 bells, one for each of the King's years, in a Whitehall covered in grey mist.

At Marlborough House, Queen Mary came to the window and stood by a bowl of flowers. The Queen Mother, the Queen and Princess Margaret leant forward in their carriage and looked up. Queen Mary watched the cortège moving slowly along the Mall, straight-backed and dry-eyed in the privacy of her sitting-room. 'Here he is,' she said, reaching for the hand of Lady Airlie.

The two Dowagers waited by the tall window. Lady Airlie remembered: 'I knew that her dry eyes were seeing beyond the coffin a little boy in a sailor suit. She was past weeping, wrapped in the ineffable solitude of grief. I could not speak to comfort her. My tears choked me. The words I wanted to say would not come and we held each other's hands in silence.'

Suddenly there was one of those moments of stillness you get on grand ceremonial occasions. The trumpeters are quiet, the rhythmic clinking of swords and the urgency of the horses' hooves stops. There was a hush, and people, 30 deep under the plane trees of The Mall, stood perfectly still until the jingling bridles of the horses of the Sovereign's Escort broke the silence.

Then the Queen Mother sat well back and the funeral procession wound its way past 145 Piccadilly, now half-demolished and gaunt, draped in black and purple with a Union flag at half-mast – the old house with all its memories of early married life, when her husband was the dutiful Duke of York, a contented younger son of the King.

George VI was leaving his capital from Paddington Station, to be buried at Windsor. The Queen, her mother and sister, in black veils, stood close together on the red carpet on platform 8. The bands of the Coldstream and Scots Guards played Chopin's 'Funeral March', swamping the emotions even more.

The final journey now was to the Castle, through the town. Shopkeepers had draped their windows with purple and black and wreaths of laurel.

A little pale sun warmed the grey Cotswold stone of the St George's Chapel as the pipers played the 'Flowers of the Forest' lament. The Queen Mother watched the Archbishops of Canterbury and York, their deep purple capes spangled with silver. The last time she had been surrounded by so many princes of the Church had been at the Coronation, when her husband had grumbled about clumsy clerics treading on his cloak.

The Dean was in crimson, and the choir, in white surplices over mulberry cassocks, sang 'I am the Resurrection and the Life' as the King's body was carried to the catafalque at the altar.

The Queen had to be supported by her mother as they faced the coffin together, swaying against each other. 'God shall wipe away all tears from their eyes' ended; the guardsmen stepped forward and, with hands as gentle as girls', removed the banner and jewelled emblems. The coffin, covered only in flowers now, was lowered into the vault. The Queen stepped forward and sprinkled earth from a gold bowl; her father now rested in the company of other Kings.

All the King's personal servants: the Palace Steward, James Ainslie, his detective, Chief Superintendent Hugh Cameron, his valets, James MacDonald and Thomas Jerran, had escorted him to the end.

There were a privileged few at St George's Chapel that day who were able to smile. They remembered a reception at Buckingham Palace, a long and formal evening. When the King and Queen withdrew with regal farewells, a foolish page forgot to close the double doors properly. The guests, still standing around with drinks in their hands, suddenly got a glimpse of the King and Queen, who, thinking they were now on their own, were hand in hand, laughing and skipping down the corridor like a couple of teenagers suddenly allowed out on their own. Everyone felt a little guilty at sharing the moment, the delight of this couple in each other and in such a special marriage.

Meticulous as always about thank-you letters, the Queen Mother wrote to Edward Seago only two weeks after the King's death. 'One can't yet believe that it has all happened,' she said, and thanked the artist for 'the heavenly pictures and particularly for the pleasure you have given the King on Tuesday 5 February'. On that day the King had appeared, ironically, 'so well', and he had been enchanted with the pictures she had collected. 'We spent a very happy time looking at them together,' she wrote.

Afterwards, she said, 'We had such a truly gay dinner'. She had thought at the time how wonderful it was that the King should once again be 'like his old self'.

15

It Must Be Saved

The telephone rang in the bungalow opposite the petrol pumps on the lonely road to Thurso. 'Is that you, Mrs Bell?' The rector's widow, Christianne Bell, ran from the garage, trying to wipe the smell of oil from her hands. 'Aye, it is,' she said, trying not to sound flustered. 'Would you like to join Her Majesty for dinner tonight, or tomorrow night, whatever suits you best?' In the past, this kind of invitation from the Queen Mother, inviting her to dinner at the Castle of Mey, would have thrown Mrs Bell into a tizzy, filling her with feminine anxieties about what to wear, and 'Oh, my hair! It's such a mess.'

'Well, tonight,' Mrs Bell said calmly. 'About eight,' the voice suggested. 'That,' replied Mrs Bell, looking at her tousled hair in the small mirror, 'would be grand.'

It is quite usual at one of the Queen Mother's dinner parties at Mey for everyone to file out of the dining-room to look for the Northern Lights over the Pentland Firth – or do the conga – and then come back to have another course. The food is imaginative, almost always the new wave cookery of France: scrambled eggs in baskets of toast with herbs on top; a hot green soup; cold chicken and ham in aspic with bowls of different vegetables, leeks, broad beans and peas simmered with sweet basil, marjoram, rosemary and parsley from the glasshouse, all served hot and buttery; gooseberries, currants or strawberries with bowls of cream so golden and rich it almost matches the rare yellow gooseberries.

Nobody is expected to dress formally. The Queen Mother will, of course, because when she is on her own at Clarence House in the evening, the dining table is prepared, candles are lit and she will be in evening dress, even if only for scrambled eggs with the corgis. But at Mey she wants her guests to be totally relaxed. The 'laird's' wife, Lady Thurso, has gone to the Castle in the same white wool dress more than once. For Mrs Bell, recently widowed, there was no problem about choosing a dress, it would be the black one again and a comb through her curly hair. No disrespect, but her hostess would not expect to see her in taffeta. The Queen Mother had admired the rector and enjoyed his sense of humour; she called at the house during his final illness with a copy of the *Reader's Digest Book of Birds* to cheer him up.

You have to go to Mey, perched on a cliff where the sky goes inky blue, to understand the Queen Mother. The resident wind has scorched the oaks, the ash and the sycamores. They bend in crescent-shapes, like hedges of question marks. A blast from this high wind could destroy in a whoosh all the Queen Mother's flowers, strawberries and plums. A high wall protects her fruit and beloved roses, called Pink Iceberg, red Silver Jubilee, Albertine and one, whisky-coloured, Glenfiddich. They are quite out of character with the uncompromising windy sweeps of Caithness.

When she walks along the beach in her blue mackintosh, her wellingtons and her battered fishing hat with its enduring feather, she is buffeted by this wind which sends the curlews shrieking and makes even the wild grey geese drop down from the sky to the shelter of the Longoe farm, where they hide behind the woolly protection of a Cheviot sheep. As the salt spray leaps from an angry sea and stings the round, powdered face, the Queen Mother will urge you to enjoy the bracing walk, cajoling with cosy 'nanny' expressions: 'Come along, this will blow the cobwebs away,' relishing the good the fresh air will be doing her friends from London.

It is her closest friends who share this mellow sixteenth-century castle. Perched in the far north of Scotland on the John O'Groats peninsula, it is the only home the Queen Mother owns. Ruth, Lady Fermoy, will play Cole Porter and Gershwin on the piano in the evening; jolly Sir Ralph Anstruther, the Queen Mother's treasurer, who lives nearby, fusses around plumping up cushions. He once earned an extra helping of strawberries and cream for his ability to match Mrs Bell verse for verse as they recited Gray's 'Elegy' round the dining table.

When the King died, a feeling of futility overwhelmed the Queen Mother. She felt vulnerable and desolate. There was no hint of self-pity. In that first year of widowhood, she went back to her roots, to Scotland where she hoped to find some peace. Perhaps she would settle and retire, going to London only when her daughters insisted. She stayed with her old friends, Lady Doris Vyner and her husband, at their home, romantically angled on a peak in Caithness and called the House of the Northern Gates. They knew her well enough to be able to inveigle her out to spend an afternoon looking at the crumbling follies, the small, turreted houses and the gaunt grey stone castles abandoned by their clans, cleverly playing on the Queen Mother's love of houses and heritage.

You need to move quickly in the spring in Caithness, because by four in the afternoon a low-lying mist can come down, and it is time to light the peat fires.

There was a danger that in her grief the Queen Mother might become like Queen Victoria. She needed somewhere to love and that place was the Castle of Mey.

As soon as they got out of the car and the Queen Mother set eyes on Mey, although it was in a bleak spot with an almost Icelandic openness, she ignored the desolation.

She walked alone on the windy beach at Dunnet, stopping to look out at white foam on the sea like the top of milk, fresh and frothy in a pail. She gathered shells and wandered through the dunes where light green lyme grass binds rafts of sand with its roots – and made up her mind. She would restore the lonely castle, which at this time looked more bleak than ever with its 'roof gone missing'. The rain was coming down on the slate cottages and great flocks of crows were twirling and wheeling, the twisted gorse bushes and purple heather the only colour, apart from the green of the few coastal farms.

'I was driving along,' she remembers, 'and from the high road saw this old castle; when I heard it was going to be pulled down, I thought it must be saved. The roof was really awful, it took twelve months to rebuild that and put in bathrooms and the electric light.' Friends and family in the South thought the Queen Mother must be *distrait* and would get over this notion, but she was indulged – for the time being.

There is nothing 'cosy' – a favourite word in the royal family – about Mey. For a woman of 51, just widowed, to want to live in Caithness more or less alone seemed foolhardy to some friends and brave to others. It was the Queen Mother's fresh beginning: Birkhall, a friendly Queen Anne house, had too many memories of the King. Royal Lodge would soon be a splash of creamy white, yellow and pink azaleas, and an even more poignant reminder of her husband, who had planned the gardens with such delight.

In July 1953, as soon as the Coronation was over, the Queen Mother set to work on her castle. Instantly, she took to the local people who were simple, direct and dignified, never ingratiating and used to hardship. Neither Celtic nor Norse, but a mixture of both, it was this truly independent spirit which the Queen Mother grew to

love. There was a respect for her and she genuinely liked the
Caithness folk, and was amused by their protective warnings about
dreadful 'whirlies', 'swilkies' and 'swelchies'. To friends staying at
Mey, these are eddying gushes of water which still slap against the
doors of the castle when there is a 'Thief-Lookan' sky.

Lord Thurso, leonine and wearing a kilt in his own weave of
Highland heathery-coloured tartan with shocking pink socks, leant
on a shepherd's crook and eyed his cattle. He felt it was typical of the
South to think it madness for the Queen Mother to come to
Caithness and live in a rather pretty 'bothy'. It filled a gap in her
life, he said, 'when she was not at all sure what her public duties
might be'. Neatly side-stepping a cowpat, Lord Thurso laughed,
showing a row of even white teeth, and was pleased to say that the
Queen Mother had done more for Caithness than Dounreay, the
Atomic Energy Authority's establishment.

A truly whirly wind had taken off the roof at Mey, so first this had
to be restored. As Lord Thurso ruefully remembers: 'At the time, we
were competing for the same builder, but as soon as the Queen
Mother's plane landed at Wick, he would mysteriously disappear.'
Lord Thurso put up with a lot of fobbing off, and Highland *mañana*,
with good grace. He later entertained the Queen Mother with a
local's view on the subject. 'The old man said there could be no
word in the Highland dialect to describe such indecent haste.'

When the Queen, Prince Philip and the children arrived at
Scrabster, the little fishing port near Mey where you get excellent
lobster, for their Western Islands cruise in 1955, they disembarked
from the Royal Yacht *Britannia* wondering what to expect.

They found a twinkling, beautifully restored Castle of Mey. It is a
rare example of a Scottish family castle, but too small to put up all
the royal family. They had tea and, when they rejoined the Royal
Yacht, the Queen felt happier about her mother's recovery than at
any time since the King died.

The castle can still look forbidding, with its two squat mock
cannons facing out – towards the Arctic Circle. When you ring the
bell, there is the sound of barking dogs, then you walk into a white-
washed hall with a double staircase. There are jugs of fresh pink and
blue flowers, a collection of walking sticks, a bowl of delicate shells, a
shepherd's crook, and an exotic little statue of a blackamoor, which
attracted much less attention in the dark brown hallway of 145
Piccadilly.

In the drawing-room there are two large china cats and a fire of wood and peat. Someone tells the Queen Mother that once it was the poor local women who carried the peat, dung and seaweed in wickerwork 'crubbans' strapped to their backs. The Queen Mother exchanges a look with Mrs Bell, who has often told her how her mother and her two sisters went to London to avoid just this kind of work. 'We both marvelled at how three simple Scottish girls made that journey all alone.'

The drawing-room is full of Caithness glass, the local craft; vases with bridges opened by the Queen Mother etched on the glass, others full of roses; and bowls of bon-bons. The strong blues and greens of local landscapes hang on the pale walls, but all you really want to do is look out at the Pentland Firth.

For a house bought in a mood of depression, Mey is light, picturesque, and full of the Queen Mother's ambience. Balmoral is formal, so is Windsor, but Mey is unpretentious. Dinner, as in London and Windsor, is never served before nine. Jane and Sandy Webster, the resident couple, do everything; he grows the vegetables and the fruit and his wife cooks them.

Artichokes, Jerusalem and globe, are great favourites with the Queen Mother, who will suggest as her guests finish eating them: 'Now, shall we all have a glass of water so we can savour the taste of rusty nails?' She always invites you to do something, never commands. Everyone at the table drinks a glass of icy fresh water. Some gulp and study the bronze firescreen cast by Lord Charteris, Provost of Eton, with its headlands, puffins and 'Willie Weet Feet', the sandpiper; even the royal yacht is in the picture. But it is not long before glasses are filled with wine supplied by jolly Scottie Taylor from the corner grocery shop, Hamish Cameron, in Thurso, with its 'By Royal Appointment' above the door. A month or so before the Queen Mother arrives in Mey, he sends cheese, wine – including Veuve Clicqot champagne – 100 Piper's whisky and crates of Scottish ale to the castle. He then gets on with the Prime Minister's monthly order of Orkney fudge: Mrs Thatcher struggles to keep her figure, but cannot resist the monthly parcel of this very sweet mix which is posted to Downing Street.

When the Queen Mother first came to Caithness, Lord Thurso asked if she would come to the Jubilee Ball. 'Oh, yes, lovely. I shall wear my tiara.' She arrived in brilliant white with a Queen's ransom of diamonds on her head. A discreet restroom had been fixed for her. But this was not what the Queen Mother had in mind at all.

As Lord Thurso remembers: 'She absolutely loves the "Dashing

White Sergeant" and the trouble was keeping the partners coming when they got winded – her stamina was incredible.' She danced until the owls had given up hooting and light was beginning to show up the funny triangular haystacks on the coastal farms.

In Caithness the Queen Mother can enjoy seclusion without isolation. She can go into Thurso in the Land-Rover, wearing headscarf, mackintosh and wellingtons. Thurso likes to think of itself as a small Edinburgh, while Wick is more commercial, with smelly fishing boats and a once good herring trade. In Wick they say: 'Thurso is tea frocks and flowers facing the window: fur coat and no drawers'.

There is a hint of cautious refinement about Miss Hattie Munro, who also has a 'By Appointment' sign outside her small Thurso shop where she sells antiques. Anyone arriving from another planet would be mystified as to why this small grey town with large drapery shops, their windows full of gloomy cardigans, woollen nightdresses and brown hats, should be so honoured. But Scottie Taylor and Hattie Munro have, in their own words, 'been looking after the Queen Mother's needs for many a year now'.

In the antique shop the need might be for another 'dear little clock', as the Queen Mother indulges her passion for them. 'Woe betide me if I haven't read the *Groat*, the *John O'Groats Journal*,' Hattie says. The Queen Mother is not gossipy but she likes to help when she can, and was concerned recently about an historic house being turned into a Pakistani restaurant.

The Queen Mother cares very much about the local heritage and customs. Every summer when the walls of Mey are pink with climbing roses, there is a tug of war between the 'strong men of the castle', her bodyguards, and the local lads. In 1983 the local youngsters managed to beat the 'strong men of the castle'.

It was a typically blustery Caithness day, a colour party from the US base was having trouble controlling their flags in the wind. The Queen Mother, who was due to meet them, stepped forward all smiles and, seeing the red-faced American who could not shake hands because of fear of losing the flag, she put both her hands over his as they both grasped the flagpole. Suddenly, this wild-eyed panicky serviceman looked at her with such relief. He forgot himself and blurted out: 'Oh, Ma'am, you've got the bluest eyes.' She remarked afterwards, 'It was well seen he was a sailor.'

The life in Caithness appeals to the Queen Mother's sense of her roots. Today, the crofters who once were so poor lean nonchalantly on the bar in Scrabster, buying their girlfriends pina coladas and talking of the latest videos. It is the television producers, actors and advertising people from the South who worry now about how to get their goat pregnant before leaving their trendy 'crofts' to fly back to London.

'She has brought to us a light,' says Sir John Sinclair, a local landowner. But, in turn, Mey has given back to the Queen Mother a lightness of spirit. Sometimes she goes walking, looking for the seals and singing 'Speed, Bonny Boat' at the top of her voice; she will come in with sand on her boots to have a warming gin and Dubonnet with whoever is staying, or just enjoy the peace on her own.

She will then go to her apartments in one of the towers. Her fourposter bed is covered in a bright flowery chintz, with pleating and piping. She has always loved fireplaces and fenders. On one of her birthdays, the King gave her a tiny white marble fireplace with a heart medallion. 'My wife,' he said with his dry smile, 'is very attached to the hearth.'

It is not an easy sentimental treasure to move, but it has now been in three homes, first Buckingham Palace, then Clarence House and now Mey. From her turret the Queen Mother loves the view in the spring as she dresses for dinner, when the lawns are white with snowdrops and daffodils are buffeted by the wind. In August, her bedroom is perfect for a last look at *Britannia* as it sails away. After tea, the family go on board the royal yacht at Scrabster, the sky is lit by the lingering fires from the castle and answering fireworks from the royal yacht. Mother and daughter are saying goodnight.

The Queen Mother knows a lot about the land, although she may not want you to think so, and she can be found amongst the tweeds, the kilts and the windblown farmers earnestly stamping along in stout brown shoes with walking sticks or crooks, walking beside them like an ice-blue delphinium, in her high heels, gloves and bag over the rough heather fields at Mey.

'Where do the stockmen live?' the Queen Mother asked Briga-dier-General Sir Keith Murray with an angelic smile when she was visiting the Highland Agricultural Society at Edinburgh. 'That's done it,' thought Murray, the Director. 'Well, Ma'am, they have a little room at the end of the pen.' 'May I see it?' she asked. He sent swift messages to the men to 'get it tidied fast'. But, far too quickly for his liking, they arrived at the stockmen's room to find the 'lads' tottering out with girlie magazines, beer, newspapers, cigarette ends, all stuffed into a hay bag. They looked a bit sheepish when the bag burst open at her feet.

The Brigadier turned puce, but the Queen Mother, with a conspiratorial smile, said: 'That must have been a very good party.' She hates humbug; she sees people clearly, understands the tensions and is receptive to atmosphere.

Anyone who thinks she is constantly swathed in chiffon and osprey feathers, flitting from a gala ballet to a day at the races, should hear her assessing her Cheviot sheep: she knows about the 'shape of the muzzle' and makes comments, spoken like a true Scotswoman, such as: 'a good long body, meat in the right places on the hips and plenty of character in the head.'

She likes the no-nonsense humour of Caithness people like Sheriff Thompson. A young thug, dressed in black leather, appearing before the magistrates in Thurso, was flexing his muscles, showing off to his friends in the gallery. The Sheriff glanced at the boy's papers and, without looking at him, remarked, 'Ah, I see you are still wetting the bed'.

Then there are the 'tinks' who call, an affectionate sounding name for beady-eyed tinkers who want to sharpen your knives or cut your trees.

She enjoys it all: the lorries nicknamed 'Wee Beastie'; the grey stone crofts with red doors; the steel blue of the white-flecked sea; the follies on top of vivid green mounds; the bare trees like the blue-grey gum trees of Australia; the reddish tinge of the peat giving a softness at summer dusk.

Caithness is not pretty, it is not cosy; it is abrasive and any woman choosing it as her favourite restoring haven has a brave spirit and is not easily frightened, least of all by her own company. For someone who loves fine architecture, even the squat little buildings and the ugly churches do not depress her. Once, when she was staying with Lord Thurso and his wife, they all went to a church near their home and the Queen Mother agreed, 'It was not a pretty church, but what a happy congregation.'

Mrs Christianne Bell was amazed when the Queen Mother turned up unexpectedly at the dedication of a lectern to her husband, the Rector, in October 1981. 'It was such a great surprise to all of us,' she said. After the service the Queen Mother went to the widow and said: 'I was so pleased I could be here.' 'She held my hand for a second so warmly, as if knowing just what was in my heart.'

In September, the Castle is barred against the winter storms and Mrs Webster tidies away the fold-up picnic chairs for another year – the Queen Mother adores picnicking at Mey. The rods are put away, no more 'riotous' parties or fishing for mackerel and hunting for crab. Sandy Webster tries to tie down all the plants, the shrubs and the roses against the gales which will come whipping in from the sea. The Websters stay on in the empty castle for the winter and pray that the roof will stay on. The Queen Mother is not expected back until the spring when the celandines are out and the salmon run again.

Some say that Mey is an extravagance, but what a small price the Queen Mother paid for restoring something 'which might have been lost forever', and, more importantly, restoring herself, healing her and, on those long walks by the sea, realizing that maybe she did have a role and should not be tempted to retire.

Everybody feels a little sad when the plane of the Queen's Flight takes off at the end of August as the Queen Mother leaves for Balmoral. On a clear day at the Castle of Mey you can almost see across to the Arctic Circle; it is not a flat landscape, and in summer it stays light until 11 at night for dancing evening reels; it clears the head and eases away anxieties.

16

Sympathetic But Helpless

Among the guests at the Buckingham Palace garden party for the Queen Mother's 80th birthday, a striking-looking couple attracted some attention. Group Captain Peter Townsend and his wife, Marie-Luce, who looks like a taller version of Princess Margaret, stood about somewhat uncertainly on the springy lawn. For him, there were fleeting smiles, hints of recognition or a sudden coldness as eyes rested on his wife. Some of the Establishment have never forgiven him.

'Go on, maybe she would like to talk to you,' Marie-Luce whispered as the Queen Mother, all smiles, came near their group. But the white chalk marker, indicating the spot where worthies are lined up, was just a few yards too far away.

In spite of a few nudges from Marie-Luce, Townsend did not push forward. It was not so much that the Queen Mother would have minded but that some of the courtiers would have shown their disapproval. He regretted his diffidence and wrote to the Queen Mother when he got back to Paris. But then, they had always been friends.

The world may have imagined that Townsend was banished from royal circles like the wicked demon in a ballet, the Fairy Queen dramatically exiling the horned villain. But Townsend had always appealed to the Queen Mother; she liked his suave jollity and tongue-in-cheek deference.

Now he lives in an elegantly rambling mansion flat in Paris, just near the Indian Embassy, his sitting-room looking out to the Eiffel Tower. He is 65 and his hair is grey and fluffy; his hands were covered in grease, his daughter's car wouldn't start. He has the casual charm and the slightly old-fashioned courtesy of a fifties Britain, captured in films like *Genevieve*.

He has a touch of the David Nivens, a dashing, low-key English style, and an understated hilarity, referring to those turbulent months when he was being pursued by the world's press as *La Chasse*. One of his several books is a loyal account of his love for Princess Margaret and his latest is about Nagasaki.

His eldest son is a Catholic priest and his other three children, two boys and a girl, are at university. He says his wife is not a bit like Princess Margaret. Marie-Luce is Belgian and he met her when he was transferred to the embassy in Brussels. She is slender and chic, like a model girl in *Elle* magazine.

She comes back into the apartment with the dog she has been exercising, her brown hair is shortly fashionable and, in her white top and smart sawn-off black trousers and flatties, looks about 20. She says her husband has time only for one more glass of red wine before she drags him to the *campagne* for *le weekend*. Townsend smiles. They love their house in the country.

Marie-Luce has a coolly Gallic attitude to her husband's romance with Princess Margaret, and, anyway, to the Townsends it is all so long ago.

Townsend had last seen the Queen Mother 13 years before in 1967, at a *Vanguard* reunion, the handsome battleship which had carried the King, the Queen, the two princesses and Townsend to South Africa.

Group Captain Peter Townsend was never the usual courtier. He had been appointed as an equerry to the King as part of a new policy which honoured officers with distinguished war records. His wife, Rosemary, thought it was marvellous: 'We're made!' she glowed to friends.

Her husband arrived for his royal duties at the Palace in the spring of 1944. He likes to portray himself then as a stuttering, inarticulate serviceman whom the Queen had to help. 'She was wonderful, always there being kind.' But it was his assurance and polish which made him ideal coping with the King who could be crotchety.

But, Townsend persists, 'One was a very shy boy who had almost just stepped out of the cockpit into the Palace. Half the time I didn't know what they were talking about, but if I had started talking about "putting the stick forward and throttling back", they would not have known what I was talking about either.' He fitted in perfectly.

There were cycling games up and down the slopes at Sandringham; solemn ceremonial occasions when the King might mutter, as he picked medals off a velvet cushion held by Townsend, 'Can't you tell that orchestra not to make so much blasted noise?' The equerry also had to soothe the King when he muttered: 'Where are those women?' until the Queen and her daughters would appear, blossomy in pink and blue chiffon.

Formal in public, there was a lot of laughter behind the scenes, and the equerries joined in. The King liked chaffing Townsend, who once got the drinks wrong: instead of mixing dry martinis for George VI and some leading businessmen, he gave them sherry instead. The captains of industry did not complain, but afterwards the King grumbled to his family, 'Do you know this dreadful fellow Townsend tried to poison me.'

They would shriek with laughter over Canasta. (The Queen Mother once said that hearing the National Anthem on television when 'one' was not present was rather like hearing the Lord's Prayer while playing Canasta.) The King liked to repeat the jokes of one of his favourite comedians, Tommy Handley, and always as soon as he heard the music of *It's That Man Again* he would turn up the volume on the wireless, with its fretwork tapestry, chuckling at Handley's 'Meet my Foreign Secretary, Signor So-So'. Then, in another voice, Handley would reply, '*Grazie, Grazie*', followed by a quick one-liner: 'The man's a Nazi.'

George VI had a sharp eye and a dry sense of humour. Once he spotted both the China Medal for the Relief of Peking and Queen Victoria's Medal for the first part of the South African War being worn by Lord Gowrie, VC. 'How on earth did he get from China to South Africa in time?' he wanted to know.

Townsend thought Princess Elizabeth was 'sweet but shy'. The Queen and Princess Margaret were good mimics, who always saw the funny side of things. Once, when the Shah of Persia was staying at Buckingham Palace, the Queen, gracious as always and making conversation with the eastern potentate, inquired, 'Have you seen *Annie Get Your Gun*?' Immediately the Shah went rather white and clasped his hip pockets. 'No, Madam, I have not got my gun.' More panic, then, 'I have left it in my room. I will send somebody to get it.'

The Shah and his wife, Farah Diba, were always favourites at the Palace. There is a photograph of Farah Diba at Clarence House in one of the sitting-rooms, and the present Queen also has one of this woman who is now a widow, living under protection for herself and her children far from Tehran and the Ayatollah who replaced the Shah. The King and Queen were always rather tickled by the reasons given by the Shah's first wife, the beautiful sister of King Farouk, when suing for divorce. She cited 'the altitude of Tehran, 8,000 feet up, too high!'

Princess Margaret has said quite openly that she was in love with

Townsend long before he knew or reciprocated. But there are those in royal circles who believe that Townsend knew very well how he appeared in the eyes of the King's youngest daughter and that he never took any steps to put a stop to what began as a schoolgirl infatuation.

The tour of South Africa in 1947 probably marked an innocent beginning for her of a love which would make her very unhappy. They were to travel on a gold and ivory train, see golden-orange sunsets over the Zambezi and feel the tingle of the spray at Victoria Falls. After a sheltered childhood, Princess Margaret was now the centre of attention. Suddenly, she was grown-up, attractive to men and eye-catching with her wardrobe of new, fashionable clothes, on the threshold of becoming a beautiful woman. Townsend has always remembered her 'large, purple-blue eyes, generous sensitive lips and a complexion as smooth as a peach'. Her sense of humour, with a lurking touch of Queen Victoria's caustic remarks, matched Townsend's own light, slightly mocking style. They were perfect foils for each other.

When Cecil Beaton took pictures of Princess Margaret as she came of age, he saw through his lens a decorative girl with 'a wonderful complexion, ice-cream pink cheeks and blue, cat-like eyes'. As she relaxed in the rose-coloured room at Buckingham Palace, with a background of Boucher tapestries showing Don Quixote adventures, she surprised the highly-strung photographer by telling him that she was quite sure that bits of potato peel had been stitched into the embroidery on her dress. It was a Dior and she was very proud of it. Clothes from France were considered highly extravagant then, not to mention that guilty feeling of spurning British couturiers.

Princess Margaret could be something of 'a holy terror'. She says of herself today, 'I'm no angel but I'm not Bo-peep either.' Once, when her parents asked her not to be so free with the sherry, she told them firmly that she would refuse to launch any more ships unless her glass was refilled; and, asked where she had learnt some modern slang, she replied: 'At my mother's knee, or some such low joint.' But in reality she got on well enough with her mother, though they are much closer now than in her adolescence. Then she was 'Papa's girl'. The King adored his daughters. He had tremendous loyalty to Elizabeth, but Margaret he spoilt. She was pretty, could be suitably grand, never forgetting her royal birth.

Few girls, and certainly not princesses, could talk really frankly with their parents in post-war days. The King and Queen were at fault in their blindness to the growing attraction between Princess Margaret and Peter Townsend. But, as often happens with couples who are happy in their marriage – as the King and Queen were – they blithely believe that all around them life is going on as sweetly as their love for each other makes the world appear. 'Peter' Townsend was such a suitable equerry and fitted in so well with the royal family that he was like a son for the King and a fun brother for the princesses.

Princess Margaret celebrated her 18th birthday at Balmoral. An admirer, Billy Wallace, in a brown check suit, escorted her 18-inch-high birthday cake, with her personal coat of arms iced on top, to Scotland, sitting beside it in the train from London. Years later, in 1956, Wallace proposed to the Princess and was accepted. He then flitted off to the Bahamas for a restoring holiday. He had been plagued by ill health and part of his recovery was aided by a Bahamian romance. When he got back, he told Princess Margaret about this morale-boosting peccadillo, thinking she would understand, but found she was far from amused. The romance was quickly concluded.

On her 21st birthday, the Princess, a magnet for all eyes, danced an eightsome reel on the lawn to the emotional wheezing of the bagpipes. Her friends and all the royal equerries stood in a long line, holding torches which spread like a lighted chain to the top of the hill where the birthday Princess lit a bonfire. It was a heady moment for any young man, even one with the resilience of a Battle of Britain pilot. Townsend, who was on duty, stayed with the King at Balmoral, not unduly worried when the Princess's excited escorts drove her off in a grey shooting brake to an impromptu dance at Birkhall.

The King liked to retire early. Sometimes he would send for his equerry and ask crossly how much longer the music would go on downstairs. Often this was a difficult question to answer even for someone with Townsend's skill, for he knew that the King's wife would dance until dawn if she was in a lively mood. To this day, the Queen Mother loves to dance, late nights never worry her and the Queen will shake her head in admiration as her mother still waves her off to bed at a Palace Ball.

Gradually, the King's health deteriorated and there were fewer parties. Soon Princess Margaret was to be psychologically isolated from her family. Her mother was hiding her anxiety behind an outwardly smiling serenity. When the Queen knew her husband was dying, it was a confidence she could not share with her daughters.

In the past, Princess Elizabeth had been a calming, protective influence, but now she was absorbed in her husband and two small children, Prince Charles and Princess Anne. She was also doing more royal tours, standing in for the ailing King who could not be available so often to his younger daughter, to walk with her and listen to her amusing talk. But Princess Margaret seemed to be coping and this was a relief to her mother.

Two months before the King's death in February 1952, Townsend was granted a decree absolute on the grounds of his wife's adultery with John de Laszlo, son of the portrait painter. They later married, but then divorced. Later still she became the wife of the elderly Marquis Camden, whose second wife died in 1978, and who died himself in March 1983.

When you talk to friends of the royal family about the Margaret–Townsend romance, they are sharply divided. Critics of Townsend say that his wife, Rosemary, became lonelier after his appointment at the Palace. She often stayed with friends and once waited in vain on Christmas Day for a phone call from her husband. She has been billed as the erring wife, but there is a sympathy for her and a refusal to believe that she wanted the marriage to break up. Left alone on her own so much with her two small sons, she began seeing the banker, John de Laszlo.

After the King's death, the Queen Mother turned to Townsend as the ideal person who could gently take over much of the strain of her move to Clarence House. Appointed Comptroller of the Queen Mother's Household, he would ease the trauma of leaving Buckingham Palace and adjustment to the shadowy role of Queen Mother. For nobody realized in those early months of widowhood how Queen Elizabeth would turn retirement into a starring role.

Her father's death left a terrible gap in Princess Margaret's life. Like many a girl who has been doted on by her father, she found it difficult to find a man who could match up to the King. Peter Townsend's new position of authority made him even more attractive to her.

The following spring, at Windsor Castle, Townsend chose a moment when everybody had gone to London to tell the Princess about his love for her. 'That is exactly how I feel, too,' she said simply. The romance developed gently. At a discreet but adequate distance from the rest of the royal party, Townsend described how they talked 'while walking on the hill, among the heather, with the breeze in our faces; or riding in the Great Park at Windsor . . . Her understanding, far beyond her years, touched me and helped me; with her wit she, more than anyone else, knew how to make me laugh.'

Both Princess Margaret and Group Captain Townsend will tell you how innocent their love was. Noël Coward wrote sympathetically in his diary that he hoped the poor dears had had 'the sense to leap into bed a couple of times at least', but very much doubted it. The fifties were still quite prim and the occasion for really private moments for them so rare that, on their own admission, they were together only at parties or formal occasions. Princess Margaret, always deeply religious and with the example of her parents' perfect marriage, was not likely to go rampaging off to the South of France for questionable weekends.

For Townsend, the Princess was an awesome responsibility. In the royal household in the fifties there were not even social pecks on the cheeks, although a courtier could kiss the Queen Mother's hand. When the Queen was attending a reception recently one of the guests noticed how many of the women were on social kissing terms with her and thought 'what an improvement'.

When Princess Margaret and Townsend told the Queen Mother that they wanted to marry, there were no objections: this was not in her nature. If there were problems, they were not really for her to solve. But there was a little stunned intake of breath; she had not appreciated how serious the romance was.

She wanted to step into the shadows. She was only 51 but had to think in her grief how best she could cope with being alone now that Princess Margaret was marrying. Deep down, she found it a delicate and very painful time, but she was glad her younger daughter seemed to have found happiness – though it was to be temporary and elusive. The Queen Mother today is much loved, gregarious and admired, but as a comparatively young widow she had few people in whom she could confide. Her friends say that it is still sometimes hard to know what she is thinking, her emotions never accessible to insensitive comment.

For a while she retreated into a protective shell, preparing for her first public ordeal after the King's death: the Coronation of their daughter Elizabeth as Queen.

But on 2 June 1953, the anxieties of friends dissolved. The King's widow sailed into Westminster Abbey, her purple train flowing out behind her, with a look of 'sadness combined with pride'. The organist played William Walton's 'Orb and Sceptre' and the eyes of the Abbey were on her. She walked slowly up the aisle with her head high, bowing to ambassadors and the crowned heads of Europe and negotiating tricky steps without once looking down.

She watched her eldest daughter in her white Coronation robe, embroidered with the rose, the thistle, the shamrock, the wattle, the fern and the lotus, seeming tiny under the Crown of St Edward but, all through the most draining royal ceremony, looking, as Queen Mary remarked later, 'quite perfect'. The young Queen was surrounded by a cluster of peeresses in their diamond 'fenders', their lace and red velvet showing up pale English complexions. The slender white arms of the duchesses looked like swans' necks as they lifted up their strawberry-leaf coronets when the choir sang out 'Vivat, Vivat', to salute the new Queen.

'The enormous presence and radiance of the *petite* Queen Mother,' said Cecil Beaton, moved elderly earls, dowagers, government ministers and young peers alike.

For her, moments that were too emotional were often saved by her grandson, Prince Charles, cherubic in white satin. He was close by her during the Coronation and she fed him restoring barley sugar when he grew restive.

After the Coronation, Peter Townsend and other members of the royal household were waiting in the Great Hall at Westminster Abbey, surrounded by ermine, diamonds and scarlet cloaks. Suddenly, out of this cluster, Princess Margaret emerged and, as she walked towards him, Townsend thought she had never looked so superb. They chatted, and she brushed a wisp of fluff off his uniform. They both laughed, and later confessed, 'We thought no more of it'.

But that proprietorial gesture was spotted by the world's press, in London for the Coronation but avid for confirmation of Princess Margaret's romance. It was the sort of thing one sees fussy wives doing outside the gates of Buckingham Palace as their husbands perspire in top hats before a garden party. It is not the kind of gesture the Queen would approve of, if she saw her daughter-in-law, Diana, picking a feather off the Prince of Wales's uniform. No one advised Princess Margaret about the implications of that intimate moment. Many years later, one courtier reminisced, with some bitterness, while standing in the rain at a Maori dance in New Zealand, 'The King would immediately have sent that fellow Townsend packing.'

Margaret and Townsend were asked to go and see the Queen. Privately, she longed to be happy for her sister, but as Defender of the Faith and temporal Governor of the Church of England, she could not agree to her sister's marriage to a divorced man. But she hit on a compromise, perhaps hoping that this would make the problem disappear: she suggested the marriage be postponed. 'It isn't unreasonable for me to ask you to wait a year?' Princess Margaret and Townsend were happy to agree, seeing no real obstacles.

But it was soon apparent that the marriage could never be. The Establishment took a disapproving view of their love, which, Townsend has said, 'took no heed of wealth and rank'. But those were precisely the things which would destroy it in the end.

These were some of the most difficult times the Queen Mother had known. She missed the King terribly. She had coped with illness, war, and his death, but now there was her wholly unpredictable daughter. Princess Margaret was never an easy young woman; and she could be moody. When things were going badly with her romance, she could be sullen and brooding, dismaying and embarrassing.

The Queen Mother was still trying to come to terms with widowhood and be very brave and busy. She became the first member of the royal family to fly around the world; she took the controls of a Comet and there are those who will cherish for always the sight of that friendly, familiar figure in blue in a pretty hat, instead of the Captain's usual short back and sides. From the cockpit of the world's first civil jet aircraft she sent a telegram to the squadron of which she was Hon. Air Commodore: 'I am delighted to tell you that today I took over as first pilot of the Comet aircraft. We exceeded a reading of 0.8 mach at 40,000 feet. What the passengers thought, I really would not like to say!'

She grew to love helicopters: 'The chopper has changed my life as conclusively as that of Anne Boleyn,' she jokes in a neat reference to the beheading of one of Henry VIII's unfortunate wives.

But, wherever she travelled, she always came back to Clarence House, and the unresolved love of her daughter for Peter Townsend. She had kept her eyes shut to the reality of her daughter's ill-fated romance, hoping in her soft, kind way that the issues would be magically resolved. The decision would be her daughter's – the Queen would have to agree or forbid her sister's marriage and then it would be up to Princess Margaret whether she took this advice or not. Criticized sometimes for being a bit of an ostrich over family problems – it is said that if she sees trouble coming she will stay apart from it, because there is polished marble under the cream – there was nevertheless on this occasion very little the Queen Mother could do.

Townsend's background was gentrified middle-class, West Country in origin, and he doubted very much if the Princess would remain happy for a lifetime as 'Mrs Townsend'. But what they both feel a little bitter about still is the lack of any guidance from the royal 'greybeard advisers' during those traumatic months. They were like children and in the hands of unemotional people like the Queen's Private Secretary, Alan Lascelles. Nobody, they say, really talked to them or spelt out the implications.

Sir Alan 'Tommy' Lascelles, who did not care for Princess Margaret, once barked at Townsend when he went to talk to him after he had seen the Queen: 'You must be either mad or bad.' The Group Captain had rather hoped for a different reaction. Lascelles did not say that marriage was out of the question, but he saw no future for the couple. Behind the scenes, he arranged to have Townsend removed from the Queen Mother's household rather speedily, like an errant footman.

Once again, the Queen Mother was sympathetic but helpless. She was now also hearing unpleasant things about friction between her daughters, how Princess Margaret had told her happily married sister, 'You look after the Empire and I'll look after my life.' She also suggested that the Queen might pay some attention to Prince Philip's private social engagements, putting a mischievous spotlight on her brother-in-law.

Some of Townsend's friends at the Palace were now deserting him. 'Perhaps they were jealous I'd got a beautiful girl,' he said. He was ultimately given a bleak choice between postings to Singapore, Johannesburg or Brussels, where he chose to become Air Attaché.

Townsend now looks back with a jaded eye to events in those final days of his doomed relationship with the Princess. Perhaps, with hindsight, he should have chosen to exit very quickly.

The Queen Mother thought the tour of Rhodesia, always a favourite place, would divert Princess Margaret's attention from her love worries. Together, they flew to Salisbury on 30 June 1953. It was a 16-day tour with 54 engagements and 1,500 miles of travelling. Princess Margaret got Bulawayo 'flu and a temperature of 103°. By the middle of July she was back in London, hardly restored, and facing the final parting.

Friends of Princess Margaret remember how much in love they were, and how desperately Townsend kept searching for texts in the Bible to show the Archbishop of Canterbury how it might be possible for him to marry the Princess.

When Princess Margaret went to Lambeth Palace to tell the Archbishop about her decision, the kindly Dr Fisher, as soon as he saw her walking into his study, reached for another esoteric text which might give her hopeful news. But those purple-blue eyes were sad and dull. 'You can put your books away, Archbishop, I am not going to marry Peter Townsend. I wanted you to know first.'

Princess Margaret and Townsend worked out between them a public end to their love. This was a communiqué on 31 October 1955:

I would like it to be known that I have decided not to marry Group Captain Townsend. I have been aware that, subject to my renouncing my rights of succession, it might have been possible for me to contract a civil marriage. But, mindful of the Church's teaching that Christian marriage is indissoluble, and conscious of my duty to the Commonwealth, I have resolved to put these considerations before others . . .

It was ironic that Princess Margaret should have made this sacrifice, since she was to become a divorcee herself. But, before that, the bonus for the Queen Mother was more grandchildren and another son-in-law. Even with all the traumas, she found more in common with Tony Armstrong-Jones's artistic diffidence than with Prince Philip's gritty no-nonsense personality.

The Queen Mother adores her grandchildren and has always had a soft spot for Princess Margaret's children, the artistic Viscount Linley and his sister, 'little Sarah', unconventional and appealing and whom the Queen virtually adopted when her sister was going through her divorce.

The Queen Mother has always felt affection for Tony (later Lord Snowdon), believing him the perfect husband for her daughter. 'I'm so pleased you are going to marry Margaret,' she said, when the royal family were all at Sandringham for the New Year of 1960 after he had proposed.

'Sshh,' he whispered. 'I haven't asked the Queen yet.' The Queen approved, though Prince Philip thought Armstrong-Jones a rum cove. But he taught him a few things, including what he should do with his hands in public. 'Keep them behind your back.'

After sleepless nights of anxiety about Princess Margaret's

unhappiness, the Queen Mother was delighted when they married in May 1960, and when Viscount Linley was born the following year and Sarah in 1964.

For such a private person, who hates people to raise their voices or lose control, the Queen Mother has found the behaviour of her wayward, beautiful daughter Margaret painful. There were tantrums like brainstorms when her marriage was breaking up, and shouting matches. Princess Margaret would throw a handbag across the room and rant and rage until four in the morning; there were sulky lunches. Friends had to be patient and tactful. Once at a lunch in the country, Princess Margaret insisted on sitting alone facing a wall, eating nothing. The Queen Mother said, 'Don't take any notice of Margaret.' Occasionally Lord Snowdon left the dining table and went into the room where his wife was looking implacably Hanoverian. When they got back to London, Lord Snowdon telephoned his host and asked if he might visit again – 'alone', he added quickly. Then came the final parting from the talented and deferential Snowdon.

The Queen's marriage had gone through a difficult time when Princess Margaret broke up with Townsend, but that was quickly healed with the arrival of Prince Andrew in 1960 and Edward in 1964.

Princess Margaret, with the temperament of a volatile actress, went through crisis after crisis in her marriage; the rows and coldness were quite alien to her mother, who probably had never had a really cross word with Bertie in 26 years. Her heart ached for her younger daughter's happiness when the marriage was going through its final agonies, which were almost worse than the actual break-up.

A holiday in Rome and staying in some of Italy's thirteenth-century castles in 1973 did not help. Lord Snowdon was found sitting sulkily cross-legged on a flat-topped chimney, refusing to come down and brooding about his career. On this final holiday with the children Sarah or David would remind him, 'Papa, Mummy is talking to you,' but all their father would say was 'I know,' until, unable to stand the atmosphere any longer, he flew home.

The Queen Mother hoped for a reconciliation with Tony, whose artistic nervousness and air of concern always impressed her.

Lord Snowdon has said that although he once married into the royal family he is still treated like any other photographer and gets a quarter of an hour to set up, a quarter of an hour to take the shot and a quarter of an hour to get out. But the family has him to thank for a hilarious picture of the Queen Mother, Princess Margaret and the Queen clowning around outside his cottage in Sussex. They pretended they were at an official opening and put buckets on their heads instead of tiaras.

When Lord Snowdon eventually married Lucy Lindsay-Hogg, former wife of the theatrical director, a serious-looking girl with long hair who had been his assistant on photographic assignments abroad, it was to her mother that Princess Margaret turned; but, if anything, she found the Queen Mother even 'more distressed' than herself. Eventually, Princess Margaret recovered some of her old sparkle and was seen in the company of a new, and unlikely, admirer.

A light whistle and the Queen Mother would dimple in spite of herself. Another whistle, as Princess Margaret stood at the window of the Garden Room at Clarence House. 'Anyone seen the gardener?' and, like one of her silky 'dorgis' – the cross between one of the Queen's corgis and Princess Margaret's dachshund – Roddy Llewellyn, wispy, fair-haired and as light on his feet as 'Fred' Ashton, the choreographer, would bound in.

Indulgent mother though she was, the Queen Mother never went to visit Roddy, son of her fox-hunting friend, Colonel Harry Llewellyn, at his commune where he liked to entertain Princess Margaret to a trendy form of what the group of hippies saw as the 'good life' in a farmhouse in Hullavington, Wiltshire. Roddy was 28 when he met Princess Margaret in 1973 and she was 43.

He was funny, attractive, had no ambition to earn a living, and was delighted to be a sort of pet for the Princess. He accepted her invitation to go to her home in the West Indies, where they sat knee-to-knee in the sunshine under a palm tree in Mustique. And whether the Queen Mother liked it or not, Roddy was a guest at Royal Lodge. 'Oh, frightfully sorry, Ma'am,' the young old Etonian in underpants and nothing else apologized. 'I was just looking for nanny to see if she would be very kind and sew a button on this shirt.' A gracious Queen Mother sailed on.

However, the Queen Mother did go to visit Tony Armstrong-Jones's tiny flat in Rotherhithe where he and the Princess played at being 'ordinary', cooking themselves dinner and entertaining Tony's mother-in-law, who walked along the street enjoying a look in the murky window of a tattooist.

Eventually, Princess Margaret's relationship with Roddy broke up; he found a wife and took up gardening more seriously. Recently the Princess's health has improved. She looks better than she has for years and has a regular and presentable escort in Norman Lonsdale, the former banker who is now a publisher. They go on holidays together with their daughters, Lady Sarah and Emma-Jane Lonsdale, who are art students together, staying at Sir Harold Acton's villa outside Florence. Sometimes the Princess travels under the name 'Harding' to Tuscany. At one time her son wanted to be a photographer, but when he left Bedales co-educational school he studied carpentry. He is a personable young man, has a BMW motorbike and is smart enough not to get his girlfriends noticed as much as his cousin, Prince Andrew. Lady Sarah cycles each day from Kensington Palace to Camberwell College of Art. The Queen Mother approves of this, though Princess Margaret has insisted that her daughter continue to live under her roof, to remind her she is royal. Sarah copes skilfully with her mother. At a John Piper exhibition at the Tate, Princess Margaret kept turning round saying, 'Where is she – where is that girl?' Her daughter had gone off to enjoy the paintings on her own. She brings friends home to Kensington Palace like Fred Ingrams, son of the editor of the satirical magazine *Private Eye*. Fred was at Camberwell with Sarah and is now at the Slade. The Queen fully approves when Sarah brings all her Camberwell student friends to the Palace to lark about in the swimming pool.

At the *Vanguard* reunion in 1967, the band was playing, and ahead was a delightful evening of war-time reminiscences and a get-together of old friends, who had been on the ship when the King, Queen and the princesses had sailed to South Africa. But it proved much more poignant than any of them had expected. As the Queen Mother walked along the line of people she suddenly spotted Townsend about two paces away. She stopped and, with a warm 'Hello, Peter', wagged her finger at him in time to the music. It had always been her signal for the hokey-cokey, a tune the royal family loved to dance to behind the scenes.

When Margaret and Townsend parted, there was a final kindness from the Queen Mother. She arranged that her daughter and Townsend should see each other in her private sitting-room at Clarence House. 'And, with the most wonderful tact and sweetness left the room so I could say goodbye. Through all the crisis, which must have been terrible for her, she never wavered.' Townsend has never forgotten this gesture.

Just as if nothing had happened, the Queen Mother had sailed above all the couple's harrowing times, not indifferent or uncaring but almost like a kindly Reverend Mother with the unworldly compassion and detachment of the cloister.

17

A Lot of Pomegranates

Clarence House is within the gift of the Queen as Sovereign but not privately owned by her as Sandringham and Balmoral. Part of St James's Palace, it is thought of as an ideal residence one day for the Prince and Princess of Wales. There is a marvellous cosiness about Clarence House, with its slightly jaded curtains and cheery staff. The footman in his dark livery beams 'what a good day!' You are shown into the sitting-room on the ground floor where there is a rather old record player, a piano, photographs of the Queen Mother with her daughters and copies of *The Times*. The house perhaps lacks tremendous care – flowers might still be there on a Monday morning, not changed since Friday – a bit lived-in you feel and a corgi's back leg may not have been a million miles away from the corner of an odd sofa. The china and silver are a dream – little silver toast racks with coronets on them – but at the same time there is a table mat from which the print is peeling. This makes the atmosphere all the more attractive.

Upstairs in the Garden Room, with its pale yellow silk walls, French Impressionist paintings and Chinese rose porcelain vases, the lady-in-waiting for the month is Frances Campbell-Preston. She studies another fan letter to the Queen Mother; this one seems genuine but, even if it is nutty, it will get a reply.

Captain Alistair Aird, the Comptroller of the Queen Mother's household, has black hair sleeked back as in the old Brylcreem advertisements and wears pinstripe suits. Everything about him is precise and neat as he sits in his gloomy office slightly below stair level, pursing his lips and wondering when the painters will finish the outside of Clarence House. They make him feel uneasy. He is the man who has to decide whether the old squashy sofas 'christened' by the corgis should be recovered and whether the Land-Rover in Scotland will last another year on the rough tracks at Mey.

The Queen Mother's money has just been increased by the Government by £12,900 to £334,400 a year. It sounds a lot but, he says, staring at the Buddha on the mantelpiece and the broken bicycle in the corner, 'we just scrape by'. She has a staff of 40.

It is 12.45, time for lunch, and Sir Martin Gilliat bounds in from his office to the sitting-room, muttering 'Where are the keys to the grog cupboard?' and pours huge pink gins. One of the ladies-in-waiting nips out to give her dog a run in Green Park.

Sir Martin exudes enthusiasm. Charm is all around when you are dealing with the Queen Mother. He has been her Private Secretary for 26 years and pretends he is still waiting to hear if he is going to be taken on permanently. He pays the Queen Mother, whom he meticulously refers to as Queen Elizabeth, the greatest compliment. He says that in all his years with her he has never once known a moment's boredom.

He is the animator, at once clever, quick, witty and sympathetic, and pretends to be absent-minded as he ambles about on gangly legs. But he is extremely astute and works with shrewd dedication in a small, cluttered office. He leafs through a huge exercise book with parchment pages; this is the engagement book for the year ahead.

When you ask Sir Martin about himself, he does not mention his experiences as a prisoner of war in Germany or his three attempts to escape from Colditz. He rather enjoys a deprecating flit over his background: Eton, the Queen Mother's favourite public school, then Sandhurst and the Green Jackets. 'I was military secretary to Earl Mountbatten when he was Viceroy of India and then to Sir William Slim, Governor-General of Australia until 1955. Then I was unemployed,' he adds. But he had been spotted as an ideal Private Secretary for the Queen Mother. 'Well, I was sure I would be sacked and sent back to Australia in disgrace.'

He is an adviser, counsellor and supportive friend. He is unmarried, has just celebrated his 71st birthday and lives in a house in Hertfordshire called Appletrees. He says the Queen Mother is not a fusspot, but she does like things to be well ordered. Privately, he has a delicious sense of humour but can be as tough as you might expect underneath all that charm.

Each morning, shortly after eleven, Sir Martin goes to see the Queen Mother. He usually has a huge tray under his arm and on it some fifty engagements to be accepted or rejected. They both love cheating officialdom. 'Queen Elizabeth has a real love of people,' he says, 'and hates it when the ordinary people are kept away from her by barriers. She knows that the humble people are kind and loving.' Perhaps the word 'humble' seems a bit patronizing, belonging more to the Victorian era of crofts and peasants than the 1980s. The Queen Mother, Sir Martin says, is always approachable, even when she is going through bad times.

When Princess Margaret had her 'unlucky break' with Lord Snowdon – a neat description of the turbulent separation – the Queen Mother turned to Major John Griffin to help her cope with the public interest in her daughter's crisis. Major Griffin has been her Press Secretary for more than 20 years. He is jolly, with a bright red face, and is married to the granddaughter of the First World War commander, Field-Marshal Earl Haig. But Major Griffin can take a rather lofty view of inquiries made after lunch and will boom disapprovingly at some innocuous question almost as if you were suggesting that the Queen Mother were a dedicated glue sniffer.

Clarence House may like to appear old-fashioned, but the small staff work with the professionalism and alertness of army officers; but then most of the men on the staff have military backgrounds. Sir Ralph Anstruther, the Queen Mother's Treasurer, is a droll old Etonian who served with the Coldstream Guards in Malaya. He is 63, also unmarried, and lives in a large house near the Queen Mother's castle in windy Caithness. His elderly mother, Madge Anstruther, used to complain she was not seeing enough of her son because he was always away on royal engagements and not at home at Pittenweem. 'Oh, I'm very sorry to hear that,' the Queen Mother replied sympathetically. 'You'd better have him back at the weekends.'

Sir Arthur Penn, a bachelor, was Comptroller of the household until 1961. A great friend to the Queen Mother, the tall man with white hair and an uproarious laugh was once tipped as the man the Queen Mother might marry. This prompted unusually forceful words from the Queen Mother, eventually watered down to a milque-toast bland official denial. She had been furious at the very suggestion of remarriage, seeing it as offensive to the memory of her husband – always referred to in the present, as the King; she never says 'the late King'.

She is very fond of her close advisers; indeed, they could be called her 'darling boys' if she had not already given that name to her horses. Sometimes, the Queen Mother likes to join in their 'jolly working lunches'. 'She is gregarious, and for some reason occasionally likes us around,' Sir Martin says, sounding surprised.

A 'recce', another military term, is always done to make sure that the Queen Mother is not accepting an invitation which might be embarrassing; the organizers must be 'above board' and checked out to prevent any devious spin-offs being linked to the royal visit. Sir Martin writes most of the speeches and Mrs Lucy Murphy, his secretary, types them on a big machine with large letters. 'Her Majesty,' he says, 'never wears glasses in public,' and, indeed, hardly at all when she is at home. There are no high-speed word processors. There is no computer to blame if things go wrong at Clarence House, the only speedy electronic gadget is the 'Blower', relaying racing results before the jockey has brushed the mud off his satin in the Unsaddling Enclosure.

The 'geese' is the unkind description given to ladies-in-waiting, not because they waddle but because of their ability to protect and quack warnings. They are usually chosen for their experience and level-headedness and come from solid, aristocratic families. In the Queen Mother's case, they are more like friends. One of the best known is Ruth, Lady Fermoy, fine-boned, good company and intensely musical. She is the Princess of Wales's grandmother.

Widowed in 1955, she holds the same views as the Queen Mother and has never considered remarrying. They were both deeply distressed when her daughter, Frances, ran away from her husband, leaving four small children – one of them Lady Diana – and a bewildered husband, Lord Spencer. Frances is now married to William Shand-Kydd and enjoys running a small shop near Oban.

Ruth, Lady Fermoy, now 76, is, a courtier suggested, 'really the Queen Mother's closest friend'. She shops in Pimlico, in the market for fresh flowers and fish, then pops into the Italian shop in Lupus Street called Big Mamma's, where Santos, the extrovert owner, offers her a glass of wine as she selects some of his home-made dishes.

The ladies-in-waiting do much more than pass hatpins on a windy day, carry the bouquets, write thank-you letters or visit royal staff in hospital. They are the antennae. In Queen Mary's day the royal family were truly insulated from the real world, and still are surrounded by anxious-to-please courtiers, standing with their hands behind their backs and eager to obey a royal command.

The ladies-in-waiting do not as a rule have left-of-centre views, being lady magistrates at heart. They can sustain conversation while delicately extracting an escargot from its shell, and not allow one provocative word to slip out as they exchange pleasantries about the weather or the height of the office block being opened by Her Majesty that afternoon. 'Oh, you are going to build a fly-over on the roof of those medieval cloisters? How interesting.' But the bureaucratic confidence will be filed away and the Queen Mother's sense of heritage aroused before the chauffeur, John Collins, has even had time to open the door of the Daimler.

The Queen Mother's ladies-in-waiting share her interests. Music is one, and Lady Fermoy runs the King's Lynn festival. The Queen Mother has been given an Honorary Doctorate of the Royal College of Music (the Diploma of the Degree of Doctor of Music *honoris causa* in the Royal College). Queen Mary was the first and only previous holder for her support for music. The Queen Mother conferred the Doctorate of the Royal College on Prince Charles in 1982. Sir Michael Tippett shares this distinction. The other holders, Dr Herbert Howells and Sir Adrian Boult, are no longer alive – dying within days of each other.

Lady Elizabeth Basset, a gentle spiritual person, has written a book about one of the Queen Mother's favourite saints, Julian of Norwich. Lady Jean Rankin was once an actress; now a widow, she likes to stay in Scotland rearing wild geese on the Isle of Mull. Olivia Mulholland is an expert on hospital management and has, through her part-American ancestry, a nice informality.

Snug beige boots, a grey and white print top and skirt and very little make-up is Frances Campbell-Preston's working outfit at Clarence House. She sits at a large desk facing Augustus John's portrait of the Queen Mother over the fireplace. This is where the artists paint, dragging their easels all over the priceless armorial English carpet.

You feel you could tell Mrs Campbell-Preston anything and your confidence would be safe. Her father was the 2nd Viscount Cowdray and her first husband, George Murray, was killed in the war in 1945 when she was 35 and had three sons. Only one, the Duke of Atholl, has survived. She remarried five years later. Robert Campbell-Preston was an eligible 41-year-old bachelor with homes in Argyll and London. They have one daughter. Mrs Campbell-Preston looks a young 74.

She tries to define the Queen Mother's effect on people and tells how they were in a neurological hospital, the patients suffering from severe mental problems or brain injuries. 'We had just finished', she remembers, 'and were saying goodbye when a door opened and there was a line of patients sitting in the corridor, nearly all in varying states of distress with heads bandaged. Taking a deep breath, I thought I'll stop and talk to one in every four.' But then the Queen Mother came forward, and she stopped to talk to every single patient, and she seemed to leave behind a warmth and cheerfulness. Her friend, the writer, Rosamond Lehmann, describes this as the Queen Mother's 'faith-healing light'.

Her staff have never been known to complain that something is a bore and this cheerful spirit permeates the household. You often hear the sound of laughter in Clarence House.

Every morning Captain Aird sees the Steward of the Household Staffs, William Tallon (who is also Page of the Backstairs), and the Housekeeper, Miss Geraldine Cockburn, who is given the courtesy title of Mrs. She has a team of eight, four head housemaids and four maids. The tasks for the young maids include grooming the two enormous clothed stone angels wearing haloes and holding staffs by the Queen Mother's four-poster bed. Every month the angels' clothes have to be washed and starched and put back on the plinths on each side of the richly carved bedhead, which is painted with an allegorical Pre-Raphaelite scene. It is almost seventeenth century in its detail. This bedroom, on the first floor, is pale blue. When the Queen Mother shows a guest her private apartments and the gambolling nudes on the ornate bedhead, she will say dryly: 'Rather a lot of pomegranates, don't you think?'

She has very high standards and expects efficiency from her staff, but she is never bad-tempered or sniffy and always makes a request rather than an order. But there are a few rules: she does not like it if the maids are hanging around the first floor with dusters when she is getting up, or if they are laughing or talking too loudly in the corridor. One senior member of staff said, 'It is expected that we do everything and not be seen and always wear black.' She likes her corgis to have their meat and cabbage cut up in identical pieces and their baskets, which look like real beds, to be kept neat with pillows and blankets not too ruffled. Flowers should look natural – gladioli, carnations and roses – and not be arranged stiffly.

The staff is small but devoted and people seldom leave. Reginald Wilcox, a 50-year-old page, has been with the Queen Mother for thirty years. 'We are getting old in her service,' members of her household have been heard to say. They are not highly paid, but they do not care for the idea of a trade union and are not keen on long holidays. They are somewhat in awe of their mistress and speak reverently of 'the presence'. 'Who will show Lady Bagwash into the presence?' a nervous footman might say.

The telephone never stops ringing and there is a list of people who can be put through directly – specials. The Queen Mother will often return telephone calls late at night. One adviser, Oliver Ford, was in a deep sleep when late one night – 11.45 P.M. – he took a call from Caithness. 'Hello, it's Queen Elizabeth here.' He shot up, wondering whether he should get out of bed and bow, for she is a stickler for formality. Once when old Queen Mary was very ill a doctor was leaving the room when he heard her say, 'I'm not dead yet. Don't turn your back on me.'

On hot summer days, a couple of pages will be out sniffing the air as early as 7.30 in the morning to see whether it will be warm enough for a picnic lunch. The final word comes from the Queen Mother herself, so they must wait until 11. As soon as she says, 'What a lovely morning,' they scurry off for the blue and white canopy, and vases of roses are put on the table with all the ornamental silver trophies and bowls brimming with dark pinky-red peaches and green grapes.

William Tallon, the Steward in charge, is a dark-haired, good-looking man in his forties who began his working life as a royal page. As a child living in the north of England he just wrote a letter to Buckingham Palace saying he wanted to work for the King. As he was only 14, they thought him a little young, but three years later, in 1951, he did get a job at the Palace. At the Ghillies' Ball that year, in the middle of the 'Paul Jones', his large brown eyes opened in horror when the music stopped and his partner was the Queen Mother – the Queen as she was then.

'Good evening,' she said, looking dramatic in her tartan sash and, seeing his dismay, suggested: 'I think this is a waltz.' It was soon apparent that there had not been a lot of time for waltzing in William's home town, so the Queen suggested, 'Shall we just walk around? What do you do?' Tallon told her, 'Ma'am, I wait on the servants.' 'Ah well,' she replied, 'we all have to start somewhere.'

Tallon later became confident enough to tell the Queen Mother how much he hates the Augustus John portrait of her in the Garden Room. He is also the person who anticipates her wishes almost before she has spoken, and she will rock back on her heels with laughter when he tells her some mischievous story. He will tip people off about her preference for Veuve Cliquot Riche and her dislike of caviare and cats. For 'cosy' evenings he will order Scotch woodcock on toast and he knows she adores bread and butter pudding. She does like nursery food.

Tallon remembers the early days of her widowhood. The turning-point was when the Queen Mother appeared at the top of the stairs. 'I am going round the world,' she announced. 'Would you like to come with me?'

On another occasion, he asked the Queen Mother a great favour.

'My Aunty Iris is coming from Sunderland today, Ma'am. Do you think it would be possible for her to stand in the hall just so she can get a glimpse of you as you leave?' The answer was, 'Of course.'

Shortly before lunch there was that familiar squeak of kid gloves against the banisters, and there was the Queen Mother. 'So you are Aunt Iris.' Before she knew what had come over her, William's aunt said, 'Oh, Your Majesty, you do look wonderful.' 'And so do you,' the Queen Mother smiled.

One or two people think that Tallon, with his Savile Row blazers, pinstriped shirts and hand-made leather shoes, is a bit too social. 'Saw Tallon in a powder blue suit,' observed Lord Drogheda, former Chairman of the Royal Opera, caustically. Old-fashioned friends of the Queen Mother believe that those below stairs should never aspire to too much daylight. Tallon adores the ballet and likes to have dinner with old friends like the ballet dancer Merle Park and her husband and is fond of soppy movies. Once he recommended *Love Story* to the Queen Mother but she thought it was too much gush.

Princess Alexandra stopped him as he whisked out of Clarence House with his smart Marks and Spencer holdall which looks like Gucci but cost £4.15. 'William, where did you get that divine bag?'

Tallon became Steward eight years ago, and has been created a member of the Royal Victorian Order. 'Long overdue,' the Queen Mother thought. He has charge of the day-to-day running of the Queen Mother's royal homes. He has a warmth and is not like one of the Prince of Wales's butlers, who once worked for Bing Crosby. An equerry was taking an artist around Kensington Palace to decide where the light would be best for a portrait of Prince Charles when the butler snapped, 'Wipe your feet.' The equerry, Major Bromhead, remarked ruefully, 'He said that to my commanding officer the other day.'

The royal servants are sometimes criticized for petulance. It is not every man who wants to wear velvet breeches all day, being continually polite, bowing and never swearing out loud. Somehow, because of the Queen Mother's personality, her staff are never put in a humiliating position. They are loyal and really enjoy working for her so that there is rarely a rebuke. In keeping with her years, she has pre-war standards. If the servants have had a late night – say at Covent Garden serving supper in the Royal Box – the Queen Mother will tell them they can have a lie-in the next morning. That usually means 7.45 A.M. and not a minute later.

Every Christmas, the Queen Mother gives her staff presents – the value is about £20 – and for the men there is often a silk tie. They cannot go wrong if they give her a box of Bendinck's mints.

She expects loyalty and in return is forgiving of any mild indiscretion on the part of her staff. But she does have a temper, which can be frightening because of her self-control. She once became cold-eyed with fury over a job not well done by one of the below-stairs staff. Yet people feel they can tell her their troubles, and they get a sympathetic ear; she conveys the sense that she understands all their worries.

Once, when she was driving to Royal Lodge for the weekend, her policeman fell asleep in the front seat beside the chauffeur. When the car suddenly stopped in a traffic jam, he woke with a start and jumped out of the car, his hand checking his gun. 'But, where are we?' the Queen Mother asked, thinking that London W6 did not look very much like the cultivated lawns of Royal Lodge, Windsor. The detective looked sheepish and she smiled: 'Hammersmith Broadway? I think we'll go a little further today.'

Nowadays, her detective is a tall amiable man, Inspector Gareth Dunn, who tells you with some pride, 'I have looked after the young lady for the last four years.'

The Queen Mother calls her household 'my little family'. Once on a plane, there was panic. 'Ma'am, I've left your speech behind.' Far from being angry, she was amused, and when she looked at the new, hurriedly written 'gracious words', remarked: 'I think we did that rather nicely, didn't we?'

Farah Diba, the former Empress of Iran, has the happiest memories of her stay in Clarence House. When she arrived the Queen Mother democratically introduced her two loyal retainers standing to attention. 'You remember William and Reg,' she said. 'They were with us in Tehran.' The Queen Mother went to Iran in 1975 and stayed with the Shah. A friendship blossomed with the Persian Queen and she has found the Queen Mother a staunch friend. 'Let us kiss as sovereign sisters,' she told the younger woman as she was leaving London at the end of a visit.

Indeed she leaves everyone wishing they could do more for her. 'In her presence,' Lord Astor of Hever says, 'everybody melts and relaxes. She has such a sense of fun.' The Queen Mother reduces everyone to cheerful sycophancy.

18

Work Is the Rent

Everyone is waiting for the Queen Mother on a cold, late-autumn afternoon at Bedford College in London. 'Quiet please,' a bossy woman shouts. 'You will all be quiet three times; once when the Queen Mother arrives, secondly when she is having tea, and, finally, when she goes.' 'Oh, Gawd, that's all the bloody time,' whispers a plump waitress in a black mini-dress, frilly apron and clumpy platform shoes, and she and her friend giggle, practising their curtsies all over again.

The waiting adds to the crescendo of tension. Suddenly, there's a whispered 'She's here, she's here,' and the Queen Mother arrives for the Golden Jubilee tea party of the Careers for Women National Advisory Centre on 10 November 1983. The room is full of serious women in stern print frocks or suits, each one, standing feet apart in sensible shoes, distinguished in her own field: engineering, science or mathematics. You could hardly call them frivolous; there are not many highlights in the hair or clothes in the season's bright reds and blues. At first, you wonder what they have in common with the Queen Mother, but the friendship dates back to 1933, when she thought talented and ambitious women needed a voice. She became their Patron, joining the pioneering Vera Brittain, Rebecca West and Virginia Woolf in encouraging this striving band of women in their search for worthwhile careers.

The Patron is dressed in parma velvet, a difficult colour for most women on a grey British wintry night, but she looks terrific. Her skin is pale, but that does not seem to matter either. There are violets on her hat, shaped like a huge scalloped oyster with a flattering veil over her face; pearls at her neck; diamond flower earrings; a diamond clip, and more violets on her lapel. It might sound too much, but it all looks perfect with the long grey gloves with tiny pearl buttons and matching grey shoes. Who says the Queen Mother has been persuaded to wear lower heels these days? Her legs may be slightly bruised looking, but she will stand for over an hour in high heels; what does that matter when you are only 84?

Her entrance is more eye-catching than that of any other member of the royal family, even the Queen. There is that irresistible smile and a pause which is timed to perfection. She walks in very slowly, smiling engagingly, and looks intently at you and then her eye travels round, mentally photographing faces; her memory is meticulous, putting people half her age to shame.

Her arrival is so good, you could describe it as theatrical, but that would be to diminish a genuinely warm 'I am glad to be here' look. Behind is the rangy Private Secretary, Sir Martin Gilliat, always a reassuring presence. He bounds into the room with such enthusiasm you would think that ever since he left Eton he had been longing for this afternoon. He is animated, springing about complimenting women on their outfits, but hardly ever taking his eye off the Queen Mother. He is not pompous, unlike one or two in the royal household. Both the Queen's Private Secretary, Sir Philip Moore, and Prince Charles's Edward Adeane rarely unbend; they add weight, while Sir Martin gives an effervescence to the most trudging visit. With that inimitable gesture of hers, the Queen Mother tilts her chin and pops her finger in the air, and asks: 'How many years is it?' pretending to count them on the tips of her gloved fingers.

'Ah, how far we've come in these fifty years,' she says, smiling at a woman engineer, who smiles back.

Mrs Mary Lloyd, a Cambridge University Careers Service Officer, has a long talk about women going into new advanced fields. 'I suppose it's progress,' the Queen Mother says dreamily, almost to herself. It would be hard to see her ladies-in-waiting working as risk assessment consultants or chemical engineers.

After a night on the sleeper from Scotland and a morning of lectures, a decorative young teacher, Alison Bailey, thought she was going to faint when the Queen Mother approached her. There was a silence and then Alison blurted out, 'We have your great-niece, Diana, at our school.' The Queen Mother looked nonplussed for a second, perhaps wondering if her grandson's wife might be secretly trying to get an 'O' level or two, until she remembered Diana Bowes Lyon at Glamis.

As the Queen Mother moves on she spots a pretty 22-year-old student photographer, Graziella Chighine, darting about taking pictures. As she deftly crept around behind the army of women with firm bosoms and permed hair, Graziella in her trendy grey balloon trousers received a sympathetic nod. 'It has to be rather artistic now. No more happy snaps these days,' the Queen Mother supposes nostalgically.

'Oh, what a lovely cake! Oh dear, it seems such an awful thing to cut it, it is such a work of art,' as if this is the first huge iced cake she has ever seen. Shaped like a book, on one iced page were all the careers for women, accountancy and architecture . . . and on top appealing golden lions with whiskers and eyebrows and bright brown eyes, guarding the cake.

'Are those lions eatable?' the Queen Mother asks, cutting into the cake vigorously with a sensible brown-handled carving knife. 'I've never seen anything so marvellous in my life,' and nearly everybody believes her.

After the cake is cut, Miss Margaret Gray, executive committee chairman, says how pleased and proud they all are that the Queen Mother should be celebrating their fiftieth anniversary with them and, turning to the glowing figure in purple, explains the reason is: 'because you are yourself, everybody loves to meet you and to greet you.'

'Oh, it is such a lovely story,' the Queen Mother tells Joan Anderson, one of the Association's historians, but although she was sitting next to her, Miss Anderson said later, 'I'm a bit deaf, you see, so I didn't hear a word of the conversation.' Some treat a royal occasion as if they have been secretly picked out by the visitor from the Palace and afterwards become tight-lipped, scurrying away and hugging themselves as if they have been told royal secrets, including the date when Prince Charles will become King.

When it is time to leave, Sir Martin gives a few eye signals, but the Queen Mother makes everyone feel that she hates to leave; hand on the table for another confidence, 'Ah, yes, women mathematicians in industry.' Not for a long time, it seems, had she been in the company of so many people with whom she had so much in common.

'Would you sign, Ma'am?' 'Oh, what a lovely book,' the Queen Mother's eyes light on the green bound leather visitors' book trimmed with gold. 'Of course I'll sign it.' There is a hush which makes her laugh. 'Listen to the silence.' Sir Martin comes forward in rather a rush with a large signed photograph and she beams helplessly. They give the impression that the afternoon has been such a delight that, at the last minute, the Queen Mother has impulsively suggested this memento. Of course, there are piles of these large photographs at Clarence House.

A modest smile from the Queen Mother, who is now on her feet, wondering if the photograph is a problem. 'But you've nowhere to put it. It's been so lovely to see you all again.' She slowly leaves, with a small wave and a soft goodbye.

It is clear from the list of royal engagements in the 1983 Court Circular that the Queen Mother is by no means cutting down.

	1	2	3	4	5
The Queen	82	60	12	141	9
Duke of Edinburgh	84	89	23	9	21
The Queen Mother	70	25	1	21	2
Prince of Wales	89	43	17	17	3
Princess of Wales	86	21	–	3	3
Prince Andrew	11	3	–	–	1
Prince Edward	6	1	–	–	1
Princess Anne	162	64	8	10	6
Princess Margaret	77	24	6	9	1
Princess Alice	26	7	1	6	–
Duke of Gloucester	89	37	14	11	5
Duchess of Gloucester	62	17	6	1	3
Duke of Kent	77	22	18	4	9
Duchess of Kent	25	6	–	2	2
Princess Alexandra	78	24	4	13	2

1. Official visits, opening ceremonies and other appearances.
2. Receptions, lunches, dinners, banquets.
3. Meetings, including Privy Council.
4. Audiences given.
5. Number of countries visited.

Compared with her diary for 1980, she is actually doing more, and still shouldering a full share of the work. In 1980 she performed 63 different ceremonies, held 14 audiences, officiated at four investitures and made ten overseas visits. By 1983 the visits abroad had dropped to two, but the total number of public appearances had risen to 117. She is patron of 300 organizations and charities, Colonel-in-Chief of 18 British regiments, Commandant-in-Chief of all the three women's services and Warden of the Cinque Ports, sharing this honour dating from the time of William the Conqueror with previous Wardens like Winston Churchill and Robert Menzies.

The Queen Mother's year is divided up carefully: February–April in London; May in Scotland for fishing; June and July in London; August–October in Scotland again; November and half December in London; Christmas and January at Windsor and Sandringham. Although she loves being in the country, her life is so circumscribed that she moves with the seasons.

The Court Circular for March 1983 gives an idea of the Queen Mother's workload. Ladies-in-waiting change over fairly often, finding the pace a little hectic.

1st On behalf of the Queen held an investiture at Buckingham Palace.
 (Ruth, Lady Fermoy, succeeded Lady Jean Rankin.)
4th Attended Dinner of the 51st Highland Division at the Army and Navy Club.
 Attended Cheltenham Races during the week.
8th Visited Queen Alexandra Home and Hospital, Gifford House, Worthing – by air.
9th Attended Reception at St James's Palace given by the Indian Army Association.
10th Received the Colonel of the Royal Yeomanry on relinquishing his appointment.
14th Opened the Duke of Beaufort Flats, Beaufort Court, Royal British Legion Flats in Gloucester – by air.
15th (Lady Angela Oswald succeeded Ruth, Lady Fermoy.)
17th Attended Irish Guards St Patrick's Day Parade at Oxford Barracks, Munster, Germany – by air.
21st With Princess Margaret was present at the Royal Film Performance in aid of the Cinema and Television Benevolent Fund at Ocean Theatre, Leicester Square.
22nd Attended State Banquet in Buckingham Palace in honour of the President of the Republic of Zambia.
24th Attended the Annual General Meeting of Queen Mary's London Needlework Guild at St James's Palace.
 Attended banquet given by the President of the Republic of Zambia at Claridges.
25th Attended Luncheon given by the members of the Grand Committee of the Benevolent Society of St Patrick at Buck's Club.
29th (Mrs Patrick Campbell-Preston succeeded Lady Angela Oswald.)
30th Attended performance by the Windsor and Eton Operatic Society at the Farrer Theatre, Eton College.

In all, she carried out 24 engagements in February and March, two of the worst winter months when most octogenarians are happy to stay tucked up with their hot chocolate.

 The Queen Mother still thinks nothing of carrying out three or four engagements in a day. They are all carefully worked out with the precision of a pilot preparing a flight path. In this case, both 'pilot' and 'navigator' are Sir Martin. Before an engagement, he likes to 'walk the course', checking possible hiccups and every little thing that could go wrong. A letter on creamy parchment writing paper, with Clarence House embossed in red, clears up any anxieties. When she is going on a visit a circular advises that Her Majesty 'would appreciate the offer of a drink'. Pink gin is acceptable, or one part gin and two parts Dubonnet, or a glass of champagne. The Queen Mother eats sparingly these days and worries about lavish food being wasted when she is a guest. She is not a 'picky' eater, but happy with very little. She would prefer a hen's egg to those of the sturgeon any day.

The Queen Mother was once dining at Gray's Inn, a favourite yearly treat with the country's legal brains. She was given a partridge and rather than upset the chef, she deftly moved the tiny bird on to Sir Dingle Foot's plate. As host, Michael Foot's brother obligingly ate a brace.

Take 17 November 1983, a week after the Golden Jubilee tea party at Bedford College. Looking at the Court Circular, it might seem just coincidence that the Queen Mother spent the day in Hertfordshire, but it had all been carefully orchestrated. Some invitations come about in a slightly unorthodox way.

Brother Benet, a remarkable member of the Roman Catholic Order of St John of God dedicated to the care of the handicapped, first met the Queen Mother at Aske in Yorkshire. Lady Zetland, 'Penny' to Brother Benet, goes to a lot of trouble to get the right blend of guests at her lunch parties. 'I like to invite people who do a lot of good in Richmond, like the local doctor and surgeon, the police, artists, and every kind of person. It makes their day to meet the Queen Mother.'

The atmosphere is unstuffy and relaxed and there is a high buzz of conversation before the first drink is poured. At lunch, Brother Benet, who has a humorous, low-key manner, was chatting to the Queen Mother and out of the corner of her eye Lady Zetland could see 'they were getting on like a house on fire'. He told her about his work for the mentally handicapped and about a new project which aimed to give these people dignity, independence and self-respect. He asked the Queen Mother simply, 'Would you come and open it for us, Ma'am?' 'Yes, I would love to,' the Queen Mother replied. The date was set, 17 November 1983 at St Raphael's Centre, Barvin Park, Potters Bar.

The Queen Mother's yearly diary takes no heed of creed; Catholic, Buddhist, Quaker or Christian Scientist, if she thinks it worthwhile, she will be glad to help. In this case, Brother Benet invited the perfect royal visitor who could handle with tact and sensitivity a delicate and moving engagement.

It was a raw day in Hertfordshire, drizzling and so depressing that even the tall, red-brick Queen Anne houses looked gloomy. At Barvin Park, a band played 'Pop Goes the Weasel', and Brother Benet, looking very much a puckish Friar Tuck, waved. A gentle soul with a crumpled and smiling face which could be 40 or 60 was hurrying along with one large white chrysanthemum in a newspaper in his hand. He took his place alongside the other mentally handicapped men to wait for the Queen Mother to open their new houses.

The Lord Lieutenant of the County of Hertfordshire, Major-General Sir George Burns, was stomping around in full dress uniform, the cold making the bristles on his florid chin stand up; he shook hands with parents, relations, nuns, helpers and residents at a great rate. Four jolly nuns joined the monks. 'We've actually touched the flowers the Queen Mother is being given.'

Police cars bumped over the soggy field, converted into a car park for the day, the grass merged into mud, and the Queen Mother's car purred into the courtyard. In a minute she was out, her light lilac outfit cheery and bright amongst the black and brown clerical robes.

Once the Queen Mother had climbed the dais, William Byrne, Barvin's oldest resident, presented her with a bouquet of pink and white flowers. 'Thank you very much, that's beautiful,' speaking very loudly because she knew he was deaf. He skipped off in his best, rather tight-fitting brown tweed suit, giving a thumbs-up sign to his friends in the crowd.

Her voice sounded as if she had a cold, her words caring. Elderly couples held on to the arms of their sons, men who had perhaps been in care all their lives; and helpers held on to others without family and they all smiled up at the Queen Mother and wanted to run up on the dais to shake her hand.

No royal platitudes drifted down to this crowd of people; instead, there was praise for 'these men of God' who created Barvin Park. They had, the Queen Mother said, 'made the vision a reality'.

It was not a day for long speeches. Quickly, the Queen Mother was off to meet the monks, telling them, 'I'm longing to see the houses.' Brother Benet asked if she would like to inspect the foundation stone laid by her Private Secretary, Sir Martin Gilliat. 'Oh, yes, I must do that.' Sir Martin is a Trustee at Barvin Park, and it is very much one of his pet causes. He was leaping around, grasping people by the hand. 'How marvellous to see you', 'oh what a lovely colour' to a woman in blancmange pink.

'Beautiful stone, beautifully laid,' the Queen Mother said with a deadly serious look in Sir Martin's direction. Then she went shopping in the craft and basket-weave workshop. 'I'd like one of those, a huge one. I'll pay. Yes, one of those picnic baskets. I'll give it as a present.' Solemnly, the residents in white coats went on working, not in the least self-conscious. 'Grand to see the work going on,' the Queen Mother said as she spotted a tiny basket-work chair for a baby, 'such lovely taste'. By now Sir Martin was getting anxious that the timetable had gone awry but, serenely, the Queen Mother went on as if she had the whole day to spend at Barvin Park.

Normally on royal engagements, there is a gracious winding up, a few dignitaries saying a formal 'thank you'. But at Barvin Park Brother Benet made no attempt to stop the residents when they surrounded the Queen Mother. He introduced them; some gave her logs with posies stuck in them, others tiny baskets or handfuls of flowers. Some of them were so excited they jumped up and down all around her; they bobbed, saluted and grinned. One tall resident was taking no chances. He stood beside the Queen Mother as his friends gave her presents and he made extravagant bows, turning his tall frame in a U and then straightening up rapidly, leaping into the air. 'Oh, how lovely, thank you so much,' the Queen Mother said, behaving as if this always happened on visits. She was being given more presents than she could possibly handle in memory of her morning at Barvin.

To Mrs Campbell-Preston, her arms filled with flowers, home-made baskets and quite large logs, the Queen Mother said as she began to leave: 'Put them all in the car, I shall treasure them always.' Then, to 'How is your grandson?' the sort of question that a member of the public would normally never ask, 'Oh, he's very well,' she replied chattily, as if talking with an old friend. Then, breaking all the rules again, another resident gave a skip in the air and triumphantly told her, 'I saw you on the television.' A smile. 'Yes, that was last Sunday, Remembrance Day, at the Cenotaph,' she replied, handling it beautifully, not in the least disconcerted by the leaping and extravagant bowing of the man who was as tall as John Cleese.

'Oh, dear, I must go,' she said as Sir Martin and Brother Benet escorted her to the car, but she now had an army of protectors, some of them trying to get into the Daimler with her. 'What a happy visit,' she waved and gave that wistful 'goodbye'. You could hardly see her face for flowers.

The watching residents were not feeling cold in the dank, chilly air because they were laughing now, still skipping and waving even though the royal car had long since passed from view.

A morning both tender and exhausting, but for the Queen Mother it was only the first of the four engagements of her day. She lunched with the Lord Lieutenant and in the afternoon she visited the Injured Jockeys Association and then on to see a new 'guinea pig' housing estate for old people in Welwyn.

That evening the royal car carrying the Queen Mother also queued in traffic jams at Mill Hill and she was late back at Clarence House. Her milliner had been kept waiting. Joy Quested Nowell couldn't help herself, 'But Ma'am, you must be exhausted.' A gentle smile, 'Well, perhaps a little tired, but it was such a good day . . . That hat is such fun,' she continued enthusiastically, as though it was the start of her day.

In the summer of 1983, the night before the Queen Mother was due to fly to Belfast for the celebrations of the seventy-fifth anniversary of the Territorial Army in the Province, the IRA threatened to mark the visit with renewed violence. The Queen Mother had vowed to take the salute at the parade at Ballymena, Co. Antrim, whatever the anxieties of the government.

The security forces were anxious and so were her advisers. But to try and stop the Queen Mother from going to Belfast was as futile as trying to persuade her to stay at home on Gold Cup day at Cheltenham. 'All right,' she said, and there were great sighs of relief that she had been persuaded to cancel her visit, until she added quickly, 'I'll compromise. I'll go a few hours earlier than planned.'

The Queen Mother flew to Aldegrove and then took a helicopter to Hillsborough Castle, once the home of Governor-Generals of the Province. She spent the night as a relaxed guest of James Prior, Secretary of State for Northern Ireland, and his lively wife, Jane, who likes to play more than a supporting role to her husband in Belfast.

It was an evening when the old residence was rather as the Queen Mother liked to remember it in the days when her sister Rose's husband, Lord Granville, was the Governor-General. 'I have such happy memories of Hillsborough,' she trilled, 'such lovely gardens.' Her bedroom overlooked Lady Granville's special rose gardens, miles of herbaceous borders, the woodland and the avenues of rhododendrons where the two sisters used to walk.

The Queen Mother was in sparkling spirits, her natural warmth making everyone feel better and less tense. Jane Prior had the old fireplace opened up and a good log fire; it was June but a typical, damp Irish evening.

The guests included the Dowager Duchess of Abercorn, another old lady who airily dismissed security-conscious 'fusspots'. 'People think it much more frightening here than it really is.' Any worries about the trip the next morning to St Patrick's Barracks, Ballymena, were left to the rubicund host, James Prior. 'My worry is that I put so many people to so much trouble,' the Queen Mother confided as they all went into the drawing-room before dinner. Her face lit up, the butler was still the same 'Harpur'; he served a light fish starter, a chicken salad and a pineapple meringue. It was a late night; the Queen Mother was having a good time. Next morning, she was off to Ballymena, but before she left she had a word with the head gardener's widow, Mrs Kirkpatrick, who was thrilled 'to talk about the old days' and thanked the Queen Mother for keeping her word. 'But I very much wanted to come,' she replied.

As far as the Queen Mother was concerned, everything was normal. She took the salute of her brave Territorials as if nothing sinister had happened, although a 30-pound bomb attached to a drum of petrol had been intercepted on its way to Ballymena.

She was full of praise for the Irish troops at a review of detachments representing 4,000 Ulster Territorials. She brought to them the gaiety of presenting shamrock to the Irish Guards on St Patrick's Day: 'One for you, and one for me.' It is that lightness of touch and spry humour which is so endearing.

Once, at a country Women's Institute, she was met by a number of rosy-cheeked ladies who had all had a fortifying drop before their President arrived. Once the curtseying and bobbing were out of the way, they offered the Queen Mother tea. She folded her hands together and, to their surprise, refused. 'No,' she said with a slight smile, 'if you don't mind I'd like to have a drop of whatever that is hiding behind the curtain.' She had spotted the bottle of sweet sherry which had been hurriedly stuck on the windowsill behind an inadequate metre of chintz.

The Queen Mother likes these rural get-togethers at Sandringham and copes well with the simple rustic jape. 'Who are you?' she was asked bluntly at the Sandringham Flower Show. 'Can your mother skin a rabbit?' Before she could reply, there was a cheeky whistle. 'But I could have answered that,' the Queen Mother remonstrated, and was answered: 'Clear off!' The Court Circular never recorded this meeting between the Queen Mother and a mynah bird in the Fur and Feather tent at the Sandringham Show.

Those who think the Queen Mother 'marshmallow sweet' would be well advised to recognize that she is not without the ability to be tart. 'I'd like to meet that young man and tell him that I don't like litter,' she said when, as the first woman Chancellor of London University, she watched the back of a dissident student who tore up his certificate at a graduation ceremony in the Albert Hall in front of 5,000 people. Once some young boys from Windsor town were throwing stones at passing cars in the Great Park. The Queen Mother's car came to a stately halt. She got out, a fearless granny, faced them and quietly suggested, in all reasonableness, that while she did not mind having stones thrown at her – they should consider 'what on earth the American tourists would think'. Collapse of vandals.

After the King's death, somebody had the bright idea that the Queen Mother would be a superb Chancellor of London University. 'It was,' said Sir Martin Gilliat, 'the spark which set off this tumultuously varied way of life.' The appointment was such a popular one that there was not an inch of room in the Festival Hall for her investiture. Eight straight-backed Royal Horse Guard trumpeters in gold laced tunics and blue velvet caps sounded the fanfare as the King's widow made a superb re-entry into public life.

A solemn young page in scarlet Court dress carried the new Chancellor's train, watched by some of the best brains of the world. Sitting amongst the academics in their robes of pink, purple, bright green, deep yellow or red velvet was the Rector of Moscow University, I. G. Petrovsky.

The Queen Mother took easily to the Chancellor's robe of black silk damask frogged with gold and her mortar board with its swinging gold tassel. Afterwards there was a lunch at the Guildhall; it was hardly a student menu – sole Walewska, roast pheasant and lemon posset. Sir Norman Birkett proposed the health of the Chancellor, her 'grace' and her warmth. She would disarm the students, even the most dedicated anti-royals, over the next 25 years, and they flatly refused to let her retire as their Chancellor until she was 80 years old.

The Queen Mother has a way with young people, so there were never any formal 'how do you do's' or waiting for her to start a conversation. It was always, 'Hello, glad to see you', or 'You are taking philosophy and theology? Very big subjects.' A student asked the Queen Mother, 'red or white?' 'I think I'll have a little glass of red wine,' she said, making a supreme effort because she drinks wine only with food, but putting the young people at ease.

The Queen Mother would come to the University about ten times a year. If she had been somewhere very smart she would arrive in a tiara. It would be passed to the Vice-Chancellor who in turn would hand it to a Fellow whose job it was to put it in the safe. He took this task very seriously indeed. But once, holding the tiara reverently in both hands, he opened the door of the safe and was trying to slide it in when the heavy door banged shut and the tiara snapped in two.

He tried to stick it together with Araldite. Holding both pieces he tapped on the Vice-Chancellor's door calling out in imitation of an ITMA character, 'Boss, boss, something terrible has happened.' From behind the door, the Queen Mother appeared with a glass in her hand and said with a huge smile, 'Yes, Sir Douglas, indeed it has.'

Sir Douglas Logan was Principal of London University at the time. He was to become a friend and was invited to the Castle of Mey to recuperate when the Queen Mother spotted him looking pale and ill after hepatitis. 'Your husband doesn't look at all well,' she said to Lady Logan, and sent them both packing to the Pentland Firth and the good cooking of her housekeeper at Mey.

On the way to the Foundation Day ceremony the following year, the Queen Mother joked over her shoulder to her lady-in-waiting. 'I wonder what the University has in store for me this year?' But the tiara incident had shown her ability to ride any disturbance with good humour. She was, says Sir Douglas Logan, 'an unqualified success'. The students put it differently; they thanked her for dancing with them and for 'all the joy you've given us'.

With the same serenity the Queen Mother goes to a Christmas party for the Westminster Children's Society at Knightsbridge Barracks and sails into a riotous afternoon of pantomime dames, magicians, games, mince pies and Christmas cake. 'What a nice atmosphere,' and then, 'Are you safe on those skates?' she asked the two pantomime ugly sisters, Ponsella and Vendetta, as they sailed past her with large cupid-bow painted lips. The children give a great cheer when they see the Queen Mother. 'Do you think it's all right?' she asks, patting the brim of her lavender feathery hat. 'I didn't think the children would want to see me in something dark today, so I fished this out. How sweet, I must just have another look,' she added, bending over the children and twiddling a pink ribbon between her fingers. The Ugly Sisters kept whirling by on their skates; there was Daisy the pantomime cow and a milkmaid with a deep voice, custard-yellow curls and a huge bosom. 'Aren't you very hot?' the Queen Mother asked this well-endowed wench, who turned out to be Ted Tiller, foreman electrician at Selfridges, doing his bit for children that afternoon.

'Isn't it lovely seeing all of them doing their own stuff?' she said, trying to undo a packet of toys without much success. It could have been an afternoon with her own great-grandchildren, except these children were far from privileged. 'Mind you don't forget to wash behind its ears,' she reminds a child dunking a doll.

'We asked her Private Secretary if there was anything the Queen Mother liked in the way of small snacks,' Molly Kaye, better known as M. M. Kaye, author of *The Far Pavilions*, explained. Her husband, Brigadier Geoffrey Hamilton, had been in the Corps of Guides like the hero of her novel. The Queen Mother was in Belfast where the Brigadier was Chief-of-Staff for Northern Ireland.

The Hamiltons' daughter, Nicola, was six at the time and, hearing that the Queen Mother had a passion for mustard and cress sandwiches, she grew some on a flannel. After the reception, the Queen Mother stopped specially to say to Molly Kaye, 'Will you tell Nicola that they were the best cress sandwiches I have ever had. I just couldn't resist them.'

Molly Kaye and her husband, like many of their army friends, still think of the Queen Mother as the last Empress of India. Brigadier Hamilton, an entertaining man, said that at an Indian Army Association party at St James's, he got so carried away he called the Queen Mother 'sir' by mistake.

All the old India hands wanted to give a party for the Queen Mother, to show their appreciation for their 'Empress' on her 83rd birthday, so she lent them five rooms in St James's Palace for the evening. She drifted through the State Apartments on the first floor, past the grand staircase designed by Wren and the William Morris tapestries, chatting to almost every guest, on her feet for over two hours. One veteran in a wheelchair and nearly 100 said he wanted to get up and walk when he saw his 'last Empress of India'.

'I was getting worried,' said Brigadier Hamilton, who was President of the Indian Army Association. 'I kept trying to hurry her along in case she got too tired, but she seemed to be having a whale of a time. There were 700 guests.'

When he introduced her to one memsahib, Hamilton said, 'Ma'am, this is Mrs Prendergast. Her husband was the first Colonel of the Guides when I first joined in 1932.' The Queen Mother put her head on one side and asked, 'Was he a wild young man?' knowing full well the flattery of her question. 'Yes, Ma'am, he was a very wild young man, but always my favourite subaltern.'

The Queen Mother is supposed to be slightly deaf, with a tiny hearing aid tucked into her collar. But the tiresome gadget can never be seen and her hearing seems very acute. When four officers were having a drink with her at the end of this party she suddenly said: 'I think I hear the corgis,' and sure enough there was the patter of those wide paws and the excited yaps as the door opened and they came rushing in. They pulled at her skirt and she said, 'they smell mother,' and, as dreadful barking and scampering began, she disentangled herself with an indulgent, 'they think it is time I went home,' and gracefully retreated.

The Queen Mother generates a feeling of happiness, but that does not minimize the strain for her. Before an engagement she will demand a tremendous amount of information, do her homework, learn all the names and pick out the salient bits from the 'bumph'. But what exhausts her is not the chat, 'How long have you been standing here?' 'Oh, really, for six years, how interesting,' but the speed with which sometimes the same people who were at the beginning of the line race along to the middle, and then to the end, so as not to miss a moment of the royal visit. Inevitably, they must hear her repeat the same things, and this makes the Queen Mother uncomfortable.

There are banks of white and purple heather, yellow chrysanthemums and frondy ferns softening the granite of Aberdeen University. In the café across the road they are selling hot stovies and treacle bread. The guests invited to the Queen Mother's graduation ceremony on 12 October 1983 dash along the cobbled streets trying to prevent the rain soaking their finery. The women seem to favour high white frilly collars and Jacobean-style hats. A handful of demonstrators shout about government spending cuts, but the protests are lost in the loud cheering for the Queen Mother.

There is a special bond between the city of Aberdeen and the Queen Mother, where she is loved not only for being herself, but also for standing in for Edward VIII in 1938 when he was preoccupied by Mrs Simpson. Now, in King's College Chapel, the University of Aberdeen has a chance to say 'Thank you'. The Queen Mother, in scarlet and blue gown and mortar board, is to be given the Honorary Degree of Doctor of Law. She comes in with the academic procession as the organist plays Bach's 'Alla Breve in D'. She looks very pleased, sitting on the edge of her chair very straight, her feet tucked one behind the other, her gloved hands resting on her lap. She looks like a student in spite of her years and comes down the steps, looking ahead, with all the grace of a girl who is light on her feet.

Whatever the engagement, opening a school or hospital; talking to old age pensioners; having fun with friends from the army; or making conversation as she is escorted by someone like Tilyenji Kaunda, the young son of President Kaunda of Zambia, at a Buckingham Palace banquet, she brings to her work the same freshness and charm.

The Queen and her mother rarely disagree; when they do it is usually about the same thing. 'Please, Mummy, you must cut down on the number of engagements you do.' 'But, darling', the Queen Mother will reply, 'work is the rent you pay for life.'

19

A Good Egg

Every year on her birthday the Queen Mother likes to go to the theatre with the same friends: 'Hugh and Fortune'; 'Ruth and Martin' and 'Fred'. They usually choose something light. One year it was the *Pirates of Penzance*, another, *Guys and Dolls*. *The Gospel According to St Matthew*, with Alec McCowen alone on the stage all evening, was not a huge success, and neither was a 'dreadful' Agatha Christie. Afterwards, they all go back to Ruth's little Eaton Square flat for a delicious summer supper, usually lobster, an excellent hock and raspberries or strawberries.

On her 80th birthday, when she got 35,000 cards and telegrams, the celebration was less private. The same six – the Duke and Duchess of Grafton; her lady-in-waiting, Lady Fermoy; the diminutive Sir Frederick Ashton and Sir Martin Gilliat towering above the Queen Mother – did not slip unobtrusively into the stalls of a West End theatre.

For ages before her mother's birthday Princess Margaret had been nagging 'Fred' Ashton, 'You must write a ballet for Mummy's eightieth.' And he did, giving the Queen Mother one of the 'nicest treats she had ever had'. After the performance of *Rhapsody* at Covent Garden on the birthday evening, she was showered with cascading silver petals, made out of milk bottle tops and the audience cheered and waved heart-shaped balloons saying 'We love you, Queen Mum.'

Old friend Sir John Betjeman's gift was a poem for her 80th birthday:

> Waves of good will
> Go racing to meet you . . .

Friends go to a lot of trouble to find unusual presents for her. She likes funny, quirky things, but she is given a lot of books on safe subjects. One friend told her about the fig tree in his garden and promised her a basket of figs. But like the Biblical fruit, the barren tree produced nothing much, except some big cabbagy leaves, useful as decoration for cream cheese. He hurried off to Fortnum and

After a highly successful tour of Canada the Queen Mother is welcomed home by the Queen. Princess Anne waits for a hug from her grandmother

The Queen has always been a devoted daughter. She spends as much time as she can with her mother. Here they are walking their corgis towards the stables in the Royal Stud at Sandringham

A Highland Fling. The Queen
Mother's stamina wears out
dancing partners. In the
background (left) Ruth Lady
Fermoy does a more sedate
version of a Scottish reel

A loving grandmother. The
Queen Mother says goodbye
to Prince Edward at Scrabster
as the royal family returns to
the royal yacht after tea at the
Castle of Mey

A rare sight of the Queen Mother wearing spectacles. Normally her speeches are written in magnified type

The widows of two Kings – the Queen Mother and the Duchess of Windsor. The Duchess was received by the royal family when she came to England for the Duke's funeral in May 1972

The Queen Mother on her 80th birthday. Children swarm into the courtyard at Clarence House with cards and flowers. Lady Sarah Armstrong-Jones and Viscount Linley look concerned as a little girl heads the wrong way, while Prince Edward and Prince Charles watch the determined boy in a hooded windcheater

Prince Charles in the paddock at Cheltenham 1981 before he rode Good Prospect in the Horse and Hound Grand Military Gold Cup. The Queen Mother reassures Lady Diana Spencer about the race; Princess Margaret looks doubtful about her nephew's chances of success

The Queen Mother does not like beards any more than the Queen does, but on his return from the Falklands war Prince Andrew was excused his whiskers

You rarely see the Queen Mother without a hat or tiara. Here she sparkles with
playwright Ben Travers on his 93rd birthday after a performance of
the play *Rookery Nook*

The Queen Mother is gregarious but she often likes to walk alone on the wild stretches of the Caithness coast or in Norfolk

The royal family always enjoy the moment on the Queen Mother's birthday when the gates of Clarence House open and members of the public greet her with cards and flowers. Lady Sarah Armstrong-Jones is with her grandmother

The royal wedding – 29 July 1981. The Queen Mother looking very happy on the balcony at Buckingham Palace with her favourite grandson Prince Charles after his wedding to Lady Diana Spencer at St Paul's Cathedral

The Prince and Princess of Wales chose the Queen Mother's 82nd birthday for the christening of their first baby, William Arthur Philip Louis. The Queen Mother holds her great-grandson in her arms in the drawing-room of Buckingham Palace on 4 August 1982

Mason and sent the Queen Mother a dozen figs. In her own pretty handwriting, on grey blue writing paper with a discreet dark blue ER on the left, back came a thank-you letter 'for those sweet foreign figs'. She appreciated the trouble he had taken but not for a minute was she fooled by the fleshy purple Mediterranean fruit masquerading as English figs.

Sir Frederick Ashton lives in a tiny house in Chelsea, just off Sloane Square, filled with ballet programmes and gewgaws. He once gave the Queen Mother a model of himself as Mrs Tiggy-winkle in the Beatrix Potter film, which she loved. On his mantelpiece there is a framed letter from the Queen Mother to her old friend, congratulating him on receiving his OM: 'Warmest hoorays . . . so thrilled your genius has been acknowledged.'

The Queen is said to be surprised sometimes by her mother's friends when she pops into Royal Lodge for an after-church aperitif on Sundays before going back to Windsor Castle. 'Oh, Mummy, why such short weekends?' Princess Margaret complains. 'Why don't you invite people on Friday evenings?' But this is only when the guests are favourite 'artistic' friends. At other times the Princess is likely to grumble, 'Last week was geriatrics' weekend.'

Normally guests arrive at Royal Lodge at about six on a Saturday evening, driving along the M4 at the quiet time. The Queen Mother flutters into the drawing-room at about eight. 'Oh, did you have a good walk? You must borrow Bertie's old walking stick tomorrow if your leg is still hurting.'

An invitation to stay arrives about three weeks ahead. Guests usually leave on Sunday evening, but sometimes the Queen Mother will say, 'You seem to be settling down here rather well. Why don't you stay on until Monday?'

Thank-you letters are difficult because one must never say 'you' to the royal family and it is best to try not to be too nauseating. And, of course, the sublime test is – will you be asked again?

The guest who is invited again never forgets, no matter how relaxed and friendly the atmosphere, to say 'Ma'am', to curtsey or to bow; the Queen Mother does not like one to forget rank. She hates being touched. One guest explained: 'I am terribly careful to ask if I may kiss her hand, and once she said to me, "There is something on your lapel, do you mind if I pick it off?"' Princess Margaret is quite different, she loves theatrical hugs and kisses on both cheeks.

The Queen Mother hates change, so her friends at Royal Lodge tend to be 'the old cosies' she has known for years: the Hugh

Cassons; former Ambassador to the United States, Lord Harlech, a good talker and son of one of her great friends, the Dowager Lady Harlech who, when she was alive, was an Extra Lady of the Bedchamber to the Queen Mother; Lord Home, who is related by marriage and whose gauntness hides a flinty wit; Norman St John-Stevas; Lord Astor of Hever; and, in the past when he was well enough, Sir John Betjeman, the Poet Laureate.

Many of the Queen Mother's friends of the same age are ill or have been gathered in or 'gone upstairs', as she likes to put it, explaining neatly the inability of some of her contemporaries to stay the course. Lord Hailsham was once cajoled into throwing his sticks away one evening at Royal Lodge when the Queen Mother inveigled him into a Welsh jig, but the miracle effects petered out when he got back to London.

Since the King's day her friends have become a more catholic collection. He would not have had a great deal in common with the delightful Sir Frederick Ashton – 'I don't crack open before 12'. George VI had a positive view of ballet: 'I like it,' he confided once, 'because you can see what is going wrong.' He would have felt more at home with the steady, landowning Graftons, who are thought a little earnest by their intellectual friends.

With their talk about salmon fishing and capital gains, the King might have enjoyed more the company of such aristocratic regulars at the Queen Mother's table as the Buccleuchs and the Abercorns, or Lord Charteris, the Private Secretary to Princess Elizabeth who carried on in the post when she became Queen. A witty, thoroughly exuberant aristocrat, he said, 'I used to get the Queen Mother to load for me; I always shot extremely well then.' Or Lady Diana Cooper, who dramatically and elegantly arrived late for lunch, her pooch 'Doggie' under her arm, and got away with the unintentional discourtesy. 'But how can I kiss you under that huge hat?' the Queen Mother said, ignoring her lateness.

When the Queen Mother went to have lunch with Lady Diana Cooper at the house in Little Venice she shares with her son, John Julius Norwich, her hostess got in a state about the parking and telephoned for an ambulance. The driver was persuaded to wait until the royal car came along. The Queen Mother went in, beaming innocently at the ambulance men while her chauffeur slid perfectly into the vacated spot.

At a house party in the country shortly after the Abdication, Sir Eric Miéville, the King's Assistant Private Secretary, remembered a group of friends were still in the garden on a warm summer night, cigar smoke drifting up to the monkey puzzle tree, the women's diamonds shining out of the darkness like fireflies, when suddenly the conversation stopped. The Queen – whom everybody was still thinking of as the Duchess of York – walked out on to a balcony and, with great aplomb and a huge smile, said goodnight: 'I don't know about you, but I am going to bed now with the King of England and nobody else.' It was not an exit line heavy with modern double meaning, but rather a boost for her husband, the new King.

Her smile becomes even more attractive with the showing of two little sharply pointed teeth, which makes it fun waiting for the next smile. Having a sturdy Scottish view about not tampering with nature, the Queen Mother has never bothered to get her teeth capped.

It is another tribute to her that she keeps her staff, because guests rarely leave before the small hours. The Queen Mother will stand up in the middle of Clarence House supper parties and say, 'Now, gentlemen, I want you to take your glasses and move round one.' Vera Lynn finds 'it makes the evening much more fun, someone new to talk to. We are doing this with our friends in Sussex now.'

The men are expected to be good company. To talk and dance well. The Queen Mother likes a true independence of judgement and does not want people to be placatory. But, on the other hand, the wise guest knows when to be quiet. It would never do to ask what the Queen Mother thinks about the Ayatollah. At the dining-table, surrounded by good food and wine, the silver candlesticks and the beautiful china, as Lord Harlech has said, 'a politician could be lulled into forgetfulness and the conversation might take off with startling momentum on a forbidden and provocative subject.'

She likes her guests to talk out and be lively and, as a skilful hostess, encourages this, but if the talk is becoming too controversial she flutters in with her irresistible smile. Her timing is superb; a little joke and a good pay-off line, or the perfect quotation as she quizzically puts her head on one side, popping her finger in the air, and astutely steers the conversation away. She has a quick wit; she speaks excellent French – and does all the Gallic gestures, with much rolling of eyes, to perfection. Her humour is never unkind, but she is a phenomenal mimic, especially of Americans. She is not, says Lord Drogheda, 'a Mike Yarwood, but she can make marvellously suitable noises.'

'I give you a toast: Idi Amin, President Carter and Wedgwood

Benn,' and she raises a glass debunking some of the people she dislikes. The former President of the United States had kissed the Queen Mother too warmly: 'He is the only man since my dear husband died to kiss me on the lips.'

But chat about her remarrying, either Sir Arthur Penn or her treasurer Sir Ralph Anstruther, has brought only laughter. No reflection on the suitability of these nice old bachelors, but the very thought of the Queen Mother's marrying for a second time is as unlikely as the Princess of Wales remaining a spinster had she not wed Prince Charles. Despite her flirtatious manner the Queen Mother lives in her own innocent world and enjoys the devoted companionship of a number of men friends.

'Come and sit here,' she says as everyone troops into the drawing-room after dinner at Royal Lodge. Although it may be after 11 o'clock, the evening is just beginning. 'Don't you think these are pretty?' she will say, patting the back of one of the matching sofas. 'My daughters had them recovered for me.'

Lord Drogheda, 'Gareth', lives nearby in Windsor and the dry humour of the elegant, tall former Chairman of the Royal Opera makes him a favourite. His wife Joan is a concert pianist and often she will play the Steinway after dinner at Royal Lodge. Sometimes there will be dancing, or a good old-fashioned singsong as the Queen Mother and her friends serenade the portraits of kings with music hall songs. Noël Coward thought the royal family got excellent free entertainment. Celia Johnson, a friend anyway, used to read to her; today it might be the actress Maggie Smith who zips down to Windsor.

The Queen Mother has crazes. A few years ago it was dancing to any Charles Aznavour record, twirling about to 'Dance in the Old-Fashioned Way'. At other times everybody has to play parlour games, 'Clumps', charades or Racing Demon, which the Queen Mother plays speedily like a lot of her contemporaries, smashing down the cards with their thin bony hands and calling 'flip-flop out'. Lord Home, sitting över tea in the House of Lords, remembers an occasion when Lord 'Bobetty' Salisbury, sitting beside the Queen Mother, picked up his hand and, with his halting lisp, cried: 'Oh, Ma'am, I am surrounded by howwible, howwible Queens . . .'

Some guests are allowed breakfast in bed and, of course, you don't have to go to church. But, as one friend said, 'By then we are all so sycophantic that of course we go.' This pleases their hostess, who has deep Christian beliefs. She appears, five minutes before, in coat, hat, gloves and handbag. 'Anyone coming?' and those who have not been in church for years except for weddings and funerals, amble along like good-natured labradors.

There is always a good traditional Sunday roast, but in the afternoon not a lot of snoozing. The yapping of the corgis means it is time for 'walkies' – and not only for the dogs. 'Anyone like to wander round the mausoleum at Frogmore?' or, 'Shall we go church crawling?' the Queen Mother will ask.

Occasionally, walkers at Sandringham or in Windsor Great Park will see a band of mackintoshed people fanning out, quoting poetry at one another. Sir Hugh Casson says the Queen Mother is very knowledgeable about country churches after exploring so many with Sir John Betjeman and Sir Kenneth Clark. She loves cathedrals and Durham is a favourite.

Lady Mollie Salisbury, who often went exploring with the Queen Mother, found this curiosity about houses and people part of the Queen Mother's charm. 'Oh, dear, I am so glad I don't have good taste,' Lady Salisbury would giggle with the Queen Mother when they had visited some self-consciously grand house with designer co-ordination and a lack of that upper-class muddle of dog leads, headscarves and green wellingtons everywhere.

Sunday evenings are the time when she loves having poetry read to her; Lord David Cecil used to read Jane Austen and John Betjeman would just talk verse.

In London there is a constant flow of people coming to lunch at Clarence House. The Queen Mother mixes the martinis herself – 'very decent' martinis – you are certainly not rushed into lunch on just a nip of sherry.

She likes intellectuals; Oxford and Cambridge academics find her unshockable with a young and lively mind, refreshingly unspoilt by an academic education, with a sense of humour – and enormous curiosity. Sir Woodrow Wyatt, a friend for years since he met the Queen Mother when he was Chairman of the Horserace Totalisator Board, says: 'She has the heart of a young girl of 18; most men are in love with her.'

When she is surrounded by the Carringtons, the Homes, the Salisburys and the Cecils, there is a feeling that this lunch party is for them a lot more fun than down The Mall. But the Queen Mother has always been at pains to make sure that she is not competing with the Palace. She never wants to outshine the Queen; their style of entertaining is totally different. But both sets of royal friends must have discretion, an ability to keep their mouths shut whatever royal secret is in their confidence. One of the Queen Mother's friends, not usually reckless, said, 'They know I would have to be put against a wall in a corner and shot first.'

In town entertaining usually means lunch rather than dinner, and the guests are different; old friends from Scotland; Jim Callaghan, the former Labour Prime Minister whom she finds delightful; the Earl of Stockton; and the late Sir Robert Menzies, with whom she shared views on the Commonwealth; and Sir John Plumb, the historian and Master of Christ's College, who likes to look dramatic under a large black fedora and whom she met when a degree was conferred on her at Cambridge.

At Sandringham, everyone is so relaxed about royalty that she can call on people with a 'Cooey, anyone at home?' to chat about pigeons, architecture, racing or the French Impressionists, and to drink instant coffee, a sherry or a cup of tea.

The food at her lunch parties is always immensely rich, mousse and Moselle, the best butter, cream and herbs. There is often a lovely egg dish to start, with mushrooms, asparagus or spinach in a rich sauce; then lamb or chicken beautifully cooked; and strawberries Chantilly. The wine is often her favourite Mouton Cadet. During the whole of lunch in the softly-lit beige dining-room of Clarence House, the Queen Mother sits bolt upright, her back never touching her chair, even if Lord Carrington has said something audacious. If it is summer they may eat in the garden, which really, by Royal Lodge standards, is rather dismal, but the Queen Mother gets a *frisson* as the traffic roars by in The Mall by presiding over a sort of *Alice in Wonderland* table as the butlers in velvet breeches pirouette round the guests. Her voice carries as she presses people to eat more.

She is rigid on politics, so guests do well to stay behind the strong blue line. Her heroes are men like de Gaulle and the late Shah of Persia and her right-wing politics belong to the Churchillian view of Empire; she sees India through the eyes of a young subaltern and disapproved of independence. She has strong prejudices, hates Britain's enemies and would never go to Japan or Germany. When Mrs Thatcher became Prime Minister someone asked, 'What do you think she'll do for the women of this country, Ma'am?' She replied: 'I think she'll have far more effect on the men.'

One of the things the Queen Mother has not quite come to terms with is the change in living standards today, particularly of the upper classes. She knows more about the other classes from television and from talking to the people she meets. After a lunch or a weekend with aristocratic friends, they see a line-up of a dozen servants and get a warm feeling that standards have not diminished. But, of course, Lady Zetland's establishment in Yorkshire is just one example of the frantic dragooning that goes on of retired retainers, getting them to come in for the day. Princess Margaret pretends she really does not understand either and will torment weekend guests at Royal Lodge, asking them, 'Why don't you ever invite us to stay?' Oliver Ford always apologizes to the Queen Mother because his house in Wiltshire is so cold. 'Ma'am, I even have to put the red wine out on the doorstep to bring it to room temperature.'

It is a perfect day in East Sussex, July 1983, at the home of Lady 'Mickey' Neville, widow of Lord Rupert Neville who was Prince Philip's Private Secretary and a good friend. The Nevilles and the royal family have been friends since Princess Elizabeth was first married. Now the Queen Mother is coming to lunch at a favourite, pretty Victorian country house where Mickey Neville has organized drinks on the lawn and a cool lunch of stuffed eggs, cold salmon with mayonnaise and a rich cold chocolate mousse, a favourite. The old servants dart about, but not in any panic, for here they are used to royalty.

The guests include Sir Alexander Norfolk; Nigel Nicolson, tall and soldierly, looking rather colonial in a linen suit, silk yellow tie and striped shirt that give a misleading impression of this gentle man; Lord Rothschild of Exbury, treasurer at Glyndebourne, chuckles as a helicopter blows all the pollen off the daisy heads on the lawn. There is no flying grass, the order goes out that lawns must not be cut later than a fortnight before a royal arrival.

'It can only be one person,' he said as, exactly on time, at 12.15, the Queen Mother, in flimsy blue and smiling, arrived. It was just an ordinary 'fun' lunch, but there were six RAF men in smart uniforms, shoulders back, to escort her as she walked the first 50 yards from the helicopter, its rotors winding down from a roar to a grumble. A car picks her up for the second 50 yards and, immediately, a glass of Pimms is offered on the terrace. 'How nice, oh, lovely,' she says and, beaming, the Queen Mother enjoys the purple clematis and masses of roses and has a minute's sadness for Mickey's having to sell this gabled house with its turrets, orangery and swimming pool. A Canadian company bought it for £750,000.

The unnerving thing about being a guest is that one can be given so many instructions about how to behave. Waiting to sit down, the eye is happily distracted by drawings of the Neville children and paintings of horses. 'First, the Queen Mother will talk to the person on her right, then halfway, she will turn to you: "Please do tell me when . . ." or, "But it is not quite like that . . ."' But long before half time, she had turned her bluey violet eyes on Nigel Nicolson and was telling him about a day she spent at Sissinghurst with his mother, Vita Sackville-West, and how she remembers his mother's little study – in the corner room of the castellated house, where she wrote about her turbulent love for her husband, Harold Nicolson, and for Violet Trefusis – and also planned a unique garden. They talked about English country houses and their contribution to art and history.

The Falklands conflict was still fresh in everyone's mind. The Queen Mother, who is always ready to be nostalgic about the Second World War, said it was exactly like 1940 all over again. Nicolson had to ask the Queen Mother, 'Did you really learn to use a rifle?' 'Oh, yes,' she said firmly, and added as she picked up her small square handbag from the floor under the table, 'Wilhelmina arrived in Britain during the war with nothing more than this.' The talk was now firmly rooted in the past. 'Oh, no, of course not, we would never have gone abroad, there were houses being kept for us in parts of the countryside I think. We could have gone to one in the Midlands,' she said, sitting up rather straight and sounding as if really it were better to be decimated by a German doodlebug than to face the road to Birmingham and beyond.

Someone idly told the Queen Mother, 'You know, Dr Coggan lives near here.' 'Ah,' she said, 'such a dear man.'

Conversation is never allowed to stay too long on a light gossipy level and the talk now was about royal influence in the selection of bishops and the conflict for churchmen between ambition and humility. 'But,' soothed the Queen Mother, 'we are so lucky with Archbishop Runcie, he is such a good egg.'

'I'd love some Perrier,' she said, and Nigel Nicolson, abandoning protocol, just reached for the sideboard and poured some so that the conversation could go on. It was the right touch. Sir Martin had a word before he left. 'HM,' he said, 'much enjoyed your little talk.'

The Queen Mother writes lyrical thank-you letters by hand. If she has been to a dinner party – or lunch more often these days – it can go on for pages, about how much she loved the food, 'Oh, those delicious bon-bons.' Letters to friends are signed 'Ever yours'; and they are always registered so, as one of the household explained, 'they don't get nicked'.

20

Darling Boys

On a wet Tuesday in winter when only the bookies and the punters are looking forward to an afternoon's racing, Tim Neligan will get a telephone call out of the blue from Clarence House: 'Queen Elizabeth would like to come to Sandown today; do you think you could arrange a snack for her? Thanks awfully.'

Neligan, who is Managing Director of United Racecourses Ltd, orders favourite royal snacks, a warm seafood vol au vent, some cold tongue and soft drinks or Dubonnet for the Directors' Box.

About an hour before the first race the Queen Mother arrives. Out shoots the electric step and there she is, wrapped in a fur-lined raincoat, clutching an umbrella and wearing funny little boots. She sets her face to the wind and goes straight to the paddock. No fuss, completely informal; so much so that some racegoers, fortified by a few whisky macs in the bar, dashing out with thoughts only of the 'dead cert' for the 2.30, practically knock her down. When they see who it is there is much raising of trilby hats; jockeys going past with urgent steps get a smile too.

It is a small tribute to the National Hunt racegoers that the Queen Mother can move around so freely and happily. But then the 'sticks' attract the military or the squirarchical, who like a bit of danger over the 'jumps', do not mind a sharp wind and a bit of mud, unlike the fashionable 'flat' racegoers who prefer fine days, a Bucks Fizz and a mention in *The Tatler*.

The Queen Mother's horses have won over 330 races. Her racing record from 1966 to 1983 totalled 343 races won and £221,961 in winning stakes. Her golden time for winners was in the early seventies with horses like Game Spirit and Inch Arran. Now she cannot afford to have more than about ten steeplechasers in training with Fulke Walwyn, her chunky, slightly deaf trainer, at Saxon House Stables in Lambourn, Berkshire. The Queen Mother may be wealthy in terms of possessions but does not have a lot of free money, so the Queen likes to help defray some of her racing expenses. After all his successful years as a trainer, Walwyn, now 73, has come round to the royal view that homoeopathic medicines, verbena or camomile sent from the royal herbalist in London, are better for ailing horses than many sophisticated vaccines. Whenever the Queen Mother is staying at Windsor it is an easy drive to the yellow and green stables tucked down Maltshovel Lane in Lambourn. She will have a word with the head lad, Darkie Deacon, about her horses, the most promising being Liffey, Sunny-boy and Sun Rising.

Sir Martin Gilliat is nominally the Queen Mother's racing manager, but, as he says, the term is misleading: 'Ma'am is an expert.' He keeps meticulous blue-bound racing records with lively commentaries such as the end-of-term report on a disappointing Irish horse, Sparkling Knight: 'After giving his rider and connections some appalling shocks he was put back to hurdling but again repeatedly ruined his chances by careless jumping.'

Dick Francis, the successful author of racing thrillers, was once a champion jockey. The Queen Mother reads all his books and tells him, 'You are getting rather bloodthirsty, Dick.' 'I don't think she minds the sexy bits,' he says. He sends her the first copy of every book of his as it comes off the press.

The Queen is one of the most outstanding owner-breeders in British racing and she longs to win a Derby, but the Queen Mother has never felt the same about the Grand National since the Devon Loch disaster. Dick Francis's memory of the 1956 Grand National is still very painful. He twists uneasily in the armchair in his Knightsbridge flat as he recalls how Devon Loch, the horse he was riding for the Queen Mother, collapsed just 50 yards from the winning post. He walked off the course in tears. In the Royal Box, the Queen Mother was very distressed. 'Well, that's racing I suppose,' the Queen Mother told him and went to see the horse. Patting Devon Loch on the neck, she said, 'You dear, poor old boy.'

At Cheltenham a little before that Grand National the former royal trainer, Peter Cazalet, had told Francis, 'The main target is the Grand National in two weeks' time; have a nice run and enjoy yourself. Don't kill him, don't give him a hard race.' But the Queen Mother, her finger touching her chin, suggested hopefully that it would be nice to win this one on the way. 'She is,' says Francis, 'the easiest person in the world, charming.'

About a week after the Devon Loch disaster, Dick Francis was invited to Windsor. It had been tactfully arranged that his wife, warm chubby Mary Francis, should be given a tour of the Castle while Dick went alone to the royal apartments. He remembers being with the Queen Mother in her sitting-room overlooking the Copper Horse and talking about the race for an hour. He had agonized over several re-runs, and he told her, 'Ma'am, I am sure it was the noise of all the people cheering. There must have been a quarter of a million that day wanting you to win. I could hear the noise.' He was given a cheque and a silver cigarette box. 'The box is silver, even underneath,' he said. 'It is inscribed "Devon Loch's National", with a private and special message which I have never told anyone.' He can offer you a cigarette at his home in Oxfordshire without raising the lid to show the message. He chuckles like a double agent, a character from one of his own books.

Perhaps racing lost some of its magic for Francis the day Devon Loch collapsed. A year later, at the age of 37, he wrote his autobiography *Sport of Queens*.

Peter Cazalet's silver cigarette box from the Queen Mother is inscribed, 'A memento of that terrible and yet glorious day'. She wrote too: 'We will not be done in by this and we will just keep on trying.' He was a stylish trainer and the Queen Mother liked to call him 'The Führer'. A friend, he had guided her racing from the start in 1949, when she had a share in a horse called Monaveen with Princess Elizabeth.

Like a true country woman, the Queen Mother loves racing but she does not ride, apart from a gentle sidesaddle canter on her pony, Bobs, as a child. She never gallops through Windsor Great Park with her daughters. Some think that Prince Charles's attempts as an amateur National Hunt jockey were purely for his grandmother's sake, though half the time her heart was pounding with anxiety, but she did encourage him and he trained in the privacy of the Lambourn stables.

Nor is the Queen Mother a golfer, tennis player or swimmer, but she does know her cricket. She told the BBC's Brian Johnston at a Buckingham Palace investiture in 1983 that she had been rather shocked by England's recent performance on the tour of Australia and New Zealand. 'I listened to every blow-by-blow account of the Test series,' she said. 'It is no good worrying about their performances, we have got to find some new people for the team.'

She enjoys the gallops, the schooling and the early mornings when the grass is still twitching; the smell of the leather saddles, the stable lads talking under their breath. But her trainer Fulke Walwyn's wife, Cath, does not expect the Queen Mother for breakfast these days; it is more often at 10.15 for the second lot. The first is out on the Berkshire Downs a little early, at seven. She is not foolishly sentimental about horses, but the racing judge Nick Locock remembers her face one winter day at Windsor when a grey she owned broke its leg. He was standing near the stewards and when the Queen Mother saw it galloping on, gamely dragging its leg, she could not hide her tears as she turned away. 'You could hear the whole crowd give a great sigh,' he said. 'The Queen Mother is adored by National Hunt people.'

She does not bet; she leaves that to her racing manager. Both of them pounce on the *Sporting Life* when it is delivered to Clarence House and also the *Racing Calendar*. Reuters may tap out urgent news about war in the Middle East or the swing of the dollar, but in Clarence House the tapes relay vital racing results and the downstairs office sometimes sounds just like a betting shop.

It was really Lord Mildmay, the aristocratic champion amateur jockey, who sparked off Queen Elizabeth's interest in racing. He was staying at Windsor after the war and talked to his hostess about the delights of young racehorses. The King enjoyed racing for 'the fun of the thing', but was really more interested in breeding horses, just as the Queen is today. This was the real start of the Queen Mother's involvement. Her registered colours, blue with buff stripes, black cap and gold tassel have been worn by a host of devoted jockeys, David Mould, Dick Francis, Bill Rees and Gene Kelly. Once the Queen Mother complained that 'the blues are not quite royal enough. I intend to have a new set, and this time the blue will be truly blue.'

Peter Cazalet also had a nice sense of humour. When the Queen Mother was in hospital in 1964, recovering from an emergency operation, huge bouquets of lilac, daffodils and tulips arrived from Double Star and The Rip, with rosebuds from Rochfort, the horses she calls her 'darling boys'. 'Please thank them from their loving and grateful owner for this imaginative, amusing and beautiful present,' she replied.

When her horse Laffy won the Ulster National at Downpatrick in 1962, and the crowd pressed round the Queen Mother, one woman got so excited she cried out, 'Would you bless us, Your Majesty?'

When Cazalet died, she gave everybody at the stables a present: Benny Dunn, the blacksmith; Joe Hills, the gallops man, and all the lads. When Fulke Walwyn had been her racing trainer for more than ten years he was created a Commander of the Victorian Order. 'I am so pleased to be able to give you this, I hope you will show it around the yard to the lads,' the Queen Mother said. A shy man with a ruddy complexion, he keeps the honour in an envelope down by his desk, really too modest to hang it on the wall.

In the years after the King's death, racing gave her a new interest. She spent many weekends at Fairlawne, the Cazalets' William and Mary Kentish ragstone house with its soft creeper and wide lawns. Noël Coward would be invited to leaven the horsiness.

Zara Cazalet ran the historic and beautiful house with a well-trained staff. As soon as the royal car arrived, Bradbrook the butler would glide out to open the door and the Queen Mother would kiss Zara Cazalet on the cheek before they had a cup of tea by the wood fire. Mrs Cazalet's French maid would unpack the Queen Mother's clothes, a couple of evening dresses and a sensible jacket and skirt for the early morning gallops. It was always so effortlessly smooth; guests were reminded of the Duke of Marlborough, who always thought that toothpaste came already on a toothbrush, until the day he had no valet and learnt the awful truth.

There was one difficult horse. Peter Cazalet confessed he could do nothing with Gay Record, a neurotic and unruly animal. The Queen Mother listened, but did not agree. She had read about an Irishman named Jack O'Donoghue in Reigate who had done wonders for an excitable horse called Trapeze II. Anyone less like a smart royal trainer than Jack O'Donoghue as he leans against a hedge admiring a sleeping cat and a huge sunflower is hard to imagine.

'Don't ask me my age,' he says in a slow Cork accent, shuffling into his tiny cottage filled with lyrical letters from the Queen Mother. His voice is so soft he can calm any highly-strung creature on four or two legs.

The first time the Queen Mother came to see him he posted a man outside the pub on the corner so that she wouldn't get lost: 'I hoped he would not go in but lead the royal car down the little track.' Jack is not an excitable man, but he certainly felt a slight nervousness when he saw the Queen Mother with her daughter as well. 'Oh, the Queen has come with me; she had a slack afternoon,' the Queen Mother explained briskly.

It was the start of a delightful and sometimes comic owner–trainer relationship. Jack liked to train cats to jump through hoops, or teach squirrels and pigs to be friends, and he worked his magic on Gay Record. He gave the Queen Mother her 100th winner and somewhere in his cottage is a telegram, saying, 'So delighted that it was Gay Record who gave me my century of wins.'

Both the Queen Mother and the Queen found afternoons at the Priory, the O'Donoghue home, delightful and quite often turned up without much warning, drinking mugs of tea in the yard surrounded by kittens and a bemused Jack.

The Queen became intrigued by O'Donoghue's skill with difficult horses. She called one day, found Jack leaning against a fence and asked if he could do anything with one of her horses, National Emblem. 'The Queen sat on a tree stump just by the entrance to my top yard and we talked. People passed by and didn't realize who I was talking with, she was so natural.' The backward and unco-operative three-year-old National Emblem was handed over to O'Donoghue for training and eventually given to him. As if granted a new lease of life, the horse then started winning. 'What are you doing letting that old rogue beat Mother's horse Sunbridge?' the Queen telephoned O'Donoghue in mock rage. 'You feel you are in heaven,' he says of the Queen Mother. 'She takes ten years off ye.' He is more interested in donkeys these days, making sure they get their pint of stout and two eggs each evening. His walls are covered with photographs of the Queen Mother, and a 19-year-old black cat sleeps on the others in an old album by a dusty bridle on the windowsill.

Racing people are not always good talkers, but Lord Oaksey is an exception. He has always regretted that, as a jockey, he has never ridden a Grand National winner for the Queen Mother. She is now starting her 35th racing season and, he thinks, 'has never looked more beautiful. Strong men would lie down and die for her.'

A visit to the Injured Jockeys Headquarters was more a pleasure than a duty, but the exhaustion of any day can be lightened by a good racing result. It is not unusual to see Sir Martin Gilliat go up to an official for an earnest conversation which has nothing to do with protocol or ceremonial: it will simply be to make sure there is a radio handy. He was once seen reversing past an astonished Lord Mayor in all his robes, edging his way along to whisper discreetly in the Queen Mother's ear the result of the 2,000 Guineas.

The latest excitement is the arrival of a new horse for the Queen Mother from New Zealand. She will rename him and visit when he has recovered from his long flight with a hundred other horses arriving in a Hercules at Stanstead in Essex. Fulke Walwyn, says the Queen Mother, has done wonders for National Hunt racing, but he says, 'She worries that people lose money on her horses – and they don't always win.'

Very often Walwyn's anxiety on the day of a race is not about how the horse will run but whether the owner will wear warm enough clothes. 'Only lately has the Queen Mother taken to wearing boots,' Walwyn says, shaking his head in disbelief. 'I'll say, "It's better out today, Ma'am," and then I see the Queen Mother at Sandown or Newbury with a bit of chiffon round her throat!'

21

My Jaunts

If the Queen Mother is not going out in the evening, she quite often goes to her four-poster bed, reads poetry and eats some of the first layer of her favourite home-made chocolates. She is, one long-standing friend said, 'an old cosy'. Another treat is watching *Yes Minister* on television and eating scrambled eggs on toasted granary bread.

She likes going to friends for 'drinkey poohs' and calling to see their gardens, doing a tour in Wiltshire and Dorset, Sussex and Norfolk. She relishes being the only woman amongst twenty-four men in the Gardeners' Club where she is not even allowed to bring along a lady-in-waiting. She is fascinated by other people's taste. Her own is Edwardian, and she has a flair for putting her private *objets d'art* in just the right places, making 'a home out of a palace'.

Oliver Ford, the interior designer, has just re-done her bedroom and sitting-room in Clarence House in blue silk with matching curtains. The sitting-room reflects her style perfectly: totally English eighteenth century with a scattering of gilded chairs, a delicate desk, a pretty fireplace and masses of photographs, some in traditional silver frames, others in gold ovals.

She adores clocks and has a French gilded wall clock in a floral frame in her bedroom, a wedding present from Princess Mary, the Princess Royal. In all her homes there is a mixture of clocks – dignified Sheraton, Chippendale or gold carriage. Although she is not too fussy about time herself, the royal clock-tender must make sure they are kept to perfect Greenwich time.

'I think you will find the Hilton is very much nicer if you look at it upside down,' the Queen Mother urges. 'Modern architecture,' she suggests drily, 'is much better seen this way.' The famous hotel in Park Lane seems rather dated now, but to the Queen Mother it was the first in a series of offensive modern buildings.

She has an eye for good art, and there are always paintings stacked against the wall in Clarence House 'in a state of considera-tion'. This sure sign of confidence, Sir Hugh Casson, President of the Royal Academy of Art, says, 'is marvellous.' It's very nouveau to

hang all your pictures at once. She buys pictures regularly and
recently went to a diamond sale at Christies.

The walls of the double drawing-room with its Aubusson carpet
on the first floor of Clarence House are covered in exciting paintings,
a mixture of modern and primitive. There are some by Nolan and
Drysdale of the burnt-out ochre Australian outback; a Lowry, not of
matchstick men but of a Lancashire farm and, more predictably
perhaps, French Impressionists. 'The Rock' by Monet and Sisley's
'The Seine near St Cloud' are exactly what one would expect to find
in the Queen Mother's house.

A whole room is given to Edward Seago. She has always loved the
work of this gentle Norfolk artist and his semi-surrealist paintings of
the marshlands, waterways and windmills in the flat land around
Sandringham. But one of her own great favourites is a very old
painting of Noah's Ark: 'Don't you just love all those animals?' She
will lead you to a Matthew Smith, a Paul Nash and Duncan Grant.
Her interest is not so much patronage but based on a true feeling for
art and an intuitive sense of what is good and what bogus.

In her London dining-room, portraits of a prune-faced George III
and his children stare down from the warm apricot walls. At night
the wall lights show up the *Point d'en Hongroise,* the Hungarian cream
and coral of the tapestry on the chairs, ready to receive the ample
seats of Lord Hailsham and Woodrow Wyatt.

Both Clarence House and Royal Lodge share the same relaxed
atmosphere. The dogs scrabble on the parquet: 'Oh, do you mind
them?' the Queen Mother will ask as evidence of a corgi is spotted
on the frilly bit of a chair. If her guest hesitates, a footman scurries in
and takes them.

The Queen Mother is 'doggy' though not in the besotted way that
the Queen cherishes her pooches. But when one of her dogs, Billy,
was dying at Windsor she left Sandringham to be with him. She was
very distressed when Blackie, the oldest and fiercest of her surviving
pair of corgis – though left with only one tooth – had to be put down
after Christmas 1983. He is now in the corgi graveyard at Windsor.

One of the crosses the royal family has to bear is sitting for
commissioned portraits for worthy causes, regiments or hospitals.
They have no say in the choice of artist and are usually rather glad
when one like Michael Noakes turns up, with a lively sense of
humour.

Annigoni was commissioned to paint the Queen Mother for the
University of London. On the day of the unveiling, the former

Principal of London University, Sir Douglas Logan, jumped in a taxi and went to Chelsea to Annigoni's studio in World's End in a state of great excitement. He was warned on the way that he might not like the painting. The Italian painter had said the Queen was a bore and that he generally found the monarchy uninspiring.

'When I got there', Logan recalls, 'I was appalled. All I could say to Annigoni was: "You have seen our Chancellor in a mood we've never seen."' Logan was so angry he wanted it sent back and suggested this to Clarence House. But the reply came: 'The Queen Mother thinks it is not too bad and, after all, it is something to be painted by Annigoni.'

Even of a downright bad portrait of a member of the royal family, she will say: 'Well, if a man has spent all those hours . . .' and makes excuses for the artist.

Most portrait painters say the Queen Mother's warmth is her beauty. There is strong feeling about the half-finished Augustus John painting in the Garden Room at Clarence House. Despite thirty sittings and lots of brandy, he still could not finish it, but he has captured a haunting translucent quality and the Queen Mother loves it. John thought her 'angelic' but did get annoyed with her once. 'Mr John was quite cross because I had been on holiday and had changed colour.' Unhappy about the painting he hid it in an attic in his studio at Fordingbridge in Hampshire. But after his death it was presented to the Queen Mother and it gives her pleasure, partly for the memory of her sittings, for John was never sycophantic. He once insisted that having arrived at the Palace sober, he must be drunk when he left. Once the Queen Mother even organized a string quartet to play for him.

Today, artists always find the atmosphere at Clarence House fun. They are given ham sandwiches and nips of gin if they seem to flag. The Queen Mother understands that the artist may be totally absorbed. Michael Noakes once heard her say: 'Oh dear, I have just dropped one of my treasured hairpins.' Of course, any normal man would say, 'Good heavens, let me get it for you,' but Noakes just muttered, 'Oh yes?' When he looked up his sitter was bending down searching the carpet. He apologized profusely, but she laughed, 'I understand, you had your mind on other things.'

The artist David Shepherd is just another in the long line of men besotted by the Queen Mother, and perceptive enough to realize that he has completely succumbed to her charm. He thinks her 'totally, wonderfully unique, incredibly royal and such a good conversationalist'. He was commissioned to do a portrait of her for the King's Regiment. When he went to Clarence House for the first sitting, he was rather appalled to find the Colonel-in-Chief in a bright pink dress ('she loves pink'), hat and gloves. 'Ma'am,' he ventured, 'I'm not awfully sure about the handbag, I'm not sure I like it,' wondering how the gouty generals of the King's Regiment would view a handbag on the lap of their Colonel-in-Chief. 'Nor do I,' she said and it was flung on to a chair. Biting his lip, Shepherd then had to say, 'Ahem, the gloves, don't terribly like those either.' 'Nor do I,' and off they came.

When Shepherd showed her the finished painting she looked pleased. 'Thank you, Mr Shepherd, I do like that.' But one military royalist at Catterick complained: 'I don't like the way you've painted her teeth.' Shepherd rightly replied that if the Queen Mother never felt she should do anything about them, why should he?

Shepherd, who is involved in world wildlife, found when he was painting the Queen Mother that they talked of Africa all the time. She was nostalgic about her first trip to Uganda. 'Winnie,' she said referring to Sir Winston Churchill, 'thought my husband and I should go and we loved it.' Prince Charles said, on meeting him recently at Buckingham Palace, 'You're David Shepherd, the man who says it's lots more fun painting elephants than my grand-mother,' a blimpish joke the Queen Mother thought rather witty.

Shepherd gave the Queen Mother a small painting of a lion and, though she must receive at least 20 gifts a day, she beamed, clutched it to her and almost ran out of the room with it, as though nobody had ever given her a present before. Nearly ten years later, Shepherd went back to show her the painting he had done of *Ark Royal*, one of her favourite ships. 'Why don't they sink it honourably in the sea instead of sending her for scrap?' He saw his gift over the fireplace in her sitting-room and, spotting his surprise, she said, 'I didn't just put it there because you were coming, it has always been there.'

It was the launching of *Ark Royal* which prompted one of the BBC commentator Wynford Vaughan Thomas's best gaffes. He had been distracted and was watching *Ark Royal* hitting the water when, not realizing that the Queen Mother was still on the television screen, he said: 'There she is, the huge, vast bulk of her.'

'Do you think you could take just a little off my waist, Mr Stone?' the Queen Mother asked another young artist, her head slightly on one side, 'just a little.' She sailed off to lunch, leaving Richard Stone in a dilemma. She has often been teased about her love of food and wine, 'gin and Dubonnet before lunch, a dry martini in the evening and Krug for tea', but she loves to entertain well. Stone altered the waist and then his conscience – and put it back.

There is a crystal triptych on the Queen Mother's desk. On one side it says 'Duties', and the artist, Lawrence Whistler, has ingeniously etched a microphone, a scroll and a foundation stone. In the centre there is a place for the typed notes of the day's engagements. On the far side, under 'Pleasures', the crystal symbols include a pack of cards, a bottle of champagne, a fishing rod and a book of poetry.

One of the Queen Mother's enduring pleasures is having friends to tea. It is served at five, and the guests – sheikhs, American presidents, a young and interesting student she has met, a friend from the country and a Bowes-Lyon grand-niece – will sit in the yellow Garden Room. The round table has an old-fashioned white, very lacy and starched cloth, with small matching napkins.

Sitting bolt upright, the Queen Mother constantly presses her guests to have more. 'But, do,' she urges as she offers another bannock, a tiny asparagus tip sandwich, lobster mousse in choux pastry, cream, iced or chocolate cakes and Highland shortcake. She never has to take her eyes away from her guests as a butler with two or three footmen leap to refill the Derby china teacups.

At six, the Queen Mother is on her feet. 'Oh, my dears, it is time we all have to go,' and the Garden Room empties.

When you hear that the Queen Mother has slipped into a restaurant, Le Gavroche perhaps, or Waltons – where the waiters made her a heart out of pimento – for mussels in champagne sauce and sherry trifle, it may appear to be completely unplanned. Well, not exactly.

John Sinclair, son of Lord Thurso, runs the Lancaster Hotel in Paris, where aristocrats spend a few days before Longchamps. He was told months ahead that the Queen Mother would be coming to lunch by Ruth, Lady Fermoy, who checked the hotel and stayed in a modest room with bath for a night. The hotel is a bit like Clarence House, with eighteenth-century clocks and excellent French furniture.

It was a perfect May day and lunch was served in the tiny pink dining-room with rosebud screens looking out on to the trellised patio. It was a small party: the Queen Mother, the Duke and

Duchess of Grafton, Sir Ralph Anstruther, Ruth, Lady Fermoy and the British Ambassador, Sir John Fretwell.

Everything was beautifully cool, though the arranged codewords were 'Help, she is here.' But the chef, who had recently deserted Maxims, was in a fury. He had created a delicate swan out of a block of ice, like a 1920s Lalique, to hold a mass of spun sugar and *soufflé* lit by battery lights. He was just perfecting the neck when it snapped; there was a dreadful crashing noise as the chef threw down the chisel, Sinclair ruefully remembers, and he literally wrung the thing's neck, shortening it by about five inches. It became a duck. The Queen Mother thought it 'absolutely lovely'.

John Sinclair saw the Queen Mother and guests into the dining-room, where separately King Umberto, Edith Sitwell and the Duke of Bedford used to dine, and went behind the service door to see – through a spy-hole – the Queen Mother having 'a most animated lunch', using the last of the hotel's distinguished Baccaret glass and Limoges plates. What a relief: 3.30 P.M. and lunch, *foie gras frais*, a lamb dish, and the swan *soufflé*, was over.

The Queen Mother loves France. In the past, she has rented a fifteenth-century house in Provence to explore châteaux; another year she took a floor of a hotel and, with some English friends, went 'house hunting'. Sometimes she stays with the Rothschilds or the Prince and Princesse de Beauveau-Craon at their castle near Nancy. The fun on her 'jaunts' is being able to go to restaurants without being spotted, although one evening a group of steel workers watched her arrive at the Capucin Gourmand restaurant in the Rue Gambetta in Nancy and tried to surround her: '*le kidnap*', the excitable French thought.

Treats at home in London include the theatre, nothing too racy because 'Everyone looks round,' she says, 'to see how we are taking it.' She has been a champion of music, loves Mozart, Haydn and Schubert and songs by Schumann and Benjamin Britten, and is fond of ballet, too.

An evening at White City watching show-jumping might be the Queen's idea of fun; her mother would prefer to see *Manon Lescaut* at Covent Garden. Her taste is not *avant garde* but the artists appreciate her genuine interest.

In seventeen years, she has never missed a gala at Covent Garden. 'Some of the most interesting men around are a bit in love with her,' says Sir Claus Moser of the Royal Opera Company; and he would not deny being in that category himself.

There is also a down-to-earth quality about her; she will not sit and beam if a performance is not good. She recognizes both excellence and *longueur*. Once, as a Spanish dancer in his black sombrero was intensely pounding the floor the Queen Mother turned to her companion and asked: 'Can we turn the hose on him?'

Benjamin Britten and Peter Pears thought it very grand when the Queen Mother arrived in her helicopter, landing on the golf links near the Maltings in Suffolk for a very special concert. She had chosen the music and there would be a little Mozart, Janet Baker would sing *Nuits d'Eté* by Berlioz and 'Ben', as she called Britten, had written something especially for her. She had known Britten and Pears when the King was alive and they used to go across to Sandringham. With friends like Noël Coward, Edith Sitwell and Ted Seago, they would play the piano, recite poetry and sing.

On her 75th birthday, Benjamin Britten composed a piece of music for her and the two men went to Sandringham to present it. He had chosen some Burns poems. Peter Pears recalls: 'It was awfully touching on that birthday. She is such a kind and loving person and wants to bring happiness. Ben was obviously very moved. He was very ill then and as we were leaving he asked, "Ma'am, may I kiss you?" and he touched her cheek.' Ten days later Benjamin Britten died. Peter Pears, who has since suffered a stroke, is still emotional when he remembers that day and the tears in the Queen Mother's eyes when he sang Schumann's *Dichterliebe*.

He remembers how she listened to a chat about pacifism with Ted Seago, the painter, at Sandringham. It was not her view, 'but she was so sympathetic'.

During the Aldeburgh Festival, the Queen Mother likes to take friends around old houses or churches or for picnics on the beach at Holkham Hall on Lord Leicester's estate. One summer, some nude bathers saw her advancing with her musical friends and, not bothering to reach for towels, thought they would surprise the Queen Mother. They were cheated when she smartly turned right up a sand dune.

She loves being with theatre people. There was a glorious meeting between the late Sir Ralph Richardson and herself – a couple of old troupers, each out-doing the other. They met at the BBC Television Centre and the Queen Mother said dreamily, 'I wonder if we shall ever have a National Theatre?' The old actor replied gallantly: 'Ah, Ma'am, I still remember the fine speech you made when you laid the foundation stone. I remember every word of it.' She put her head on one side, 'Do you really? Can you say some of it for me now?' In his marvellous voice, Sir Ralph was forced to make one up.

Words flowed that had certainly never been written by the cautious hand of Sir Martin Gilliat; Sir Peter Hall and Arnold Wesker were stunned. The Queen Mother herself looked rather delighted at her eloquence about 'the sounding board of English drama for generations to come'. 'Ah, yes,' she said. 'It's coming back to me now.'

When she left, Sir Ralph, feeling much in need of a stimulant at the Garrick, said with a wink to Sir Peter Hall, 'That was a close one, cocky.'

22

Ma'am, Darling

Balmoral, August 1983. Panic, a royal diary records 'no grouse'. Prince Charles had gone 'awf', the family said, to find a fish; Prince Philip was with the Factor so that leaves the Queen, Princess Margaret, the Queen Mother and one or two jolly cousins having a skittish picnic behind the shelter of a hessian screen.

'Mummy, why do you wear those awful combs in your hair?' Princess Margaret teases and her mother pats her grey curls. 'Because if I don't my hair will fall down.' Princess Margaret persists, 'I wouldn't mind, but why can't you wear grey ones to match instead of tortoiseshell?' 'Right,' says the Queen Mother, 'you buy me some, darling.'

The Queen chuckles and lays out the picnic, opening her house present, an 'Eskie' Australian wine cooler holding the slimline tonic water for her and the white wine for her mother, sister and cousins.

Joining the picnic, another member of the royal family watches mother and daughters and smiles: 'Those three ladies are in constant touch, they are devoted and share everything. They talk a lot about clothes and telephone each other every day.'

Today, all three royal ladies are dressed in the Balmoral tartan of red, black and heathery blues, white ankle socks for the Queen and the favourite squashy felt hat with a red feather for the Queen Mother. She gets her kilts made by Hartnell and somehow never looks windswept, although she likes a blast of Highland air on her cheeks.

One young royal said: 'Normally you have to change umpteen times; in the morning a skirt, then a dress for tea and an evening dress for dinner.'

'Oh, no shooting pudding or butteries for me,' says Princess Margaret with mock distaste, reaching for a glass and a cigarette. Shooting pudding has been a tradition with the royal family in Scotland since Queen Victoria. It is a 'you'll never walk again' heavy plum pudding mix the colour of black soil. Butteries are little airy rolls like croissants only slightly less fattening.

The Queen Mother loves being in Scotland and says the corgis like it. Mother and daughters have great contests about whose corgis are the most vicious. All three are probably at their happiest in Balmoral on a good summer day in the 'shiel', a log hut given to the Queen Mother by her friends and household as a birthday gift that looks down through the pine forests to the boulders by the fast-flowing River Dee, which with the sun on it can turn the colour of good Scotch whisky.

Although the Queen Mother casts one of the most skilful rods in that élite stretch of fishing, she liked to pretend that often she went only for the sake of her old ghillie, Jimmy Pearl. 'I just go along to please Pearl,' she would say as she landed another plump salmon. Since his death in 1980 the family have persuaded her to cut down on her fishing.

Balmoral is a funny, comfortable Victorian mixture. ' "Tartanitis" everywhere,' an aesthete sniffed. 'Even the linoleum in the servants' quarters is tartan.' After the Abdication, the King and Queen tried to make it 'cosy', but it is fairly unchanged, with lots of blond-pale maple wood cupboards, a pastel drawing-room and Landseer paintings of shaggy Highland cattle and Queen Victoria looking immovable on a small pony. In 1952, the Queen Mother was quite happy to move back to Birkhall, the large white Queen Anne house which Victoria used for poor relations.

To get to Birkhall you drive through Ballater, that royal village where the baker makes the 'butteries' and where the café owner complains because Prince Philip has set up a rival teashop at the gates of Balmoral. Ballater is like a skiing village, grey and sharply cleaned by the snow. The Princess of Wales and Lady Sarah Armstrong-Jones buy their toffees there. On the road to Birkhall, past the pines and sweeping valleys, Range Rovers travelling at speed flit by carrying a prince or two up the valley to shoot or fish.

The house is perched high up above sloping lawns, white heather and Giant Himalayan lilies. 'Isn't it a delicious garden?' the Queen Mother says as she shows you the clumps of cornflowers, larkspur and blue and purple Michaelmas daisies she planted herself.

Usually the Queen Mother and Princess Margaret will drive over to Balmoral, but not before about mid-day. After lunch muddy dogs, children, the Prime Minister, anyone who is staying with the Queen, will climb into the Land-Rovers and go off for a picnic and a good hearty walk. If it is raining, the Queen Mother seems to like it even better.

More talking is done by the royal family when they go to Scotland for their two-month holiday than at any other time of the year.

Somehow for them, London and Windsor are busy places and they are rarely in Sandringham. When the Queen Mother is telling people about a family picnic or a tramp through the heather, she refers unstuffily to the Queen as 'my daughter' or to Prince Charles as 'my grandson'.

It is not unknown for the Queen Mother to burst into song as she sits in the heather with a cup of something warming. And Prince Philip, if he is barbecuing, will grin and concentrate on the sausage as the Queen joins in some old-fashioned song like 'I know where the flies go in winter time', their voices carrying across Ballochbuie and making the red deer perk up their antlers.

'It looks so special and beautiful today,' the Queen Mother says as if she were seeing the Dee Valley for the first time; and then, to a grand-niece, 'Oh, Liza, that was such a lovely lunch, those simply delicious quenelles,' remembering a lunch party given by Lady Elizabeth Anson at her tall house in Holland Park. 'I hate quenelles,' Princess Margaret says. 'They are boring.' Then, as she tells her cousin she has put on a lot of weight, the Queen Mother soothes, 'Now Margaret, you have a bee in your bonnet about weight.' All the time the Queen is playing house, setting out the knives and forks, boiling kettles and talking to the corgis.

The Queen Mother is not a spartan person; and the young royals often escape to Birkhall for tea, first using the footscraper in the dark, pine-log porch. It was here that Lady Diana Spencer sank gratefully into one of the armchairs and worked on her needlepoint as only a Sloane Ranger could on the verge of falling in love. Prince Charles came to collect her for a game of hide and seek on the banks of the River Dee, teasing photographers heavily disguised as ghillies, then they would scamper back to Birkhall for one of the Queen Mother's teas: Earl Grey tea; chocolate cake, her favourite Black Bun, a rich Highland fruit cake.

Prince Charles is like a son to her; she adores him. Very often at Royal Lodge on summer weekends when the doors are open on to the lawns and fat, drowsy bees skim over the Queen Mother's favourite Laddie carnations and pale pink roses he will arrive hot and sticky in his polo gear. He will put his head round the door and guests tactfully scatter after a few pleasantries, picking up copies of *Country Life* and disappearing to the paved terrace with its scented lavender hedges. The Queen Mother mixes a couple of Pimms and she and her grandson chat and 'hoot with laughter together in a corner'.

They may talk about who is going to catch the biggest salmon in Scotland or whether the 'Hairy Mary' or the 'Black Doctor' are the best salmon flies. The Queen Mother taught him to fish, but he is now as worried as his mother about her wading into the River Dee. They both love to recall the incident when another woman fishing in breast-high waders was casting on the far bank when she suddenly spotted the Queen Mother on the other side. She automatically did a deep curtsey but, unfortunately, slipped into the deep water and was last seen floating towards Aberdeen.

Prince Charles gets his salmon flies from a vigorous old character called Miss Megan Boyd, who has cropped hair and wears a collar and tie. Fishermen from all over the world come to her hut on the Sutherland coast for her inimitable bright yellow and red jungle cock feathers. In 1971, she was awarded the British Empire Medal but, she apologized, she could not go to Buckingham Palace to collect it – because of her dog. She later made a little shrimp fly brooch for the Prince of Wales to give to his wife with a note: 'Dear Prince Charles, will you please give her the brooch. Tell her you have the best catch you'll ever have.' Soon afterwards he invited her to have a 'dram' with him. 'I had a wee martini and he had a sherry, but all he wanted to know was: was I charging enough to make a living.'

Prince Charles and his grandmother also talk seriously. It was she who suggested to the Prince that he should not become a Freemason, though his grandfather, George VI, and his father joined the brotherhood – although Prince Philip describes the secret society with its 700,000 members as a 'bit of a silly joke'.

The Queen Mother has often joked when she is complimented on her youthfulness, 'Oh, I want to live to be a hundred so I can get a telegram from the King.' But at present it is Prince Charles who turns to his grandmother for guidance. He asks her about the King and how he handled political pressures. Few understand so well the Prince's need to go into the Kalahari Desert for ten days, to be quiet and have time to think with the guidance of the philosopher and explorer, Sir Laurens van der Post, one of Prince William's godparents. Both grandmother and grandson are sensitive enough to appreciate that they cannot see each other so much now that he is married. But the Queen Mother is also the best person to guide the Princess of Wales; they are terrific friends. The Queen Mother was delighted about the second baby the Princess had last September.

The Queen Mother understands better than most how the

Princess of Wales feels about a lifetime ahead in the public eye and sympathizes with her dislike of grand State occasions. An Italian diplomat bowed to the Princess of Wales and told her he had been coming to the Queen's Corps Diplomatique receptions at Buckingham Palace for the last ten years. The Princess rolled her eyes and pulled a face: 'Oh, to think I have another fifty years ahead of me,' she replied.

Some of Prince Charles's earliest memories of his grandmother are of eating chocolate cake while she did conjuring tricks for him, pulling funny faces and sometimes wearing a moustache.

Princess Anne was never quite so close to her grandmother. 'The Queen Mother is a wonderful family person,' she says. 'And when I was a child and up to my teens, I don't think I went along with the family bit. So my appreciation of my grandmother probably developed later than anybody else's.' The Princess has developed her own uncompromising personality, her hair drawn back severely and with little time for frivolity. She and the more frivolous Queen Mother can hardly be soulmates. For her work for the Save the Children Fund, it is expected that the Queen will honour her daughter shortly with the title 'Princess Royal'. Once, during a family New Year in Sandringham the Princess and Captain Mark Phillips stayed in a caravan to be near their horses. Inviting some locals to 'first foot', she joked, 'Do come. Papa has put us over a sewer.'

The first time the Queen Mother saw Prince Andrew was in a cream-coloured cot lined with pink satin. He was one day old. He, too, is very tender towards her and you will sometimes see this brisk young man take his grandmother's hand as she gets out of a car and then, rather endearingly, hold on to it if they are about to negotiate steps.

Yet the Queen Mother remains extremely fit. She almost runs up the stairs in Clarence House, leaving companions 30 years younger out of breath and forced to sit down. Shortly after her 80th birthday, when the Queen and Prince Philip were in Australia, Mrs Sylvia Grey, the chairman of the National Federation of Women's Institutes, suggested to the Queen Mother after she had opened a new teaching block at Marcham, Berkshire: 'I do hope, Ma'am, you can take it easy tomorrow for a change.' The Queen Mother looked amazed. 'Take it easy? This weekend I have the boys on my hands. I shall probably be playing cricket most of the day.' No wonder the more mature young royals say, 'Ma'am, darling, must you do so much?'

The young in the family often find they get a more sympathetic hearing from the Queen Mother than from their parents. When Prince Richard of Gloucester, always an independent spirit, wanted to marry a Danish commoner, Birgitte van Deurs, whom he met at Cambridge where he studied architecture, there was a little uncertainty about how she might fit in. But the Queen Mother liked the girl's freshness and became her champion. She went to the wedding; the Queen regretted she had previous engagements and stayed away. Prince Richard, who became the Duke of Gloucester in 1972 when his brother, William, was killed in an air crash, says: 'I can't tell you what the Queen Mother means to all of us. You only have to be loved by her, and to love her yourself to know that no matter what, you could never let her down.'

But the Queen Mother will never interfere too much, and this may be seen by outsiders as a weakness. Her strength is in her calm and good nature.

'She has been the most marvellous mother,' the Queen says, 'always standing back and never interfering.'

Once, when the Queen was lunching at Clarence House at a small table set for two in the library, a vase of the Queen Mother's favourite lily of the valley in the centre, she relaxed and said she thought she might have a glass of wine. 'Is that wise?' her mother inquired. 'You know you have to reign all afternoon.'

Her admiration for her elder daughter is quite open. It is very rare for her to be angry, but she was, it is reported, in 'a total fury' when an intruder broke into Buckingham Palace and got into the Queen's bedroom.

The Queen Mother never ceases to be thankful for Prince Philip as a son-in-law. They have a mutual respect; he loves the way she zips around in helicopters and, on one of her birthdays, he flew low over Clarence House dipping the plane's wings. Their only real disagreement is not about the correct altitude for touchdown at Windsor Castle, but about Gordonstoun, a 'dreadful place', she thinks. But Prince Philip is pleased with the mark his old school has made on his three sons.

In the evening at Balmoral the pipers play and there is vigorous dancing, Prince Philip and his sons clapping as the Queen Mother is swept along in a reel while the Queen slips off to bed.

Any girl setting her heart on marrying Prince Andrew or Prince Edward would be advised to make sure she can do some Highland dances even though they may not be the thing in 'Tramps'. Douglas

Sutherland, descended from an old Scottish family and author of several books on what makes a gentleman north and south of the Border, says, 'You feel an awful fart if you can't do a reel and it simply means you are not socially acceptable.'

At the end of the evening, the Queen Mother and Princess Margaret are driven back to Birkhall, talking and laughing for most of the seven-mile journey. Princess Margaret seems happier as a divorcee and much better company. But she can still be exasperating, as when she refuses to go to church. 'You know I don't care for the Church of Scotland.'

The Queen Mother handles her moods cleverly. Once, during fire practice at Royal Lodge, Windsor, Princess Margaret would not get out of bed for a mock 'rescue'. The staff were in a dilemma when they met the Queen Mother coming down the stairs, a serene picture in chiffon but clearly ready for any emergency.

'Oh well,' she said sweetly when she heard about her daughter's refusal to get up, 'she'll just have to burn, won't she?'

23

A Super-confident Glorious Lady

The Duchess of Windsor lies in her house in Paris, slipping deeper and deeper into a state of unconsciousness. Sometimes she will ask pathetically: 'I wish someone would put a sweet in my mouth,' stir to some dance music or convey displeasure to her two nurses. She is a shrunken old lady sadly wasting away from a nervous disease. She is washed and brushed, but she is no longer able to sip vodka from a silver cup or enjoy old photographs of herself and the Duke of Windsor wearing paper crowns in the 'El Morocco' night club at New Year in 1953 – the year of the Queen's coronation.

The Queen Mother rebukes Lord Home youthfully for his lack of enthusiasm for the latest space programme. 'If you think it futile,' she says, 'you will never get anywhere.' The former Tory Prime Minister, only three years her junior, gives in.

Lord Harlech has told a story against himself. It was the end of a dinner party at Royal Lodge: 'Ladies, shall we?' the Queen Mother suggested and, first, the women rose and then the footmen pulled back the chairs for the men.

For what seemed an eternity, Lord Harlech's feet desperately searched under the table for his evening shoes. He always likes to push them off when he is relaxed; it is a family habit. Fearfully embarrassed, he could not stay at the table a moment longer. The Queen Mother was on her way out and he had to pad behind her across the dining-room in his stockinged feet.

Dreading the drawing-room, and Princess Margaret's disapproval, Lord Harlech was saved as the Queen Mother stopped, turned to him and, with a wave of her hands, held up a pair of black monogrammed slippers. 'David, is this what you are looking for?'

It is hard now to think of Wallis Simpson as a *femme fatale*. A friend of the Windsors in Paris thought their marriage had been happy, though it was a mother–son relationship. 'You see, David never had a mother.' Mrs Simpson, with her brittle style, her grooming and her tautness, gave him a happiness – and he had no regrets. They were never as rich as people imagined, and although friends like Lady Mosley say she had flair their house in the Bois de Boulogne was perhaps a little too Newport, Rhode Island – rather too glossy and comfortable for a French house. It has stunning *trompe l'oeil* and eighteenth-century French furniture but some of the older visiting English aristocrats took a poor view of candles which switched on and off. Normally, a gruff voice answers the intercom at the great black gates, and an upside-down red and white *Interdit* sign lies on the grass. It is like a fortress.

American pilgrims to the Bois report to New York that the Duchess is a 'mushroom lying in a gilded ghetto'. The pug dogs are dead.

Her mind was already fragile when she returned at last to Windsor, for the Duke's funeral in 1972. The Queen Mother, who feels sorry for the Duchess of Windsor now, sat by her and tried to give words of comfort: 'I know, I have been through this myself.'

Ludovic Kennedy went to Clarence House to talk about a television programme on the Queen Mother's life. 'Ma'am, with respect', he pleaded, 'to do a programme about your life and not mention the Abdication would be like talking about World War II and not including Churchill.' But she was adamant. There could be no mention of the Abdication. 'As this was the central event which pitchforked her on to the throne, I felt I could not accept her stipulation,' Kennedy said, and the idea was scrapped. Tactful friends who have photographs or paintings of the Duke and Duchess of Windsor will make sure that they are out of sight when the Queen Mother is visiting.

When the King died, Lionel Logue, the speech therapist who had helped her husband with his stammer, sent the Queen Mother the tall, ugly Victorian chair from his rooms in Knightsbridge used by his royal patient. Logue was also instrumental in putting the royal widow in touch with a medium, Mrs Lilian Bailey.

Friends had admired her strength and thought how well she was bearing up, but the Queen Mother told them, 'Not when I am alone.' On her own admission she felt 'engulfed by great black clouds of unhappiness and misery'.

She turned to the world of spiritualism for comfort. When Logue had told George VI about Mrs Bailey, who had put the therapist in touch with his dead wife, the King had told him quietly: 'My family are no strangers to spiritualism.' Queen Victoria, he said, had maintained contact with her beloved Albert, for whom she mourned for 30 years, through her ghillie, John Brown. There have been ribald stories about the relationship between the Queen and the crusty old Scots ghillie. But Gordon Adam, son-in-law of Lilian

Bailey, said: 'Brown was a medium. All records of sittings were ordered to be destroyed at the time of her death, but through the ghillie Albert ruled the country at a distance.'

Adam, a director of *Psychic News*, remembers his mother-in-law as tall and serene with silver hair. 'If our children were crying in the middle of the night, she would walk into the room and they would stop at once.' She particularly liked to help people who were in mourning and there was no question of payment.

Out of the blue, Lilian Bailey received a telephone call at her home in Wembley, asking her to go to an address in Kensington. When she got there, she was blindfolded and then taken to another house.

She always remembered the rustle of skirts as the other sitters took their places. When Mrs Bailey came out of a deep trance, the blindfold was taken off and before her were the Queen Mother, the Queen, Princess Alexandra, the Duchess of Kent and Prince Philip.

There were several private sessions afterwards for the medium with the Queen Mother. Then one day the Queen Mother pinned a piece of costume jewellery which she had taken from her dress on Mrs Bailey's shoulder. 'You know we do not have many possessions, but I would like you to have this.' It was a thank-you for her discretion and for restoring peace to the Queen Mother. She came back into public life almost immediately.

Many of the Queen Mother's friends get credit, too, for helping to restore her: Lady Doris Vyner and Sir Winston Churchill, for example, who cajoled her with almost war-time rhetoric: 'Your country needs you, Ma'am'. The academics at London University who persuaded her to become their first woman Chancellor helped, as did the pilots who flew her round the world; the jockeys who nearly broke their necks to ride winners for her; the painters like John Piper, and the devotion of the composer Benjamin Britten.

In her early days of mourning, the Queen Mother insisted on going to Scotland. She is Colonel-in-Chief of the Black Watch and the regiment was leaving for Korea. She flew north and was entertained well in the officers' mess. After the late night it was assumed that the Queen Mother would have breakfast in bed. In the morning the battalion marched off, just before five. The soldiers had been a dismal downcast group of men. Suddenly, through the rainy mist, they saw a smiling face in a headscarf peering through a gap in the hedge. Their Colonel-in-Chief was in her wellies and a woolly coat. The men did not even have time for an 'eyes right', but suddenly the mood lifted and they set off 'almost elated', as one later said.

Back in public life, the Queen Mother made it a policy never to admit to being cold or tired. To her 'illness is a bore'. But in 1966 she had to admit defeat when no homoeopathic remedy could help. She went into hospital for the removal of an internal obstruction, a colostomy. Even then, her sense of humour never left her. A bulletin had been issued by the surgeon, Sir Ralph Marnham, saying that she was comfortable. But, as she ruefully suggested, 'There is all the difference in the patient's meaning of the word and the surgeon's.' For a few months she was a little wan and peeky; she had to eat more vegetables and wholemeal bread; but there were no disagreeable after-effects which might have prevented her from enjoying such a busy life.

That was nearly 20 years ago and since then her only illnesses have been the odd cold, a leg ulcer and a runaway salmon bone lodged in her throat. Hugh Cavendish, a kinsman of the Duke of Devonshire, who was a guest at Royal Lodge that night, said it was all he could do to get the Queen Mother to stop being polite. 'I could see she was in great discomfort and I had to persuade her to stop trying to make conversation before I gave her a slap on the back.' After the bone was removed from her throat, she did admit as she was leaving the King Edward VIII Hospital for Officers, 'I feel I am suffering from jet lag,' and joked about 'the Salmon's Revenge'. It had been a severe shock to the system of an 82-year-old, but eight days later she was beaming her way round an inaugural meeting of the Court of Patrons of the Royal College of Obstetricians and Gynaecologists.

Nevertheless she can be sympathetic about other people's illnesses. Vera Lynn tells how once at a supper party at Clarence House the Queen Mother spotted that she was a little preoccupied. 'She is such a darling and, as always with her, you get around to talking about the family. When I told her about my mother's being in hospital, she said, "Now what can we send her?" She scooped up some *marrons glacés* from the sweetmeat tray and said, "Give these to your mother with my love."' Three days later the telephone rang in the kitchen and Vera Lynn's husband, Harry Lewis, answered. 'Windsor Castle?' he asked. 'Is that the pub, then?' 'No,' the operator replied sniffily. 'It is the Queen Mother inquiring about Miss Lynn's mother.'

This 'super-confident, glorious lady', as an artist once described her, is simply keeping a promise she made when the King died: 'Now that I am left alone, to do what I can to honour his promise to his people.'

Whenever the Queen is passing Clarence House in a ceremonial procession, she dips her head and looks up for an instant from her State coach to the sitting-room window on the first floor. Nearly always she sees the reassuring figure of her mother smiling and waving a large white handkerchief. The Queen always bows to her mother at the Trooping the Colour ceremony, and the Queen Mother has never failed to be moved by her daughter's grace.

She has planned her own funeral, every detail, even down to the candles for her lying-in-state. 'I'm afraid I don't awfully care for yours, do you mind if I supply my own?' She will occasionally pop into the Infirmary at the back of Westminster Abbey to watch the good ladies of St Faith, all voluntary expert needlewomen, take finest silk thread from scarves and delicately repair a royal funeral pall, restoring Tudor roses and the tree of life.

She has been a widow for 32 years, longer than she was a wife, and she has a deeply held faith. She enjoys the company of churchmen and lunches about once a year with the Papal Nuncio, Archbishop Bruno Heim.

A plump contained Swiss with a dry sense of humour, Archbishop Heim's hobby is designing coats of arms and he keeps an amusing and colourful Heraldic guest book. He designed the Queen Mother's coat of arms. They appear with a credit in the Guide Book to Glamis Castle.

She has chuckled at his coats of arms for other guests as they sit together on a hot summer day on the lawn, she in pink and the Papal Nuncio in black with a purple beret. 'Here's Agatha Christie's. I told her I learnt all my English from her books, so for her, a feather and a hatchet.' Mrs Thatcher said briskly that as a grocer's daughter from Grantham she had no coat of arms. But instead of designing a box of matches, a bar of soap or a loaf of bread, the prelate has drawn an iron sword cutting through a hammer and sickle, an idea he took from a cartoon in a Russian paper.

When the Queen Mother first went to lunch with the Papal Nuncio, she asked if she might go into the kitchens afterwards to thank the cook for 'such a delicious meal'. She often does this, but was surprised this time to find a little nun bent over the cooking pots rather than some nice, fresh-faced Cordon Bleu girl ready to drop a curtsy. The Queen Mother thought the kitchens rather Victorian and, that afternoon, visited her own in Clarence House again to make sure they were not too bleak.

The Queen Mother will continue to use helicopters like taxis; when she was in an emergency landing in a Wessex, she joked, 'The wretched little thing has broken down'. An RAF officer tried to look correct as he carried her spare shoes and umbrella. 'Oh, well, it's a lovely day for it,' she joked. She would love a trip on Concorde.

She will continue to debunk, but never unkindly. Once, on a liner, a nosy passenger thought he knew her face: 'You advertise something, now what is it?' With a smile, the Queen Mother answered: 'Oh, it would be too unprofessional to tell you.' It is the sort of story her favourite author, P. G. Wodehouse, would have loved.

She will go on putting people at their ease, like the unfortunate waiter who dropped a sardine in her lap at a Mansion House banquet. It was deftly removed, 'I promise not to say anything about it, if you will bring me another.'

And she will continue to make entrances with all that 'creamy English charm' which entranced Evelyn Waugh. On her wedding day, Princess Marie Louise turned to Lady Strathmore and said: 'How lovely Elizabeth looks.' Lady Strathmore glowed. 'Elizabeth not only looks lovely, she is lovely. I do not believe she has ever had an ugly thought or said an ugly thing in all her life.'

While she has to cope nowadays with the deaths of her friends, and even of her nieces and nephews, as they all grow older, the Queen Mother herself looks forward to even more trips abroad. 'She does not enjoy idleness,' one of her household says, 'and takes the view that as long as she is fit and well, she wants to be doing things.' Even so, it seemed a bit steep that on a perishing day in March 1984 it was the Queen Mother and not any of the strapping young men of the royal family who turned up at the Wembley Stadium for the Milk Cup soccer final. She cheerfully watched as the mud and curses flew and Liverpool battled Everton on a rain-sodden pitch to a disappointing draw without score.

When her leg was bandaged after an injury recently – 'I refuse to tell you what happened it was so foolish' – she insisted that it be covered in pink, blue and white ribbons to match the evening dress she was wearing to the Waterloo Banquet at Windsor.

'Oh, Mummy, I do like your chariot,' Princess Margaret remarked as the Queen Mother arrived at the banquet in a wheelchair. But it was no ordinary wheelchair the Queen Mother had commandeered for her entrance. It was a vintage model once used by Queen

Victoria; the Queen Mother wrinkled her nose at all the dust it had gathered.

If you want to ask the Queen Mother to come to open a new wing of a hospital, it is unlikely that she will be free before 1986; her diary is very full.

Her daughters and friends fear that her good nature will wear her out, but the Queen Mother, who loves to prove them wrong, is planning her very own turn of the century. When Lady Jean Rankin, one of her ladies-in-waiting and Woman of the Bedchamber since 1947, gently suggested her own retirement, there was an appalled silence. Then the Queen Mother said, 'Oh, please, no, you can't possibly. Look at me, I have to go on.' Lady Rankin, five years younger – a mere 70 – smiled and asked what time the Queen Mother would like the car, as they had a heavy day ahead.

Years ago it was suggested that the Queen Mother might become a Governor-General; the Queen immediately put her foot down: 'Oh, I am afraid not, we could not possibly spare Mummy.'

Index

Index